T0350615

COUNT YOUR BLESSINGS AND STOP STRESSING

365 DAILY DEVOTIONS

Ray Comfort

BroadStreet
PUBLISHING

BroadStreet Publishing® Group, LLC
Savage, Minnesota, USA
BroadStreetPublishing.com

Count Your Blessings and Stop Stressing: 365 Daily Devotions

9781424566556 (faux)
9781424566563 (ebook)

Stock or custom editions of BroadStreet Publishing titles may be purchased in bulk for educational, business, ministry, fundraising, or sales promotional use. For information, please email orders@broadstreetpublishing.com.

Cover and interior by Garborg Design Works | garborgdesign.com

Printed in China

24 25 26 27 28 5 4 3 2 1

Foreword

Stress has become part of contemporary life—from fluctuating gas prices to sickness, pressures at work, and financial problems that only add to tensions in the home. We are tempted to stress every day. But circumstances or feelings should not sway our joy. Childlike trust in God as our Father is the antidote to stress. This means trusting in his comforting promises and trusting that his commandments are perfect, right, and good. The old hymn had it right: "Trust and obey, for there's no other way to be happy in Jesus but to trust and obey." Here are three proactive actions that help us stress less:

- Believe God's Word. Trusting in the exceedingly great and precious promises of God can give us a refuge from the storm.

- Battle sin. Jesus calls us to lay down our lives, follow him, and imitate him. When we obey his commandments and pursue righteousness, there is less and less room for doubt and fear to cling.

- Help others. It's hard to be worried about yourself when your thoughts are occupied with how you can bless someone else. And the most important help we can provide is that which we offer to unbelievers when we share the good news and snatch them from death.

That's why this devotional has three elements: comfort to soothe anxiety, encouragement to fight your sin, and exhortation to bless those around you. Devotions with these topics are mixed throughout the year. I pray that this cycle of personal growth and blessing others helps you see another perspective—life in the light of eternity.

Kind regards,

Ray Comfort

September 2022

January

The Goodness of God

Every good gift and every perfect gift is from above.
JAMES 1:17

Familiarity certainly breeds contempt. When we become accustomed to something, we tend to take it for granted. Nobody appreciates the "gift" of lungs until they struggle to breathe. We don't truly appreciate eyesight until we start losing it. We don't recognize the blessing of having enough food until we suffer from hunger. We take for granted the blueness of the sky, the sound of the birds in the morning, the cool breeze, the warm sun, the wonderful taste of food, and the joy of love and laughter. We rarely stop and smell the roses or thank the one whose hand created them. We take for granted the clouds that carry the rain that waters the earth and gives us life. The old hymn carries such a wonderful truth: "Count your blessings, name them one by one; count your blessings, see what God hath done."

Every good gift comes from the hand of our benevolent Creator, who graciously gave us life. Having such an attitude of appreciation will produce joy in our hearts—even in the middle of our daily trials. We can count our blessings because God will always lead us into that which is good and never into evil. And knowledge of his blessings will keep us from stressing.

Father, today I will stop and count my blessings and name them one by one.

Prepare His Way

"Prepare the way of the Lord;
  make his paths straight."
MATTHEW 3:3 ESV

John's message was for sinners to prepare the way of the Lord. He told them to make the Lord's paths straight. Perhaps the greatest gift God has given to humanity is the gift of free will. We can choose to sin, or we can choose to serve. We can stay in the pigsty, or we can return to the Father like the Prodigal Son and ask to be made a hired servant. Nothing is impossible for God. He could prepare the way for himself and make his own path straight. But he's left that up to you and me.

Today we have a choice. It can be a day when God has access to our thoughts and the choices we make. We can allow him to have his way in our lives by doing that which is pleasing in his sight. This will be much easier for us if we have already obeyed the admonition of Scripture: "Present your bodies a living sacrifice, holy, acceptable unto God, which is your reasonable service. And be not conformed to this world: but be ye transformed by the renewing of your mind, that ye may prove what is that good, and acceptable, and perfect, will of God" (Romans 12:1–2 KJV).

Father, today I affirm that I am no longer my own. I have removed every hinderance. I am yours.

We Are Never Alone

"The voice of one crying in the wilderness…"
MATTHEW 3:3 ESV

Sometimes we can feel as though we're a mere voice crying in the wilderness when we share the gospel. We are nobody special, and nobody is listening; we are just a voice crying out to this world—wanting every man and woman to know that God is deadly serious about sin and that he has appointed a day on which he will judge the world in righteousness. We sow in tears and complain with Isaiah, "Who has believed our report?" (Isaiah 53:1). However, even though Scripture calls John the Baptist a voice in the wilderness, his labor wasn't in vain. His voice was certainly heard. The crowds came to the wilderness: "Then Jerusalem and all Judea and all the region about the Jordan were going out to him" (Matthew 3:5 ESV).

Never believe the lie that you are ever alone. If you are trusting in Jesus Christ, you have his promise that he will never leave you nor forsake you. Ever. We truly have a friend in Jesus, and that friendship will be as rich as we make it. Enrich your prayer life with gratitude, appreciation, thankfulness, praise, worship, and love, and this will flow if you never lose sight of the cross. It will keep your joy full and your cup running over—into this world.

Father, thank you for always being with me as I share the good news with others.

Who Has Warned You?

"You brood of vipers!
Who warned you to flee from the wrath to come?"
MATTHEW 3:7 ESV

John the Baptist and Jesus both aimed messages at the religious leaders because of the leaders' hypocrisy. The leaders couldn't be trusted. Never trust a viper. Don't even get close to it because it has a deadly bite. Jesus told the disciples to leave the Pharisees alone because they were the blind leading the blind. There is something wonderful about the scathing words of God against religious hypocrisy. It is such a stumbling block for so many. The hypocrisy of professed Christians emboldens some to sin. And how grievous it is to see robed men and women professing to speak to God and perverting the Scriptures and deceiving the hearts of the simple.

John also asked who warned them to flee from the wrath to come. But although we may also have a history of hypocrisy, if we are trusting in Jesus, we don't need to fear that wrath and can take comfort in the Scriptures. This is why we should regularly pray: "Search me, O God, and know my heart: try me, and know my thoughts: And see if there be any wicked way in me, and lead me in the way everlasting" (Psalm 139:23–24 KJV).

Father, thank you for seeing the depth of my sin yet still forgiving me through Jesus and leading me to eternity by your side.

Worthy of Repentance

"Bear fruit in keeping with repentance."
MATTHEW 3:8 ESV

John the Baptist told his listeners to mean business with God. He told them that they should have *evidence* that they had truly repented. The evidence that we have an apple tree in our garden is the apples. If the tree does not bear fruit, we will likely cut down the tree. And if we profess faith in Jesus—if we have truly repented of our sins—there should be evidence. This evidence was clearly seen in the repentance of Zacchaeus: "Zacchaeus stood, and said unto the Lord: Behold, Lord, the half of my goods I give to the poor; and if I have taken any thing from any man by false accusation, I restore him fourfold. And Jesus said unto him, This day is salvation come to this house, forsomuch as he also is a son of Abraham" (Luke 19:8–9 KJV).

If we are saved, we, too, should bear the fruit of repentance—along with fruit in keeping with righteousness, praise, thanksgiving, and the Spirit. This is the biblical way to examine ourselves and see if we are in the faith. Part of that fruit is to have the peace of God, which passes all understanding, and that peace guards our minds in the midst of daily stress (see Philippians 4:7).

Father, may I be a fruit-bearing Christian, and with my life, may I bring glory to your name.

Unquenchable Fire

"The chaff he will burn with unquenchable fire."
MATTHEW 3:12 ESV

John the Baptist was not afraid to talk about hell. Neither was Jesus. Neither should we be. However, we live in a day and age when it's not politically correct to say anything that would offend. But I would far rather that someone be offended by hearing about hell than feel its flames. If pastors and preachers spoke of the reality of hell with tears in their eyes rather than a holier-than-thou finger in the face of sinners, more people would come to the Savior.

God is the judge of the universe, and he has set aside a day on which he will judge the world in righteousness. If we are true and faithful witnesses, we will not hesitate to warn every man about the reality of that terrible and most terrifying place. Hell makes no sense when we do not precede the sharing of the gospel with the law to show sin to be exceedingly wicked. There is a hidden blessing here. The more we see our sin, the more we will see God's mercy, and that increases the joy of our salvation and our love for God. He who is forgiven much, the same loves much (see Luke 7:47).

Father, never let me compromise the gospel because I fear man.

Pleasing the Father

"This is my beloved Son,
with whom I am well pleased."
MATTHEW 3:17 ESV

What son isn't moved to tears by the commendation of his father? It's also common to see a grown man tear up when he talks about how his father never praised him when he was a child. But here we have the ultimate commendation. God himself says that Jesus is his beloved Son, and in him, God was well pleased. Jesus, in thought, word, and deed, caused the heart of his Father to rejoice.

But once a sinner is born again, God says, "This is my beloved son, with whom I am well pleased." Not because of the sinner's own righteousness but because of the righteousness of God in Christ. What a wonderful consolation it is to think of the Prodigal Son coming back to his joyful father. There is a type of God's love for us—when we come to him with a contrite heart. We think of the prodigal's father calling for a robe to clothe his son and a ring for his finger and commanding a great celebration because his son was once dead but was made alive. What comfort it is for us to think that God has rejoiced in our salvation, covered us with a robe of righteousness, giving us an inheritance in Jesus Christ. Such comfort and joy sustain us through the trials of each day.

Father, keep me in the palm of your loving hand.

Faith's Key

"Therefore I say to you, whatever things you ask when you pray, believe that you receive them, and you will have them."

MARK 11:24

The context of this promise is that Jesus had just cursed the fig tree, which then withered. After that, he spoke of believers removing mountains and casting them into the sea. He then said "therefore" and told his disciples to make sure they mix faith with their prayers. When we pray, we should always mix our prayers with faith. In other words, we should trust our heavenly Father to supply our every need. Here is the qualifier: "Let him ask in faith, with no doubting, for he who doubts is like a wave of the sea driven and tossed by the wind. For let not that man suppose that he will receive anything from the Lord; he is a double-minded man, unstable in all his ways" (James 1:6–8).

Need is the key word in interpreting such an open promise from the Scriptures. If we pray that God will supply our greed rather than our need, we are going to be disappointed. But the apostle Paul gave us another great promise: "My God shall supply all your need according to His riches in glory by Christ Jesus" (Philippians 4:19).

Father, I thank you for knowing my every need today—both small and great—and I trust you to supply them.

Spiritual Muscle

I bow my knees to the Father…that He would grant you,
according to the riches of His glory, to be strengthened with
might through His Spirit.

EPHESIANS 3:14, 16

This is Paul's earnest prayer for every Christian—that God
(through the power of the Holy Spirit) would make us strong
in Christ—"according to the riches of His glory." We need
strength for the many trials that life brings our way. And the
Lord has the ability to do just that—to build up the muscle
of godly character so that life doesn't crush us. The first
principle of gaining the strength we need is to believe that he
will faithfully keep his word. He *will* give us strength "with
might" exactly when and where we need it: in the inner man.
That is the battlefield where we fight the good fight of faith.
While the "outward man is perishing, yet the inward man is
being renewed day by day" (2 Corinthians 4:16).

He will give us the necessary spiritual muscle to
overcome sins that so easily beset us. And sin *easily* besets
us. That's why we, minute by minute, need his Spirit within
us. Without his continuing help, we would be overcome by
sin and consequent death. But victory is ours because Jesus
dwells in our hearts. We are sealed by the Holy Spirit. We
belong to him.

*Father, today let everything I do be for your glory and be
rooted and grounded in love.*

The Present Reality

Faith is the substance of things hoped for,
the evidence of things not seen.

HEBREWS 11:1

The ignorant think that faith is for the weak. But it is for the strong. Faith just *is*. It is an ever-present reality right now because of where it is directed. It is centered on the moral character of God. It is strong because of what is arguably the most profound truth in the Scriptures. And that immovable rock upon which faith sits is the marvelous fact that it is impossible for God to lie (see Hebrews 6:18; Titus 1:2). God will not and cannot ever deceive. It's not within his holy nature to do such an evil thing. And so our faith in Jesus sits upon the unchanging integrity of our Creator. If we let that truth permeate our soul, every divine promise becomes an instant and constant light in the darkness of this world. It becomes a deep well from which we draw cool and life-giving water in this dry and barren land. When all else fails, faith stands triumphant because it sees him who is invisible.

However, we must constantly remind ourselves that faith is only ours if we take hold of it. The Scriptures tell us to "take" the shield of faith (see Ephesians 6:16).

Father, today I take the shield of faith and believe every precious promise you have given me in your Word.

Fit for Use

We walk by faith, not by sight.

2 CORINTHIANS 5:7

Our eyes can easily fool us. We believe we see water on the road on a hot day. The sun seems to spread as it rises over the horizon. Ask any sleight-of-hand magician if the human eye can be fooled. Their profession rests on our gullibility. That's why the Christian walks by faith and not by sight.

Few would deny that regular walking is good for our health. It keeps our body fit for use. And it is spiritually healthy to "walk" by faith. We who walk as Christians do so because we want to go somewhere. There is a planned destination that keeps us moving. We walk through this world because it's not our home. Faith instead sets its gaze on the heavenly home for which we yearn, and the Scriptures help to energize our walk. But we don't want to go to heaven alone. While we walk through this world, we also reach out to it with the gospel. The book of Psalms begins by promising the blessing of God will be upon those who refuse to walk in the counsel of the ungodly. Our walk is away from this evil world because our destination is a city of God that cannot be moved.

Father, let this day be a day in which I draw closer to you and walk in faith every moment.

Hope-Filled Faith

May the God of hope fill you with all joy
and peace in believing.

ROMANS 15:13 ESV

The apostle Paul's desire was that the God of hope would fill believers with "all" joy and peace as a result of believing. Our joy and our peace shouldn't be subject to our surroundings. We must hold on to both in the storms because that peace guards our hearts and minds (Philippians 4:7) and the joy of the Lord is our strength (Nehemiah 8:10). But Paul didn't stop there. He wanted those who believe to then abound in hope. In other words, he desired that their faith would magnify their hope. The word *hope* in the English language is a weak word, but biblically it is an anchor to the soul. It keeps us steadfast in Christ.

The Bible calls God "the God of hope." He is the One in whom we put our expectation. Faith is like a great helium balloon that quietly lifts us above our trials so that we can see our destination. It is what we then see that gives us peace and joy in believing. Our faith in Jesus isn't lifted by our own effort. It is lifted above this life because of the power of the Holy Spirit, who works in and through us.

Thank you, Lord, for giving me the help of the Holy Spirit—to give me power to live in this life and prepare for the next.

A Tossed Sea

Let him ask in faith, with no doubting,
for the one who doubts is like a wave of the sea
that is driven and tossed by the wind.

JAMES 1:6 ESV

A driven and tossed sea has no form. It is an entirely unpredictable mess. It's the very opposite of the quiet and still waters promised to those who don't doubt the promises of God (see Psalm 23:2). Faith rests its head in sleep in the storm while doubt panics in fear. And so it should. If we doubt the integrity of God, our whole faith crumbles in a second. Scripture warns, "He who does not believe God has made Him a liar" (1 John 5:10). In contrast, we are promised "perfect peace" if we keep our mind on God (see Isaiah 26:3).

When we doubt the exceeding great and precious promises of God, our hope vanishes, and our joy and peace leave with it and slam the door. May our faith always be like perfectly tranquil water, reflecting the glorious heavens and the shimmering sunlight of the love of God. It is in that calm and quiet that we come before God knowing that he hears our every prayer. This is our example: "Jesus lifted up His eyes and said, 'Father, I thank You that You have heard Me'" (John 11:41).

Father, I ask today that you grant me faith and keep my mind peacefully on you.

Without Faith

Without faith it is impossible to please Him,
for he who comes to God must believe that He is.
HEBREWS 11:6

Contrary to popular worldly opinion, the Bible tells us that an atheist isn't wise. It says that he is a fool (see Psalm 14:1). To believe that there's no God is to believe the scientific impossibility that nothing created everything. It is easy to believe that God "is" because creation is. It is stark evidence of his creative genius. Eyes, not faith, are all we need to know that God exists: "The invisible things of him from the creation of the world are clearly seen" (Romans 1:20 KJV).

Without faith it's impossible to please anyone. Try it sometime. Tell your boss that you have no faith in him or her and see how long you keep your job. Tell your spouse you don't have any faith in him or her, and you've sowed seeds that could end in a divorce. Lose faith in a friend and you will lose that friendship. Faith is the glue that holds jobs, marriages, and friendships together. Telling a friend or associate that you are full of faith at the conclusion of a letter was once standard practice. "Yours faithfully" meant that you wanted their trust. God wrote "Yours faithfully" to us in the blood of his Son.

Father, may I be ever faithful. I live to hear the words, "Well done, good and faithful servant."

Seeing God

Jesus said to her, "Did I not say to you that if you would
believe you would see the glory of God?"
JOHN 11:40

In today's verse, Jesus was telling Martha to remember
what he had told her. She would see the glory of God. The
apostle Paul said that he wanted to stir up his hearers by
way of remembrance (see 2 Peter 3:1). Remembering can
strengthen our faith in times of trial and relieve us of the
stress of worry. The glory of God in this case was the raising
of Lazarus from the dead. That was glorious.

The moment any of us truly believes is like seeing the
first rays of the early morning sun. The reality of God dawns
on us as we look at his handiwork. He opens the eyes of our
understanding so that we see the Maker through what he
has made. But the most glorious hour will come when the
sun fully rises. On that day we will see him face-to-face. The
gospel made us pure, and Jesus said that the pure in heart
will actually see God (see Matthew 5:8). It is on that day that
we will remember his words: "Did I not say to you that if you
would believe you would see the glory of God?"

*Father, I long for the day when I will see you, but meanwhile,
I will joyfully walk by faith knowing that day will come.*

I Shall Not Want

"If you can believe,
all things are possible to him who believes."
MARK 9:23

While it certainly is true that all things are possible to those who believe, it doesn't necessarily mean that we are going to get everything, as some preachers affirm. Jesus spoke these words to the desperate father of a demon-possessed child. Jesus was saying that if we believe, anything is possible, but he was not giving us a blank check—an unconditional promise that whatever we want we can have if we can just muster up enough faith. The Savior puts to death monster of continually wanting more, bigger, and better. It's crucified with Christ.

The Scriptures warn, "You ask and do not receive, because you ask wrongly, to spend it on your passions" (James 4:3 ESV). The key to understanding what seems to be an open promise is that when we come to the Savior, our desires completely change. Our "wants" become the same as what God wants. We whisper, "Not my will but yours be done." He writes his law upon our hearts and causes us to walk in his statutes. So instead of selfishly wanting things, we now say, "The LORD is my shepherd; *I shall not want*" (Psalm 23:1 ESV, emphasis added).

Father, you alone are my heart's desire. I want only you and what you want for me. Help me to be free from greed.

The Testing of Our Faith

Knowing that the testing of your faith
produces patience.

JAMES 1:3

The word *knowing* is very telling. It speaks of an ongoing knowledge that all believers should expect regular problems. In Acts, Paul was "strengthening and establishing the hearts of the disciples; encouraging them to remain firm in the faith, saying, 'It is through many tribulations and hardships that we must enter the kingdom of God'" (Acts 14:22 AMP). We should always be knowledgeable as to *why* trials come our way. If we don't know the reason, it won't be long until we are discouraged.

The testing of our faith reveals to us the depth of our godly character. If our faith is strong, we will be patient, and we will even be able to rejoice in tribulation. But if our faith is weak, we will become impatient, prone to complaining, frustrated, and stressed. Therefore, we must be careful to remember that negative trials produce a positive end. They produce that which is highly prized in the sight of God and that will give us comfort in our lion's den. And in that fiery trial, we can rejoice knowing that all things work together for good because we love God and are called according to his purpose (see Romans 8:28).

Father, may I be mentally prepared for today's trials, small or large, knowing that you allow them because you are the lover of my soul and wish to see my faith grow.

Whom Having Not Seen

Though now you do not see Him, yet believing,
you rejoice with joy inexpressible.
1 PETER 1:8

A skeptic could well ask, "How can we love someone we cannot see?" True, we can't see Jesus with our natural eyes. He dwells in blinding light that is unapproachable (see 1 Timothy 6:16). But we can see the love of the cross. We can see his love expressed in that supreme sacrifice, and we love him because he first loved us.

He first loved us in creating us. He loved us by giving us eyes to see his marvelous creation—the sunlight, the deep blue skies, and big puffy white clouds. He loved us by giving us ears to enjoy good music and the sound of the birds in the morning. He loved us by giving us puppies and kittens, trees and flowers, fruits and an endless array of delicious food, and the stars in the heavens. He made us in his image and gave us the joy-filled ability to reproduce after our own kind. And he loved us by giving us a glorious hope of the future— because of the cross of Calvary. How could we not return that love with all of our heart, mind, soul, and strength?

Father, I love you. You are my Lord and Savior, my God and King, the lover of my soul.

The Glorious Hope

"I am the resurrection and the life.
He who believes in Me, though he may die, he shall live."
JOHN 11:25

If we believe that Jesus is the Christ and trust him with our eternal salvation, it changes everything. We are made new in Christ. Our faith slams shut the gates of hell and swings open wide the doors of heaven. It means we will live because he lives. We have a glorious hope in Christ, and we don't sorrow as this world sorrows in the face of death. Scripture says of the believer, "Though he may die, he shall live!" No other religion dares promise any such thing. And what other religion could back such a fantastic claim with power? But Jesus does.

Think of what he said: "I am the resurrection and the life." That is utterly profound. He is the resurrection. He is the one who will call all humanity from their graves with his voice (see John 5:28). He is the life source. The life we possess is ours because he gave us part of himself. He breathed life into us. "All things were through by Him, and without Him nothing was made" (John 1:3). Such thoughts are mind-boggling but true. If we believe that Jesus is the Christ, it changes everything…in this life and the next.

Father, I believe that Jesus is my only hope of resurrection, and my trust is entirely in him.

This Is Our Victory

Whatever is born of God
overcomes the world.

1 JOHN 5:4

This evil world, like a massive tidal wave of filth, seeks to overcome the Christian—to drown every one of us in sin. Soap operas, watched by millions of people, are neither operas nor are they clean. They drip with lust because it sells. It gets attention. The Bible says, "By means of a harlot, a man is reduced to a crust of bread" (Proverbs 6:26). And we see lust everywhere from billboards to social media to television, movies, book covers, and magazines. Add to that the incessant battle we have with the demonic underworld, and we can easily feel overcome by the tidal wave—from without and from within.

But when faith makes its entrance, it lifts us above the world, the flesh, and the devil. The Scriptures tell us that we have "escaped the corruption that is in the world through lust" (2 Peter 1:4). A living trust in the living God takes us like Noah's ark and lifts us high above the ocean of filth, and it will eventually lead us to ultimate victory of a new world wherein dwells righteousness.

Father, I long for the day when the evil that surrounds me comes to an end. Thank you for the hope we have in Jesus.

He Who Is Weak

Receive one who is weak in the faith,
but not to disputes over doubtful things.
ROMANS 14:1

Part of being a peacemaker is to know when not to speak. Our mouths are often the cause of unwanted trouble. The Scriptures warn, "Whoso keepeth his mouth and his tongue keepeth his soul from troubles" (Proverbs 21:23 KJV).

Godly wisdom is peaceable. It doesn't push its own pet doctrines that have proven to cause division within the body of Christ. How easy it is to be a spiritual bully when I'm speaking to a new Christian. If I want him to believe as I believe, think as I think, and do as I do, it can lead to disputes over things that aren't important. A new Christian may have a conviction that God doesn't want him to eat meat while those of us who are stronger in the faith know that every creature of God is good and that we shouldn't refuse anything if we receive it with a thankful attitude (see 1 Timothy 4:4). Rather than bully others and push our convictions on them, sometimes it's best to hold our tongue and be gentle because the new Christian is a babe in Christ who will mature in time.

Father, help me to always have my speech seasoned with salt, especially toward those who are new to the faith.

Running from Sin

You, O man of God, flee these things and pursue righteousness, godliness, faith, love, patience, gentleness.

1 TIMOTHY 6:11

Paul has just said, "The love of money is a root of all kinds of evil, for which some have strayed from the faith in their greediness, and pierced themselves through with many sorrows" (v. 10). And now he instructs the Christian to run from the deception of greed. It promises pleasure, but in the long run, it brings pain. Greed is spiritual gluttony, and it comes with special problems.

But as Christians, we are no longer our own. We now belong to God, and so we don't indulge. We are different from this money-obsessed and evil world. We are fleeing from it and at the same time earnestly looking forward to the next life. Like Lot and his fleeing family, we are quickly leaving Sodom. We have been warned to flee from the wrath that is to come. And God forbid that we should ever turn around and, like Lot's unwise wife, longingly look back at this sinful world. Instead, we look for a city whose Maker is God (see Hebrews 11:10). And we set our sights on righteousness, godliness, love, patience, and gentleness. We always strive to do that which is right in God's eyes. These are the good fruits of loving and knowing God.

Father, help me to keep my eyes on you and on the kingdom that cannot be moved.

Go Your Way

Jesus said…"Go your way; your faith has made you well."
And immediately he received his sight.

MARK 10:52

Go your way, dear Christian. You are no longer a prisoner of
sin and death. Go your way because in Christ, your Maker
has allowed you your freedom to do what you will. You
are a unique individual whose faith in Jesus has made you
whole. It's your way, and it's your life. That's God's gift to you
because he's good and kind. It is therefore your choice to
sing, dance, love, laugh, work, and play.

But something special happened when Jesus opened
your eyes. Although you have the freedom to live out your
life as you want, the eyes of your understanding have been
enlightened as to what really matters, and you, therefore,
don't want to go your own way. You want to serve the Master.
Your desire for legitimate pleasure has been tempered with
an overwhelming desire to follow Jesus. The blind man who
received his sight could have gone to his house, but he chose
not to do so. He wanted to be with Jesus—to follow him and
to see what he was going to do next. That's our choice today.
Do we stay home, or do we reach out to the lost and see what
God does? Do that and you'll experience the abundant life.

*Father, nothing gives me more joy that belonging to and
serving you.*

There's No Confusion

As many as received Him, to them He gave the right
to become children of God.

JOHN 1:12

The world wrongly assumes that all human beings are
naturally God's children. While he is our Creator, the Bible
tells us that he's not our Father. We are not his children until
we are supernaturally born into his family, and that happens
when we are born again through faith in Jesus.

A Christian is someone who has received Jesus
Christ. Receiving him isn't the same as receiving a message
or a compliment. Salvation is when we receive him as a
person. When that happens, we pass from death to life. The
Scriptures speak of salvation being in the person of Jesus. We
are told that "Christ…is our life" (Colossians 3:4) and that
"He who has the Son has life" (1 John 5:12). The Scriptures
say that those have the right to become God's children "who
were born, not of blood, nor of the will of the flesh, nor of
the will of man, but of God" (John 1:13). We are all born of
the flesh through natural birth, but when we are born again,
we are born of God. It is then that we are sealed by the Holy
Spirit as one of his own. This experience is the difference
between life and death, heaven and hell. Therefore, all of us
must make sure that we are one of his.

*Father, thank you for sending your Son so that I can be truly
born again and sealed by your Holy Spirit.*

Bruise His Heel

"He shall bruise your head,
and you shall bruise His heel."
GENESIS 3:15

Way back in human history—at the tragic entrance of sin and death—we were given the hope of the gospel. Here is the first promise of our redemption, the promise of the coming Messiah. Jesus would fatally bruise Satan's head, and Satan would bruise the heel of the Savior through the suffering of the cross. It was because of the consequent resurrection that Jesus then ripped from the devil the keys to death and hell and set the captives free. The Scriptures say, "Since therefore the children share in flesh and blood, he himself likewise partook of the same things, that through death he might destroy the one who has the power of death, that is, the devil, and deliver all those who through fear of death were subject to lifelong slavery" (Hebrews 2:14–15 ESV).

Look at who now holds the keys: "I am He who lives, and was dead, and behold, I am alive forevermore. Amen. And I have the keys of Hades and of Death" (Revelation 1:18). Satan was always behind Jesus. When he tempted Jesus, Jesus told the devil to get behind him (see Luke 4:5–8). Satan couldn't stop Jesus from the mission to bring us salvation. All the devil could do was bruise Jesus' heel.

Father, I praise you for Jesus' victory and power over death and the devil. I have no need to fear.

The Beautiful Reminder

"I set My rainbow in the cloud, and it shall be for the sign of
the covenant between Me and the earth."

GENESIS 9:13

The number seven has special significance in Scripture. It
signifies completeness. There are seven continents, seven
seas, and red, orange, yellow, green, blue, indigo, and violet
make up the seven colors of the rainbow. Think about its
amazing design. The same colors, like a curved colorful,
seven-lane highway, always manifest in the same order.
These seven colors arc across the heavens when there is
moisture in the air and remind us of the faithfulness of
our Creator. Wherever there is a cloud (if there is sunlight
present), we can catch a glimpse of a rainbow because the
light reflects off tiny water droplets in the air. This is why
rainbows always form directly opposite the position of the
sun in the sky.

The rainbow extends from the earth, up to the
heavens, and back down to the earth, reminding us that (as
the Scriptures say) it is the sign of the covenant between
heaven and the earth. May you and I (as tiny parts of the
church) be a colorful rainbow in this dark and cloudy world.
May we always reflect the character of the one who is light
itself—his seven virtues of love, mercy, grace, righteousness,
justice, truth, and goodness.

*Father, even in the midst of a thunderstorm, the rainbow
reminds me of your faithfulness.*

The Promise to Abraham

"I will make you a great nation;
I will bless you and make your name great."
GENESIS 12:2

One of the most wonderful and unique properties of the Bible is its incredible continuity. Where it creates a theme, for thousands of years, multiple writers uphold that theme, whether it's faith, morality, the character of God, righteousness, or the sin of man. The Scriptures from beginning to end also speak of the faithfulness of God to keep his word. Our very salvation rests on this truth—that he cannot lie.

This was God's steadfast promise to Abraham, but it is just one of thousands of promises that Scripture calls "exceedingly great and precious promises" (2 Peter 1:4) that are open to every believer in Jesus. These are exceedingly great and precious because they are trustworthy. Any promise is only as good as the one making the promise, and God is the promiser. When he gives us a promise of provision in this life—to supply all our needs according to his riches in glory—we can believe it. And when he gives the promise of life in the next, we know it to be true. This is why we preach the gospel with great boldness. We know that God backs up his word with power.

Father, thank you for your powerful, reliable promises. Help me to share the gospel and those promises with others.

God Came Down

"I have come down to deliver them
out of the hand of the Egyptians."
EXODUS 3:8

The Bible makes a big deal out of God delivering Israel from the hands of those who had enslaved them. Their deliverance from the hands of the enemy is repeated throughout the Psalms. There's good reason for this. What happened to Israel foreshadows our redemption from death. We were once enslaved by sin. It is a hard taskmaster, making us make bricks without straw (the Scriptures say the way of the transgressor is hard [see Proverbs 13:15]).

But in Christ, God came down to deliver us from the hand of the enemy. And he did so in the same way he delivered Israel from Egypt. He sent the Ten Commandments to reveal his glory and to show us our sin (Romans 3:19, 20; 7:7, 13). When we apply his blood (the blood of the Lamb) to our lives, death passes over us. In Jesus, death loses its terrible sting: "O death, where is thy sting? O grave, where is thy victory? The sting of death is sin; and the strength of sin is the law. But thanks be to God, which giveth us the victory through our Lord Jesus Christ" (1 Corinthians 15:55–57 KJV). And now, we are heading toward the promised land of the coming kingdom.

Father, thank you for coming down to this sinful earth to deliver me from sin and death.

The Headwind

"I will certainly be with you."
EXODUS 3:12

When I was a child, I unfortunately lived on the wrong side of town. Almost every morning, I would have a headwind as I rode my bike three miles to school. And almost every afternoon the wind would change so that I had a headwind as I rode my bike home. It was disheartening. Before we come to Christ, God is against us. We cannot please him while we are still in our sins; life is a continual headwind. However, when we are born again, we move to the right side of town. God is no longer against us because of our sins. He makes us "accepted in the Beloved" (Ephesians 1:6). We are no longer enemies in our minds because of wicked works. He will certainly be with us. We have proof of that through the cross: "What shall we then say to these things? If God be for us, who can be against us? He that spared not his own Son, but delivered him up for us all, how shall he not with him also freely give us all things?" (Romans 8:31–32 KJV).

While it may seem as if life is a continual headwind, we must never forget that God is for us. And that's all that matters.

Father, when the winds of adversity blow against me, help me to remember that you are always on my side because of the cross.

The Little Big Word

"If you diligently heed the voice of the Lord your God
and do what is right in His sight…"

Exodus 15:26

The word *if* is often used in a negative sense. When
something terrible happens to us, we look back and say, "If
only I had done this differently." However, the Scriptures
often use that same little word in a positive sense. God told
Israel that *if* they diligently listened to his voice and did that
which was right, certain positive things would happen. Jesus
used it in a positive way when he said, "If ye continue in my
word, then are ye my disciples indeed; and ye shall know
the truth, and the truth shall make you free" (John 8:31–32
KJV). Peter told believers, "If ye do these things, ye shall
never fall" (2 Peter 1:10 KJV). Jesus also said, "If ye love me,
keep my commandments" (John 14:15 KJV).

If always has consequences, sometimes good and
sometimes bad. Therefore, we should make sure we don't have
an "if" moment at the end of our lives, lamenting, "If only I
had served the Lord with more of a commitment." Today, use
if in a positive way. Look at all the wonderful promises of God
and say, "If I do my part, then God will do his."

*Father, all I desire is your smile on my life. May I be quick to
fulfill conditions that guarantee your blessing.*

On Eagles' Wings

"How I bore you on eagles' wings
and brought you to Myself."
EXODUS 19:4

God carried Israel on eagle's wings, and he had a destination. He carried them to himself. If the lion is king of the beasts, the eagle is doubtless king of the birds. God created the eagle in a majestic form, along with a kingly profile, and he crowned it with superior strength. An eagle's eyesight is around five times better than human vision, and it has the ability to see up to almost two miles away. Although eagles can soar at altitudes of fifteen thousand feet, they fly in long glides to conserve energy and can reach speeds of up to one hundred miles per hour.

But there's more here than the amazing wonder of the eagle. We can find comfort in the fact that it was God himself who lovingly took Israel in his capable hands and carried them to himself. And our Creator carefully and capably both carried and preserved us in Christ. He sought us, saved us, keeps us, and promises to never ever leave us or forsake us. On top of that, his Word tells us that nothing can separate us from his unfailing love. Not even death itself: "Nor height, nor depth, nor any other creature, shall be able to separate us from the love of God, which is in Christ Jesus our Lord" (Romans 8:39 KJV).

Father, take me high on eagles' wings and carry me closer to yourself.

February

Commandment with Promise

"Honor your father and your mother,
that your days may be long."
Exodus 20:12

The law was given to stop every mouth and leave the whole world guilty before God (see Romans 3:19). And this commandment is a mouth-stopper. Which of us, particularly in our teenage years, hasn't in some way dishonored our parents—through disobedience, a bad attitude, or back talk? But violation of the ordinance can be indirect. When David sinned with Bathsheba (by committing adultery and murder), he also dishonored his parents' good name. Many a son or daughter has publicly shamed his or her parents because of sin. Or we can dishonor them in their old age through neglect or by a resentful or contemptuous attitude. This commandment comes with a promise that the New Testament reiterates: "Honour thy father and mother; which is the first commandment with promise; that it may be well with thee, and thou mayest live long on the earth" (Ephesians 6:2–3 KJV).

If we want all to be well and to live long lives, we should carefully note the promise of long life and well-being. And we would be wise to always honor our parents not only because they deserve honor but also because God himself has commanded this.

Father, thank you for giving me a promise with this command. Help me to always honor my parents in deed, in attitude, and in memory.

God Is Love

"God so loved the world
that He gave His only begotten Son."
JOHN 3:16

Ask anyone to describe the nature of God, and most will say that he is love. And they are right. The Bible does say that God is love (see 1 John 4:8). However, to believe that he is love but to then deny that he is a God of justice, of truth, and of righteousness is to make a great mistake. If he is only love, then there is no need for a judgment day. Any human being who is said to be all love with no sense of justice would be unbalanced. Human love cannot be separated from a love of justice.

John 3:16 tells us that it was love that moved God to give his only begotten Son to be crucified at the hands of a cruel world. Jesus was manifest because the Father loved justice, and he also loved the world. Love of justice mingled with a love of mercy resulted in the horror of the cross and our salvation. "God, who is rich in mercy, for his great love wherewith he loved us, even when we were dead in sins, hath quickened us together with Christ" (Ephesians 2:4–5 KJV). It was because God is rich in mercy that we became rich in Christ.

Father, may your love in me cause me to give myself for this world. Help me to reach others with the gospel.

Use Your Stress

How long, O LORD?
Will You forget me forever?
PSALM 13:1 NASB95

The Pharisees at the time of Christ dishonored the law so that it lost its power. In the Sermon on the Mount, Jesus lifted up the law and showed us that God requires truth in our inward hearts. In the same most famous of sermons, he spoke of being free from worry and stress by trusting in God. However, not all stress is bad. Leonard Bernstein said, "To achieve great things, two things are needed: a plan and not quite enough time." Sometimes stress can push us to achieve great things. More often than not, life's pressures can send us to God for the peace that only he can give. Therefore, it's not the stress that is good or bad but what we do with it.

Psalm 13 is typical of David's approach to stress in the psalms. The beginning of Psalm 13 shows that David was going through a rough patch. He was full of sadness (v. 2) and was in great stress, in fear for his life, in fact (vv. 3–4). But this stress pushed him to cry out to God, creating this psalm. By the end of the psalm, David still had not been delivered yet, but he was expectantly awaiting it, trusting in God: "I have trusted in Your lovingkindness; My heart shall rejoice in Your salvation" (Psalm 13:5 NASB95).

Father, remind me to always let stress drive me closer to you.

Lord, I Believe

"He who hears My word and believes in Him who sent Me…
has passed from death into life."

JOHN 5:24

To call myself a "believer" and not believe that I am saved from death is an oxymoron. A believer has faith in the promises of God. And the natural fruit of believing is peace. We have peace in the knowledge that the Beloved has accepted us, that we have passed from death unto life, and that our names are written in heaven. To not believe God's promises is to accuse him of being a liar (see 1 John 5:10). Childlike faith (faith without question) is the first principle of Christianity: "I assure you and most solemnly say to you, unless you repent [that is, change your inner self—your old way of thinking, live changed lives] and become like children [trusting, humble, and forgiving], you will never enter the kingdom of heaven" (Matthew 18:3 AMP).

We may question many essential doctrines and interpretations of prophecy to make sure we believe correctly, but we should never question the integrity of our Creator. "Without faith it is impossible to please him: for he that cometh to God must believe that he is, and that he is a rewarder of them that diligently seek him" (Hebrews 11:6 KJV).

Father, I will never doubt your integrity. I believe every promise you've made.

Abiding Satisfied

"I am the bread of life;
whoever comes to me shall not hunger."
JOHN 6:35 ESV

While common, everyday bread is a staple of life, Scripture tells us that man does not live by it alone, "but by every word that proceeds from the mouth of God" (Matthew 4:4). Those who eat natural bread will perish, but those who eat the bread of life will live forever. Without coming to Jesus and spiritually eating the bread of life, sinners will perish.

Until we came to the savior, we directed our energies at the attainment of happiness. That's the goal of most in life. No one in his or her right mind wants to be unhappy. We commit ourselves to entertainment, or watching sports, making money, or raising a family. These things are legitimate and can give a measure of satisfaction. However, Solomon achieved all the successes and pleasures in life and came to the conclusion that they were all just chasing of the wind. They were vain pursuits because of the reality of death. Until that ultimate problem is solved, we will be chasing the wind. And it's solved when we fear God and partake of the bread of life. In Jesus the hunger stops: "The fear of the LORD tendeth to life: and he that hath it shall abide satisfied; he shall not be visited with evil" (Proverbs 19:23 KJV).

Father, I am satisfied in you. I no longer hunger for life because you are the life of my soul.

We Are No Longer Slaves

> "If the Son sets you free,
> you will be free indeed."
> JOHN 8:36 ESV

Be careful of those who maintain that you can be a Christian and still serve sin. When the Bible speaks of being "free indeed," it is speaking of being free from the power of sin. Just before Jesus spoke of the Son making us free, he said, "Truly, truly, I say to you, everyone who practices sin is a slave to sin. The slave does not remain in the house forever; the son remains forever" (John 8:34–35 ESV). When we come to the Savior, he saves us from our sins. We are new creatures in Christ. Old things pass away and all things become new (see 2 Corinthians 5:17). We, of course, battle sin daily, but we never surrender to its power. The Amplified Bible says of John 8:34, "I assure you and most solemnly say to you, everyone who practices sin habitually is a slave of sin."

If we fall into sin, we quickly rise up. We are quick to confess our sins and turn from them in sincere repentance. To fail to do so is to play the hypocrite. Through the new birth, God has given us a new heart that is now turned toward obeying and pleasing him rather than ourselves (see 2 Corinthians 5:9; Romans 8:5–6). We are no longer slaves.

Father, thank you for setting me free from sin. Never let me serve sin again.

We Can Say "Never"

"Most assuredly, I say to you, if anyone keeps My word
he shall never see death."
JOHN 8:51

What a great stumbling block the words of Jesus are to
a proud soul! How could they be true? These are even
offensive words because they offer false hope to the simple.
Only a fool would believe such folly when death is so
evident, so says the skeptic.

Jesus obviously knew that his words would be
offensive because he began with "most assuredly." Then he
opened up salvation universally. He said "anyone." Anyone
who keeps his word will never see death. How good and
kind God is to reach out his hand in Christ and save us from
death. Our salvation is more than a quick decisional prayer.
It is a total yielding of our lives on the altar of sacrifice.
Those who repent and give Jesus their all will keep his word
because God has given them a heart to do so. Then notice
the word *never*. Those who trust alone in Jesus Christ will
never see death. Never. In Christ, death has been swallowed
up. It has been destroyed, and we are more than conquerors
through him who loved us. Oh what an amazing Savior!
What glorious consolation. Thanks be to God for the
unspeakable gift.

Father, I will never see death because of your amazing grace.

They Know His Voice

"He goes before them, and the sheep follow him,
for they know his voice."
JOHN 10:4 ESV

As we travel through this pain-filled life, the Good Shepherd goes before us. He knows our future, and in his great faithfulness, he directs our paths. This happens because we long to do his will and are, therefore, committed to follow him. And we can follow him because we know his voice. This doesn't necessarily mean we hear the audible voice of God.

When God spoke to Israel, they were terrified. When he spoke to Jesus, those nearby thought they had heard thunder. While some maintain that they have heard the audible voice of God, it is more common to listen to his voice through his Word. The Scriptures say that God's Word is a lamp to our feet and a light to our path. He directs us through his Word. God also speaks to us through the voice of our conscience. It tells us if something is right or wrong. We can also learn the mind of God through listening to godly council. The wisdom of the godly can help us hear his voice, and we can know what is acceptable to God through good old-fashioned common sense. The Scriptures tell us, "The lips of the righteous know what is acceptable" (Proverbs 10:32).

Father, help me to always be sensitive to hearing your voice and knowing your will for my life.

The Only Door

"I am the door.
If anyone enters by Me,
he will be saved."
JOHN 10:9

Saved is a word many Christian's hesitate to use because the word has negative connotations. It insinuates that some people are *unsaved*. And even if we acknowledge that some people have been saved, confusion often exists about what we are saved from. Some testify about being saved from drug abuse, some from a life of drunkenness, and others have been saved from a life of crime. The result has been that for many, Christianity is nothing more than some sort of philosophical life improvement.

The Scriptures, however, make it clear that when we come to the Savior, we are saved "from the wrath to come" (1 Thessalonians 1:10). That message is offensive because it paints God as being angry at sinners. Offensive though it may be, we must never waver in our testimony to this world that Jesus saves from death and consequent damnation in hell. And the world seems even more offended when we say that he is the only door to salvation.

But those who are offended by this miss the point: God gave us a door. What undeserved kindness and love!

Father, thank you for giving me a way to you. Help me to be a true and faithful witness of your love.

Our Blessed Assurance

"No one is able to snatch them
out of the Father's hand."
JOHN 10:29 ESV

Misunderstandings are the landmines of Christian warfare.
One landmine that we often step on and that has caused
great damage within the church is the doctrine of "once
saved, always saved." To address this belief, we must step
carefully to avoid misunderstandings. Some take this to
an extreme by maintaining that anytime someone walks
forward at an altar call, they can be assured of their salvation
even if they never truly repent and live a new life. In other
words, they believe you can sin your heart out and still be
assured of salvation.

The way to remove the landmine is to change the
phrase to "*If* saved, always saved." Many who profess faith
in Jesus are false converts. But if someone truly repents and
puts their trust in Jesus, they will bring forth fruits worthy
of salvation, and that means that they will continually turn
from sin. In doing so, they can have absolute assurance that
they have been saved, are being saved, and will be saved.
They can have total confidence that God who has begun a
good work in them will complete it. No one will pluck them
out of God's hand because the evident fruit shows that they
are truly born again.

*Father, I thank you for keeping me safe and for the knowledge
that no one can snatch me out of your hand.*

Seeking the Honor of God

"If anyone serves Me,
him My Father will honor."
JOHN 12:26

When the Prodigal Son returned to his father, he pleaded with his father to employ him as a servant. He came destitute, with the knowledge that he had sinned against his father and against God: "The son said unto him, Father, I have sinned against heaven, and in thy sight, and am no more worthy to be called thy son" (Luke 15:21 KJV).

This knowledge produced deep sorrow for his sin and humility of heart. Sadly, many today don't see their sin and, therefore, come to see God as their servant. He becomes the means by which they succeed in life. He is the key to their prosperity. In reality, when we are born again, we become servants of Christ, and our mission is to take the gospel to this lost and dying world. The questions we should ask ourselves each day are, "What am I going to do today to serve Jesus? Am I going to live for myself or for his will?"

It is in service of the Master that we find freedom from stress even in weakness and in the midst of trials. Paul said, "I am well content with weaknesses, with insults, with distresses, with persecutions, with difficulties, for Christ's sake; for when I am weak, then I am strong" (2 Corinthians 12:10 NASB95).

Father, help me today to serve Jesus by seeking to save that which is lost.

Safe in Jesus

"Now is the judgment of this world."
JOHN 12:31 ESV

Jesus was speaking of the cross when he said this. His next words were, "Now will the ruler of this world be cast out. And I, when I am lifted up from the earth, will draw all people to myself" (vv. 31–32 ESV). Because I am a believer, my judgment day is over. My case has been dismissed. Because Jesus was lifted up from the earth and crucified from my sins, I have "Paid in Full" stamped across my file. The accuser of the brethren can't point a finger at me because I am safe in Jesus.

The moment Jesus cried, "It is finished," Satan was finished also. The prince of this world was cast down because of the cross and the consequent resurrection of the Savior. And so every believer in Jesus can have boldness on the day of judgment: "Herein is our love made perfect, that we may have boldness in the day of judgment: because as he is, so are we in this world" (1 John 4:17 KJV). And that boldness can be exerted in prayer. The Bible says that because we trust in Jesus, "Let us therefore come boldly unto the throne of grace, that we may obtain mercy, and find grace to help in time of need" (Hebrews 4:16 KJV).

Father, it is with great confidence in the finished work of the cross that I seek you in prayer.

The Spotless Lamb

"I did not come to judge the world
but to save the world."
JOHN 12:47 ESV

We must never forget the reason that Jesus came to the earth the first time. He did not come in flaming fire, rendering his anger with fury upon this wicked world. He didn't come as the judge of the universe. He came as a harmless and spotless lamb, to die for the sin of the world. His words were gentle. His actions were loving because he came for the salvation of the world. This was the promise of the Old Testament, and its fulfillment was seen in the New Testament, culminating in the cross of Calvary. The law came by Moses, but grace and truth came by Jesus Christ. It is in that wonderful grace that we find not only peace with God but also the peace of God. However, the stress of daily life can easily steal our peace.

Listen to Isaiah 26:3: "Thou wilt keep him in perfect peace, whose mind is stayed on thee: because he trusteth in thee" (KJV). We have to stay our minds on God, trusting in him. That takes a continual discipline not to be distracted by the many little and sometimes big trials.

Father, help me to keep my mind on you and not be distracted by trials.

God's Will

"I will come again
and receive you to Myself."
JOHN 14:3

Whenever we say, "I will," we should always be quick to add, "if God wills." As fallible human beings, we are not always able to fulfill that which we desire to or to say what we will accomplish. Lions' dens, Red Seas, and other annoying circumstances can get in the way. But when God says, "I will," it is done. Jesus will come again. He will accomplish what he said he would do.

We can apply that certainty to every other statement in the Scriptures. When God says something, we can bank on it. Read this Scripture passage: "Be careful for nothing; but in every thing by prayer and supplication with thanksgiving let your requests be made known unto God. And the peace of God, which passeth all understanding, shall keep your hearts and minds through Christ Jesus" (Philippians 4:6–7 KJV). That means, if we give a problem to God in prayer, we leave it in his hands. And we can trust that the peace of God will keep our hearts and minds. God said so.

Father, I cast all my cares on you today.

What We Can Do

"Without Me you can do nothing."
JOHN 15:5

This is the reason each of us must continue in prayer. Prayer is a humble acknowledgement of our dependence on God. Trusting in the Lord is the only way to achieve that which will last. The most capable of us will eventually prove to be helpless and hopeless in the face of death without that dependence. Whatever we may think we achieve in life on that day will be futile. Understanding that truth is perhaps the greatest revelation any of us can have.

The context of today's verse is that Jesus is the true Vine and we are the branches. A branch that's not connected to the vine will in time wither and die. Therefore, our first and greatest priority in life must be making sure that we are in the Vine—that we are born again and trusting alone in Jesus. We must then make sure that we always acknowledge him in all our ways that he might guide our paths. "In all thy ways acknowledge him, and he shall direct thy paths" (Proverbs 3:6 KJV).

Remember today that Jesus is your Vine, giving you life and nutrients. He guides your paths and is with you to give you all you need. Trust in these truths today.

Father, never let me forget that without you, I am nothing and can do nothing.

The Word of Christ

If ye abide in me,
and my words abide in you...
JOHN 15:7 KJV

It is good to commit Scripture to memory, especially the words of Jesus. This is not only for our own edification and comfort but also for the sake of the unsaved to whom we testify. Scripture tells us that temple officers who were sent to arrest Jesus returned empty-handed, saying, "Never man spake like this man" (John 7:46 KJV). To commit the words of Jesus to memory and quote him to sinners will leave them saying the same thing. How could they not? His words are without precedent. The apostle Paul spoke of committing the words of Jesus to memory. He said, "Let the word of Christ dwell in you richly in all wisdom; teaching and admonishing one another in psalms and hymns and spiritual songs, singing with grace in your hearts to the Lord" (Colossians 3:16 KJV).

The psalmist had another reason for us to memorize God's Word in our hearts: "Thy word have I hid in mine heart, that I might not sin against thee" (Psalm 119:11 KJV). Jesus said, "If ye continue in my word, then are ye my disciples indeed; and ye shall know the truth, and the truth shall make you free" (John 8:31–32 KJV). God's Word is wisdom, keeps us from sin, teaches truth, and brings freedom. What a wonderful resource and beautiful gift!

Father, help me to discipline myself to continue in your Word and be a disciple indeed.

Joy That Remains

These things have I spoken unto you,
that my joy might remain in you.
JOHN 15:11 KJV

It's very interesting that when the Bible speaks of joy and peace, it gives their ownership to the Lord. Jesus said, "Peace I leave with you, *my* peace I give unto you: not as the world giveth" (John 14:27 KJV, emphasis added). The peace we have that passes all understanding is the peace of the Lord. And in today's verse, Jesus speaks of "my joy" being in the believer. The joy that dwells in us is the joy of the Lord, and the joy of the Lord is our strength (see Nehemiah 8:10). It is joy that helps us to overcome daily trials.

It was the words of Jesus that kept the joy within his disciples. It was when he spoke to two disciples on the road to Emmaus that their hearts burst with joy: "They said one to another, Did not our heart burn within us, while he talked with us by the way, and while he opened to us the scriptures?" (Luke 24:32 KJV). So as you walk with Jesus, soak your soul in the four Gospels. Read his words over and over and let the Spirit of Christ who dwells within you (see Romans 8:9) open the Scriptures and bring you joy.

Father, may I follow closer to Jesus and hear his voice, and may his joy give me strength to glorify your name.

All Who Live Godly

"If they persecuted Me,
they will also persecute you."
JOHN 15:20

This world harbors a lot of hate. Politicians are often hated because of their policies. Rich people are hated because of their riches. And Christians are hated because they love God and because they stand for righteousness. Jesus was persecuted from the moment he opened his gracious and eloquent mouth. The hatred came because men loved darkness rather than light, because their deeds were evil. If we belong to Jesus and we are unashamed of him, we will suffer persecution. If we are letting our light shine, somebody somewhere should be speaking ill of us. The Bible says, "*all* who desire to live godly in Christ Jesus *will* suffer persecution" (2 Timothy 3:12, emphasis added). However, it is an honor to be persecuted for Christ, and God even gives blessing and great reward to those who endure such difficult times.

Read the assurances of Jesus: "Blessed are they which are persecuted for righteousness' sake: for theirs is the kingdom of heaven. Blessed are ye, when men shall revile you, and persecute you, and shall say all manner of evil against you falsely, for my sake. Rejoice, and be exceeding glad: for great is your reward in heaven: for so persecuted they the prophets which were before you" (Matthew 5:10–12 KJV).

Father, I'm honored to suffer persecution for your name's sake.

Commanded to Rest

On the seventh day God finished his work that he had done, and he rested on the seventh day from all his work that he had done.

GENESIS 2:2 ESV

This day's gold nugget of a quote on how to live today without stress comes from Sydney J. Harris. He said, "The time to relax is when you don't have time for it." It reminds us of how the stresses of the day can be cumulative. We can overthink the cause of stress when all we need is to take a day off and take the time to relax. If God took the time to rest, so should we.

God made us to work, but he also knows our weakness: "He Himself knows our frame; He is mindful that we are but dust" (Psalm 103:14 NASB95). His commands are never a burden, but they are life. In Genesis he gave us his own example of resting, and in Exodus and Deuteronomy he commanded it: "Six days you shall labor and do all your work, but the seventh day is a sabbath of the LORD your God; in it you shall not do any work" (Deuteronomy 5:13–14 NASB95). In his law, he graciously required the rest that we need. This is a necessity for our bodies. And obeying this command is a faithful witness to the unbelieving world around us.

Father, never let me forget to be a true and faithful witness.

The Work of the Spirit

"He will guide you into all the truth."
JOHN 16:13 ESV

Who would deny that we are living in the last days, when Bible prophecy is lining up and pointing to the second coming of Jesus? Because of that glorious hope, these are exciting times. But they are also perilous days of darkness and deception—days where evil people will become worse and worse. That's why we need to listen closely to the voice of the Holy Spirit and persist in prayer. Jesus said that the Holy Spirit is the spirit of truth, and he will guide us into all truth. And the way to know the difference between truth and error is to know God's Word. Jesus said, "Your word is truth" (17:17 ESV).

As lowly human beings, sometimes we are at a loss when it comes to knowing how to pray. But we can trust the Holy Spirit to help us when we pray. The Scriptures enlighten us as to the work of the Spirit in our prayers: "Likewise the Spirit also helpeth our infirmities: for we know not what we should pray for as we ought: but the Spirit itself maketh intercession for us with groanings which cannot be uttered. And he that searcheth the hearts knoweth what is the mind of the Spirit, because he maketh intercession for the saints according to the will of God" (Romans 8:26–27 KJV).

Father, please guide me into all truth and help me to pray effectively.

Life's Continual Trials

"In the world you will have tribulation;
but be of good cheer, I have overcome the world."
JOHN 16:33

We have been born into a world of war. Millions have lost their lives when wicked men decided to attack another country. But the moment we were born again, we found ourselves in another type of warfare, spiritual warfare. In that war we have a threefold enemy: 1. The world with all its evil pleasures attracts our sinful heart. 2. The flesh craves the pleasures of sin. And 3. The devil tempts us and provokes us to give our flesh to the sinful world.

Every moment of every day is a battle. That's why in this world we will have tribulation. We will have trials that never seem to end. But God allows tribulation to come upon us because it causes us to grow in our faith. Harsh winds send the tree's roots deep into the soil. But our consolation is that this is a battle that has already been won. It was won the moment Jesus rose from the dead, defeating our greatest enemy, death itself. That's why of all the people in this world, we should be the most cheerful. Jesus said be of good cheer. Because he has overcome the world.

Father, help me to be cheerful in every situation because I know that you're working all things out for my good.

The Search for Eternal Life

"This is eternal life, that they may know You, the only true God, and Jesus Christ whom You have sent."

JOHN 17:3

Since the beginning of time, humanity has vainly searched for, hoped for, and craved for immortality. They have looked to the wisdom of men, secular science, man-made religion, cross-legged gurus, and vain worldly philosophy, but nothing has ever delivered. Death remained king. The grave kept its victory. Even though the gospel is a loud trumpet saying, "This is eternal life!" they refuse to listen. Tragedy of tragedies, little do they know that if they reject God and his Savior, they reject eternal life and embrace death.

In this one verse, Jesus clearly defines immortality. It isn't found in Eastern religion, worldly philosophy, or through men of science. It is found in a relationship with the Creator, the only true God, who revealed himself to Moses on Mount Sinai, thundered out his law, and then sent his Son, Jesus Christ, to fulfill the law, die in our place, and rise again, giving his righteousness to all who believe. Simple though this may be, it is a huge stumbling block to the proud of heart. Unless we humble ourselves and become as little children, we will not enter the kingdom of God. It's so simple and yet complex. So plain and yet so hidden.

Father, thank you for sending Jesus of Nazareth, the Savior, to save me from my sins.

Seeing Isn't Believing

"Blessed are those who have not seen
and yet have believed."
JOHN 20:29 ESV

Thomas refused to trust Jesus. He chose sight over faith. He said that unless he put his hand into the side of the Savior and his fingers into the nail holes in Jesus' hands, he would not believe. He robbed himself of the divine blessing. When we trust God in fiery trials, it honors him. Peter speaks of the blessedness of this trust: "That the trial of your faith, being much more precious than of gold that perisheth, though it be tried with fire, might be found unto praise and honour and glory at the appearing of Jesus Christ: Whom having not seen, ye love; in whom, though now ye see him not, yet believing, ye rejoice with joy unspeakable and full of glory" (1 Peter 1:7–8 KJV).

We haven't seen Jesus, and yet we love him, and we prove the reality of our love by trusting in his promises. Those who do so are blessed. "Beloved, we are [even here and] now children of God, and it is not yet made clear what we will be [after His coming]. We know that when He comes and is revealed, we will [as His children] be like Him, because we will see Him just as He is [in all His glory]" (1 John 3:2 AMP).

Father, I trust you today but long for the day when I will see you face-to-face.

Your Adversary, the Devil

"I will be an enemy to your enemies
and an adversary to your adversaries."
Exodus 23:22

God told Israel that if they walked in obedience to his will, he would fight for them. He would side with them and be an enemy to their enemies. The Israelites refused to keep his commandments and broke God's covenant with them. But God mercifully made a new covenant with all who will believe in his Son. Therefore, the heart of God expressed in this promise to the Israelites holds true for us today. As Christians, we are called to "love [our] enemies and pray for those who persecute [us]" (Matthew 5:44 NASB95), but we do have one enemy. The Scriptures call him "your adversary, the devil," and warn us that he "prowls around like a roaring lion, seeking someone to devour" (1 Peter 5:8 NASB95).

This passage in 1 Peter urges us to "resist him, firm in your faith" (v. 9 NASB95). We are called to war against this enemy. Ephesians 6 describes the battle armor we have: the "belt of truth," "breastplate of righteousness," "shield of faith," and "sword of the Spirit, which is the word of God" (vv. 14, 16, 17 ESV). Paul also tells us that we should be "praying at all times in the Spirit" (v. 18). Fight diligently against your enemy, with faith in God's promises and salvation and with constant prayer to him. And when you feel overwhelmed in this battle, remember: God is fighting for you as well, and he has already won the battle.

Father, keep me diligent in my spiritual battle.

The Life to Come

> "I will take sickness away
> from the midst of you."
> EXODUS 23:25

God promised Israel that if they would serve him, he would bless them with health and strength. The land wouldn't be barren, no one would experience the heartbreak of miscarriage, and there would be no sickness. Who in his right mind wouldn't want to embrace this promise? Imagine a life with no cancer or the thousands of other diseases that plague humanity. If only the world could see that sin is a deadly enemy and not a comforting friend. If only they would believe the Scriptures—that righteousness exalts a nation, followed by the blessing of God: "Blessed is the nation whose God is the LORD" (Psalm 33:12 KJV).

But the gospel is more than the promise of God's blessing in this life: godliness is profitable unto all things, "having promise of the life that now is, and of that which is to come" (1 Timothy 4:8 KJV). The godliness given to us in Christ gives us wonderful promises for this life and for the next. And even when we find ourselves in suffering, we can say with the apostle Paul, "I reckon that the sufferings of this present time are not worthy to be compared with the glory which shall be revealed in us" (Romans 8:18 KJV).

Father, thank you for the comfort of your promises for this life and for the life to come.

God's Presence

[The Lord] said, "My Presence will go with you,
and I will give you rest."
Exodus 33:14

While God is omnipresent (he dwells everywhere in the
universe and beyond), he could cause his presence to
actually go with Israel. The psalmist said of his presence:
"Whither shall I go from thy spirit? or whither shall I flee
from thy presence? If I ascend up into heaven, thou art there:
if I make my bed in hell, behold, thou art there. If I take the
wings of the morning, and dwell in the uttermost parts of the
sea; even there shall thy hand lead me, and thy right hand
shall hold me" (Psalm 139:7–10 KJV).

The Scriptures tell us that there is fullness of joy in the
presence of God (see Psalm 16:11). And here he promises
Israel that he will go with them and give them rest. Jesus
said, "Take my yoke upon you, and learn of me; for I am
meek and lowly in heart: and ye shall find rest unto your
souls" (Matthew 11:29 KJV). It is the presence of God in us
that gives us rest from our labors. Coming to Christ means
that we no longer have to labor to please him. We have
ceased from our labors because of the cross. What a burden
it is for those who are trusting in their own religious works
to save them. But for the Christian, it was enough when
Jesus said, "It is finished."

Father, I rest in the finished work of the cross.

Set It on a Pole

The LORD said to Moses, "Make a fiery serpent,
and set it on a pole."
NUMBERS 21:8

Any of the Israelites who looked at the fiery serpent were
healed of its bite. This is a wonderful picture of the coming
Messiah who would be lifted up onto a cross. Whoever looks
to him on that cross for their eternal salvation is healed from
the deadly bite of sin and death. Perhaps Jesus opened this
particular verse to the two disciples on the road to Emmaus:
"Beginning at Moses and all the prophets, he expounded
unto them in all the scriptures the things concerning
himself" (Luke 24:27 KJV). He certainly referred to this
verse with Nicodemus: "As Moses lifted up the serpent in
the wilderness, even so must the Son of man be lifted up:
that whosoever believeth in him should not perish, but have
eternal life" (John 3:14–15 KJV).

The curse of the law fell on Jesus, and whoever looks
to him in faith is freed from the curse. "Christ hath redeemed
us from the curse of the law, being made a curse for us: for
it is written, Cursed is every one that hangeth on a tree"
(Galatians 3:13 KJV). The "fiery serpent" is a reference to
the serpent's burning and painful bite. And that's what Jesus
endured on the cross for us—a terrifying baptism of fire.

Father, thank you for the cross of your only begotten Son.

The Blessing of Work

"Six days you shall labor
and do all your work."
EXODUS 20:9 NASB95

One of the primary sources of stress in most of our lives is
our work. The scope for stress at our jobs can be endless: we
have a boss to please, coworkers to collaborate with, clients
to satisfy, logistics to manage, or deadlines to meet. Work
is hard, no matter what occupation we work in. That's part
of living in a fallen world. The Scriptures make that clear
right away in Genesis when God cursed the ground and told
Adam that he would live by toil and sweat (Genesis 3:17–19).
Although a job well done provides satisfaction, it is still
difficult. It's toil. It causes stress.

But it's important to thank God for the gift of
employment and work. Our jobs allow us to provide for
ourselves, and hopefully they allow us to help others as well.
We should thank God for providing jobs to take care of our
needs. We should be grateful for the blessing of employment
and how it supplies our daily food.

*Father, thank you for my job. Please help me glorify you in my
work today.*

The Coming Law

Have no fellowship with the
unfruitful works of darkness.
EPHESIANS 5:11

Picture a father walking with a smile on his face toward his child who is eating a cookie. How does the child feel as he approaches? Perhaps the child is happy to see his father or curious about what he will say, but the child isn't fearful because he's not doing anything wrong. But how would the child feel if he'd been told he can't have a cookie until later, and his father was walking with a frown and the empty cookie jar in hand? No doubt the child will feel anxious to a point where he might want to hide.

This is why sinners run from God. Their guilt keeps them in the darkness, fearful of coming to the light because it exposes their evil deeds: "For every wrongdoer hates the Light, and does not come to the Light [but shrinks from it] for fear that his [sinful, worthless] activities will be exposed and condemned" (John 3:20 AMP). This is why we must be gentle when we speak to the lost. In a sense we use a light dimmer rather than a bright light as we talk to them about sin, righteousness, and judgment to come. May God give us courage to confront this evil world and help them to see their sin and the salvation in Jesus.

Father, help us to warn every man.

March

Love that Gives

God is love.

1 JOHN 4:8

Love gives. It gives of its own volition. The word *volition* comes from the Latin verb *velle*, meaning "to will" or "to wish." The word *voluntary* comes from the same source. Love doesn't give because it is forced to give. A man who loves gives flowers. He gives his beloved a ring, and then he gives of himself to the one he loves in holy matrimony. That's the nature of love. And yet human love has a measure of selfishness. We give to get. We want the affection of the one we love in return.

And that's the difference between human love and the love of God. God loved the world, but his love wasn't drawn out because we were attractive. We were the opposite. The Scriptures tell us that Christ died for us while we were still sinners (see Romans 5:6). Nothing in us was worthy of such love. But he loved us because he is the essence of love. And it was because of that great love that he gave his only begotten Son (John 3:16). He gave Jesus to suffering and death so that we could live forever. The Father displayed his love for us like the light of the noonday sun. Such is the love of God.

Father, help me to remember your love today, every moment.

The Lord Your God

> "The LORD your God will raise up for you
> a Prophet like me from your midst."
> DEUTERONOMY 18:15

When we count our blessings and name them one by one, number one in the blessing count should be for the fact that the Lord our God raised up a prophet like Moses from the midst of Israel. Thousands of years later, God kept his promise to raise up that prophet. He did it through his people, and he did it in a way that was similar to the way he raised up Moses.

Moses was almost killed as a babe. So was Jesus when Herod slaughtered all males under the age of two in the region of Bethlehem (see Matthew 2:16). Moses spent forty years in the wilderness being prepared to lead the children of Israel out of Egypt. Jesus spent forty days and forty nights in the wilderness being tempted of the devil—being prepared for ministry. God used Moses to open up the Red Sea and deliver Israel from their enemies. And God used the Messiah to open up the ultimate enemy, death, so that we could pass through it and be delivered from its power.

Thank God for the unspeakable gift of the glorious gospel. May we never forget the blessing that God kept his promise to raise of a prophet.

Father, today let me be bold in my proclamation of your gift of Jesus.

What the Proud Know

He is proud, knowing nothing.
1 TIMOTHY 6:4 KJV

Here is the summation of the knowledge of a proud man who disagrees with the words of Jesus and of "the doctrine which is according to godliness" (6:3 KJV). He knows nothing. Of course, a proud and godless man has a measure of knowledge. He may know something about history or about mathematics, politics, or motor vehicles, or how to build a house. However, when it comes to that which matters—the things of eternity—he knows nothing. We, however, are blessed beyond words because God has given us the Scriptures, which are a lamp to our feet and a light to our path (Psalm 119:105). But more than that, God gave us Jesus, who is the light of the world. The unsaved don't know where they are going, but we do. Listen to the wonderful, words of our Savior: "I am the Light of the world; he who follows Me will not walk in the darkness, but will have the Light of life" (John 8:12 NASB95).

It was the brilliant Thomas Edison who rightly said, "We don't know a millionth of one percent about anything." That's why we should come to Christ as little children and stay as little children—with humble, inquiring minds. That is the key to continued learning.

Father, teach me your ways. Help me to grow in my understanding of things eternal.

Hold On to What You Have

Godliness with contentment is great gain.
1 TIMOTHY 6:6

The verse before this one spoke of evil men who were destitute of the truth, who supposed that gain was godliness. Their supposition was incorrect. There is no gain—even when a man gains the whole world but loses his soul (Matthew 16:26). This is because without godliness, we have nothing. But godliness with the addition of contentment is great gain. Contentment is an attitude. It is the good fruit of living a life of self-denial. The apostle Paul said, "Not that I speak in respect of want: for I have learned, in whatsoever state I am, therewith to be content" (Philippians 4:11 KJV). Paul learned to be content. It was an attitude of mind. And once we have that, we must hold on to it with both hands because each year, businesses pour billions (if not trillions) of dollars into advertising to create discontent.

The world wants us to want their worldly products. That's the principle of selling. The key to keeping ourselves content is to realize what we have in Christ. We already have great gain. What could be greater than the knowledge that we have everlasting life? We have treasure in earthen vessels. Therefore, dear Christian, "Let us hold fast the profession of our faith without wavering; (for he is faithful that promised)" (Hebrews 10:23 KJV).

Father, I know that you are faithful and that you will never let me go.

We Carry Nothing Out

We brought nothing into this world,
and it is certain we can carry nothing out.

1 TIMOTHY 6:7

We all know that we brought nothing into this world, but it's the greatest of revelations for the Christian to know that he will carry nothing out. This helps us to realize what matters in life. Jesus spoke of a man who didn't have this revelation. He said that he would build bigger barns in which to put all his goods. He wasn't rich toward God. Jesus called that man a fool because that night the Grim Reaper was going to come for him (see Luke 12:20). Such thoughts sound depressing, but in reality, they can be a huge blessing because they help us to get our priorities straight. As English missionary C. T. Studd once said, "Only one life, t'will soon be past, only what's done for Christ will last."

The Scriptures say that when we are in Christ, our works follow us. So in a sense, we leave this world with nothing except what we do for the Master. I take great consolation in the fact that I came into this world with nothing but I leave with my hand in the hand of Jesus. What a wonderful blessing it is to have hope in our death.

Father, help me to hold on to the things of this world with a loose hand and to you with my tightest grip.

Don't Set Yourself Up to Fall

They that will be rich fall into temptation and a snare.
1 TIMOTHY 6:9 KJV

The Bible doesn't condemn us if God has blessed us with riches. Abraham was rich. David was rich. So was Solomon. The Bible tells Christians who are rich to be "ready to distribute" (1 Timothy 6:18 KJV). A rich person can be a blessing to those who are in need. They can assist the widow and the fatherless. They can feed the hungry and clothe the naked. Today's verse doesn't warn us against riches. It rather warns us against covetousness. It speaks of those who want to be rich. It addresses those who are consumed with greed. These are the ones who set themselves up to fall.

Jesus said that we "*cannot* serve God and money" (Matthew 6:24 ESV, emphasis added). We only serve the Master, but if the love of money is our master, it will in time lead us into many foolish and hurtful lusts. We do ourselves a great favor when we are satisfied in Jesus. He told us how we can fortify ourselves from taking that path: "First and most importantly seek (aim at, strive after) His kingdom and His righteousness [His way of doing and being right—the attitude and character of God], and all these things will be given to you also" (Matthew 6:33 AMP).

Father, please keep my heart from the subtleties of greed.

Fleeing to a Destination

Thou, O man of God, flee these things.
1 TIMOTHY 6:11 KJV

Paul has just spoken about hurtful lusts, evil people, and the subtlety of covetousness drawing the godly away from the love of God. Then he tells Timothy to flee these things. This is genuine repentance. We continually flee from that which will harm us. We perpetually turn from lust, greed, selfishness, hatred, bitterness, and other sorrows. All these things are not only sinful, but they also are destructive to the human soul. However, we don't simply flee for fleeing's sake. We run toward that which will strengthen us. We quickly move toward and follow after righteousness, godliness, faith, love, patience, and meekness. We flee from evil to good in the same way we would flee from a roaring lion that was intent on devouring us: "Be sober, be vigilant; because your adversary the devil, as a roaring lion, walketh about, seeking whom he may devour" (1 Peter 5:8 KJV).

The devil cannot devour us when we give ourselves wholly to righteousness and live in godliness. Neither can he take our joy and peace when we embrace faith and love. When we completely submit to God, the lion backs off. "Submit yourselves therefore to God. Resist the devil, and he will flee from you" (James 4:7 KJV).

Father, I submit to you afresh this day, knowing that this is the key to my victory.

Fight the Good Fight

Fight the good fight of the faith.
Take hold of the eternal life.
1 TIMOTHY 6:12 ESV

If we want to grow in our faith and experience the blessing of walking in the perfect will of God, we should become involved in the most noble of causes—to fight the good fight of faith. It's not only noble, but it's also the ultimate just cause. People often use this verse out of context to justify political and other agendas. But our fight is good because we are warring against evil, and we are fighting for the salvation of human souls. We are continuing the work Jesus began. Through his cross and the resurrection, he put salvation within the grasp of every human being that sat in the shadow of death. And now, whosoever will may lay hold on eternal life.

The Bible tells us not to be passive in this battle. We're not here simply to hold our ground against evil. We are told to fight. That means we are to move forward. We are to possess the land, and we do so by proclaiming the gospel of Jesus Christ. It is the gospel that "is the power of God unto salvation" (Romans 1:16 KJV). It is when a sinner comes to a place of repentance and puts their faith in Jesus that we gain ground in this battle. We defeat the enemy when someone comes to Christ.

Father, help me to fight the good fight this day.

In the Sight of God

I urge you in the sight of God
who gives life to all things.
1 TIMOTHY 6:13

When Scripture says "in the sight of God," it is speaking of his omniscience. It is a good thing to ask non-Christians how it feels to know that God knows them by name, that he knows how many hairs are upon their heads, that he sees them in darkness as if it were pure light, and that he sees their thoughts and intents of the heart. Christians feel a sense of comfort in knowing that God knows all about them. But unbelievers like to think that God can see some things but not others, and this complacency will take them to hell.

The way to remove such complacency is to open up the divine law. It is to do what Jesus did in the Sermon on the Mount and show unbelievers that God considers lust to be adultery, hatred to be murder, and that lying lips are an abomination to the Lord. No sinner should take comfort in knowing that God sees everything. Rather, they should fear and flee to the cross of Jesus Christ to shelter from God's wrath. It is only then that they can take comfort because their sins are washed away and they have peace with God.

Father, you are the God of all comfort, and in Christ, I can have the ultimate consolation.

The Good Confession

Christ Jesus…in his testimony before Pontius Pilate
made the good confession.

1 TIMOTHY 6:13 ESV

Jesus didn't say too much to Pontius Pilate. He was as a
lamb before his shearers. He submitted himself to the will of
God—and that was to suffer for our sins. Pilate questioned
Jesus about his silence, urging Jesus to speak because, Pilate
said, he had the power to take Jesus' life. But Jesus answered,
"Thou couldest have no power at all against me, except it
were given thee from above: therefore he that delivered me
unto thee hath the greater sin" (John 19:11 KJV).

He also said,

My kingdom is not of this world: if my kingdom were
of this world, then would my servants fight, that I
should not be delivered to the Jews: but now is my
kingdom not from hence. Pilate therefore said unto
him, Art thou a king then? Jesus answered, Thou
sayest that I am a king. To this end was I born, and
for this cause came I into the world, that I should bear
witness unto the truth. Every one that is of the truth
heareth my voice. (John 18:36–37 KJV)

That was his good confession, and it should be ours.
Our kingdom is of another world, and that confident hope
helps us endure the struggles of this world.

*Father, help me to focus today on my true home in heaven and
on my true King.*

In His Own Time

He…is the blessed and only Potentate,
the King of kings and Lord of lords.
1 TIMOTHY 6:15

We cannot begin to imagine the magnificent glory that
will be seen at the coming of Christ. The same verse tells
us that the Lord Jesus will manifest himself "in His own
time" (v. 15). He isn't in a hurry. He waits for sinners to
repent because he's not willing that any should perish (see 2
Peter 3:8–10). The only reason evil remains in this world is
because of his amazing long-suffering toward sinful people.
But the time will come when the sky will roll back and the
world will suddenly see him who is the blessed and only
potentate. The supreme ruler of the universe will manifest
himself as the King of kings and the Lord of lords.

What does this mean for those who belong to Jesus
Christ? It is the hope of every Christian. It means that we
should never be cast down or discouraged because we know
that we win in the end. We know that death has lost its
terrible sting and the grave its victory. And so we look to the
heavens; we look up as Jesus told us to (see Matthew 24:33)
because we serve the King of kings. Oh dear Christian, never
let the enemy take away your courage. Discouragement
should have no place with such a glorious hope set before us.

Father, may I live every day as if it is the day of Christ.

He Alone Has Immortality

[He] alone has immortality,
dwelling in unapproachable light.
1 TIMOTHY 6:16

It's good to ask an unsaved person why billions of people seek after God. In every nation, multitudes of men and women follow their religion. Why? And the answer is clear. They have had the revelation that they are dying and that God alone has immortality. And so they try to reach out to the Creator in the hope that he would grant them everlasting life.

We are born into this life with the thought that we aren't going to die, but it slowly dawns on us as we mature that we will one day die. That revelation is the first step for a sinner to come to Christ. The problem with most is that they don't think this terrible dilemma has an answer. That's why we as Christians must step up and proclaim the good news of the gospel—that Jesus Christ "has abolished death and brought life and immortality to light through the gospel" (2 Timothy 1:10). When David famously said, "My cup runneth over" (Psalm 23:5 KJV), he wasn't just speaking of an overflow of material blessings. What we have in Christ— our stress-free peace, our strength-giving joy, our knowledge of his love, and our faith in God—should bubble up and run over into this world.

Father, help me to see the multitudes who are lost, to pray for them, and to reach out to them with the gospel.

Who Will See God?

[He] whom no one has ever seen or can see.
To him be honor and eternal dominion. Amen.
1 TIMOTHY 6:16 ESV

If we are told that no one has seen God at any time, why does the Bible say that certain patriarchs in the Old Testament saw him? The answer is that when Moses "saw" God, he saw him as a manifestation of the burning bush. When Moses asked to see God's glory, God himself said that Moses couldn't see him and live. His holiness would have consumed Moses in a second. When Abraham encountered the Lord, he encountered him in the form of angels. When Jacob was in the presence of God, he saw him in a dream—as a ladder reaching up into the heavens.

The apostle Paul "saw" the Lord Jesus on the road to Damascus as blinding light, and that experience blinded him permanently but for the healing grace of God. And yet Jesus told us in the Sermon on the Mount, "Blessed are the pure in heart, for they shall see God" (Matthew 5:8 ESV). The good news of the gospel is that wretched sinners are made pure in heart by the grace of God through the cross of Jesus Christ. That means we will get to see something no man or woman has ever seen. We will see God.

Father, I praise you for your incredible glory, and I am grateful that one day I will see you.

The Kindness of God

Trust in…the living God,
who gives us richly all things to enjoy.
1 TIMOTHY 6:17

As a result of the Genesis fall, life is so full of suffering and death that we can lose sight of the kindness of God. Think of how each day begins as a gift to humanity. The glorious sun rises over the horizon—often surrounded by magnificent clouds—and the birds sing songs of praise to the God who has given us this day. The air has become fresh and clean overnight as the dew cleanses it and refreshes the flowers, the grass, and the vegetation across the face of the earth. Babies are born. Children receive puppies and kittens as gifts. The table is lavished with food that boggles our eyes and delights our taste buds. We turn on music that gives us joy and can move us to tears. We enjoy love and laughter, friends and family, and all these, plus much more, are tokens of God's love for sinful humanity.

He gives us richly all things to enjoy. And he has iced the cake by destroying death through the glorious gospel of Jesus Christ. Oh how we should fall at his feet in praise and adoration for his absolute kindness to sinful wretches such as ourselves.

Father, open my eyes to see your hand that gives me so much to enjoy in this life and a glorious hope in the next.

Oppositions of Science

[Avoid]…oppositions of science falsely so called.
1 TIMOTHY 6:20 KJV

Be careful not to take it seriously when sinners reject the Bible because they say they believe in science. It's as though saying "science" covers all their bases and, therefore, justifies their rejection of the Scriptures—when saying that actually means nothing. The world often points to Darwinian evolution, thinking that it is scientific when it's certainly not. It is nothing but the imaginations of sinful people, evidenced by the fact that it doesn't even pass the scientific test. To do so, any theory must be testable and observable. But the theory of evolution cannot be either. It is "science falsely so called."

But notice the wording of this verse—"oppositions" of this so-called science. The philosophy of this world is set up in opposition to God. When any thought opposes the Bible, that's the "science" we should reject, and we need not reject it hesitantly. Genesis passes the scientific test. What we read in the creation story we can also observe and test. We see morning and evening, just as Scripture says. We see every animal bringing forth after its own kind. We can observe and test trees and plants that bear seeds after their own kind. And we see the reality of suffering and death… just as the Scriptures teach. No, we need not be intellectually embarrassed by God's Word. It is truly scientific in the exact sense of the word.

Father, thank you for your true and reliable Word.

Guard Truth

Some professing have erred concerning the faith.
1 TIMOTHY 6:21 KJV

The Christian walks and lives by faith. Just as currency is the means of exchange between us as human beings, so trust in God is the means of exchange between us and our Creator. We trust him and his exceedingly great and precious promises with all of our heart. "Without faith it is impossible to please him" (Hebrews 11:6 ESV). If you try removing something from a store without the exchange of currency, you will be arrested. So we must never be tempted to move away from the currency of trust in God.

In the above Scripture verse, Paul has just admonished Timothy to "keep that which is committed to thy trust, avoiding profane and vain babblings" (v. 20 KJV). In other words, guard with diligence the godly truth with which you have been entrusted. Faith is the shield we are told to hold up against the arrows of the enemy (see Ephesians 6:16). Be diligent to keep your faith and avoid the world's babblings that often come disguised as the words of experts. And in this command we see God's love for us: this command he gives is a sure path to peace of mind. Leaning wholly on God's Word as our standard gives our hearts and minds a steady, stable rock of truth to stand on amid the chaos of the world and its opinions.

Father, I again affirm my faith in your impeccable integrity and in your Word.

Life and Good

"See, I have set before you today life and good,
death and evil."

DEUTERONOMY 30:15

When the Scriptures say to the children of Israel to "see,"
they are saying to look and to see. Some people can
physically look, but they don't see. Their mind is preoccupied
with other things. But the Bible is telling Israel to weigh up
the issues and contemplate what is at stake. Who in his right
mind would reject life and good and instead choose death
and evil? However, those things always go together. Life
and good are bedfellows, as are death and evil. If we choose
to follow evil because it seems good, we follow death. If we
choose that which is good, we choose the way to life. The
word *good* in biblical terms means "moral excellence." And
only God is good. That's why we follow Jesus. He makes us
good (righteous) in the sight of God through his shed blood.

Every day we stand before a crossroad. In a sense,
every day, God sets before us a way of life and good or death
and evil, and we have a choice to follow that which is good
or to follow that which is evil. Every temptation to sin is a
signpost with those words on it. We have those choices today.

*Father, help me to make wise choices this day by walking in the
fear of the Lord and the light of your Word.*

Be of Good Courage

"Be strong and of good courage,
do not fear nor be afraid."
DEUTERONOMY 31:6

The sort of strength today's verse is referring to here is a strength that we "take." We're told to be strong. In modern language we would say, "Get a grip. Take hold of yourself!" Saying that is the equivalent to a sobering slap on the face of a hysterical person.

When fear confronts us, we must come to our senses and be strong because to do so is an attainable attitude. It's attainable by simply trusting in God, and anybody can trust him, irrespective of their age, talents, or intellect. It is that strength that will produce a courage that will not be afraid. Notice the verse speaks of a good courage. Some exercise courage to do evil, such as robbing a bank. Some exercise courage to risk their lives for an adrenaline rush. But when we trust in the Lord, that trust results in courage that is good because it dismisses fear. Today we need to be strong in the Lord for whatever is ahead of us. Be strong, be of good courage, and fight the good fight of faith.

Father, help me to be strong, of good courage, and not afraid.

He Will Testify of Me

"He will testify of Me.
And you also will bear witness."
JOHN 15:26–27

Way back in the 1960s, it was very common for the ungodly to call Christians "Jesus freaks." This was because Christians were Christ-centered. While the term was meant to be derogatory, to those of us who were Christians, it was an honor to know that we were being biblical. The Holy Spirit testifies of Jesus. And if we are born again and have the indwelling Holy Spirit, we will do the same. We are to be a witness of Christ, of his words, of his life, of his death, and of his resurrection. In other words, like the apostle Paul, we should not be ashamed of the gospel (see Romans 1:16).

An encouraging biblical truth is the fact that God always gets what he wills. Scripture tells us that the Holy Spirit will testify of Christ. It also tells us that we will be witnesses. Nothing can stop us from doing his will. The world may battle us, but we will overcome because if God is for us, nothing can be against us. So this day, make sure you redeem the time, testify of Jesus, and be a good and faithful witness to the truth of the gospel. This day will never come again. Seize it—because it is your opportunity to tap into eternity.

Father, today I am willing to do your will. Please open doors and give me a divine encounter.

Things to Come

"He will tell you things to come."
JOHN 16:13

While the world professes to know the future, it doesn't. It can't tell us what will happen one minute into the future. They may make calculations, guesses, and estimates, and they may predict what they believe the weather will do, but many a parade has been rained upon because they have gotten it wrong. If someone knows the future, they need only go to a casino and become a millionaire overnight because they can predict the roll of the dice. But they can't. Only God knows the future. And the Holy Spirit-inspired Scriptures have told us the future before it comes to pass. Any skeptic who studies Bible prophecy with a humble heart will have his mouth stopped. In Matthew 24, Luke 21, 2 Timothy 3 and in many other places, we see the future written down so that we can know that this library we call the Bible is indeed the inspired Word of God.

Take comfort in the fact that although you do not know the future, your loving heavenly Father does. And he has shared enough of it with you that you can live a life of peace and security. Read stories from Scripture today and trace God's providential hand at work in the lives of his people. Read Revelation 21 and 22 and remember that you already know the final resolution of this world, and it is beautiful beyond words.

Father, keep me focused on the joy of the future restoration you promise.

You Will Receive

"Ask, and you will receive,
that your joy may be full."
JOHN 16:24 ESV

Here is a blank check to the bank of the will of God. We need only to fill in the blank. Ask and you will receive. However, Christians are those who have submitted themselves to God's will. We have laid our own will on the altar and said with Jesus, "Not my will, but yours be done." In doing so, we read this verse with the knowledge that when we pray, we're not motivated by selfish desires. When Jesus said to ask and added that we will receive, he was saying that we will receive an answer to our prayer. But the answer may not be a yes. Sometimes God says no, and other times he will tell us to wait.

No wise parent gives a child everything he wants. This is because not everything is good for the child. And God answers the prayers of his children according to whether the request we make will be for our good. We are limited to the past and present, but God makes his decisions according to the future. He knows what will happen if we get our request. It is in this knowledge that we are joyful and have learned to be content whether we live in abundance or we live in want.

Father, my joy is full in the knowledge that you are the lover of my soul.

This Present Evil Age

He might deliver us from this present evil age.

GALATIANS 1:4

These words were written two thousand years ago, and yet they are applicable nowadays. The apostle Paul lived in an evil age. It was an age of great cruelty and degradation. It was age when men loved darkness rather than light because their deeds were evil. It was a time when Christians were hated for the name of Jesus because they stood for righteousness. And yet the promise of God's deliverance was as real for them as it is for us today.

Since the fall in Genesis, men and women have been evil. They have been cruel, wicked, and selfish. And yet, it seems that humanity's capacity to do evil has exploded in recent times because of technology. We can now travel faster to do evil. We can now expediently kill millions with the blessing of the government. We can commit adultery without any sense of shame. We even find entertainment in watching the evil acts of others. And yet, God in his kindness has continued to deliver from this present evil age those who trust him. When Jesus said, "It is finished," our salvation was complete. It was signed in his blood. May we rest in this deliverance today.

Father, today help me to live as one who has been delivered from the evil age.

No One Shall Be Justified by the Law

By the works of the law no flesh shall be justified.

GALATIANS 2:16

Most people believe the opposite of what the Scriptures tell us. They think by keeping the Ten Commandments (God's law) they will be saved. As long as they try to be good people, they will be fine on judgment day. They do have some minor sins, but they are nothing serious. Besides, whatever bad thing they do, the good they do will outweigh the bad.

But try that in a court of law. Say to the judge that you did commit serious crimes, but you want him to take into account all the good that you've done. He will probably laugh at you and say that he's not there to judge you on your good works. He's there to judge you on your crimes. That's how justice works. And if that defense won't work on a judge in a court of law, it's not going to work on judgment day. The only way we can be justified (have our case dismissed) is to forsake the law as a means of righteousness and simply trust in the mercy of God provided to us through the cross. The Bible says that the moment we put our faith in Jesus, we are justified. We are made right with God. We're given the righteousness of God in Christ.

Father, I'm not saved because I am good but because you're good.

A Brand-New Person

> "I have been crucified with Christ;
> it is no longer I who live."
> GALATIANS 2:20

How foolish the Scriptures seem to the natural mind of man. Here the apostle Paul says that he has been executed with Jesus Christ and that he no longer lives. It's only when we are born again and God opens the eyes of our understanding that we can comprehend the things of the Spirit. This is a legal statement, and if you and I are trusting in Jesus Christ, we, too, have been crucified with him on that cross two thousand years ago. We, too, no longer live because that old sinful Adamic human being that we were before we came to Jesus Christ is dead as far as God is concerned. We were executed and have been raised in newness of life, being born again with a new heart, new desires, and a completely new life.

When we were born into this world, it was a radical experience. We didn't exist, and then we did. And the new birth is just as radical. If any man exists in Christ, he is a new person. Old things truly pass away and all things become new (see 2 Corinthians 5:17). That's what it means to say that I have been crucified with Christ; it is no longer I who live.

Father, I am grateful that I am a new person and that my old sinful life no longer exists.

Adopted by God

You are no longer a slave but a son,
and if a son, then an heir of God through Christ.

GALATIANS 4:7

The metaphor of adoption in Scripture is a beautiful one.
It describes how we've gone from having nothing to having
everything. Previously we were destitute, but now we have an
inheritance. We have "a living hope through the resurrection
of Jesus Christ from the dead, to obtain an inheritance
which is imperishable and undefiled and will not fade away,
reserved in heaven for you" (1 Peter 1:3–4 NASB95).

This metaphor also shows the heart of God for
us: that of a loving Father, who cares for us, protects us,
disciplines us, and longs to give good things to us. Read the
words of Jesus: "Or what man is there among you who, when
his son asks for a loaf, will give him a stone?…If you then,
being evil, know how to give good gifts to your children,
how much more will your Father who is in heaven give what
is good to those who ask Him!" (Matthew 7:9, 11 NASB95).
How should we respond to this great love? "Beloved, now we
are children of God…We know that when He appears, we
will be like Him, because we will see Him just as He is. And
everyone who has this hope fixed on Him purifies himself,
just as He is pure" (1 John 3:2–3 NASB95). In gratitude, we
strive to become ever holier, just like our Father.

*Father, thank you for adopting me. Help me to live as a true
child of God.*

They Were Finished

Thus the heavens and the earth were finished,
and all the host of them.
GENESIS 2:1 KJV

The heavens and the earth were finished. Creation was complete. The horse was finished. It had two eyes, two ears, one mouth, four legs, and a curve in its back to fit a human rider. The dog was also finished. It had two ears, two eyes, four legs, one tail, and one bark. Both the horse and the dog also had all the necessary parts to breathe air, digest food, see sights, hear sound, and reproduce after their own kind. Plus, both had male and female. Everything was finished. Complete. Ready to go.

Because of Adam's sin, we are physically fallen. Paul called this body "vile" (Philippians 3:21 KJV). But the Bible says that when we come to Christ, we are complete in him (see Colossians 2:10). Even though our redemption was complete the moment Jesus said, "It is finished," our fallen nature still pulls us down. However, we don't live after the flesh. We live after the Spirit. We don't look to the things that we see because the things that we see are temporary. We look to that which is eternal. That's where we find the secret place of the most high, and that's where we find freedom from daily stress.

Father, thank you for giving me your Word so that I can live as you desire me to.

The Beginning

In the beginning God created the heavens and the earth.

GENESIS 1:1

To the ungodly, the origin of life is a mystery. But for those who believe the Bible, the mystery is solved in one sentence. God created the heavens and the earth in the beginning. We know that only God is eternal and that he has stated in his Word that the heavens and the earth (as we know them) had a starting point. The psalmist points to the eternality of God before the Genesis creation, before the beginning, when God dwelt from everlasting to everlasting: "Before the mountains were born or before You had given birth to the earth and the world, even from everlasting to everlasting, You are [the eternal] God" (Psalm 90:2 AMP).

Eternity is the dimension of time with both ends removed. Such thoughts are too much for the human brain to entertain, and yet they leave us in awe of our Creator. And that awe explodes when we think of the incarnation. This eternal Creator became flesh and dwelt among us. But the awe grows even greater when we think of what happened at the cross. All because of God's kindness, we can now look forward to pleasure forever: "You will show me the path of life; in Your presence is fullness of joy; in Your right hand there are pleasures forevermore" (Psalm 16:11 AMP).

Father, thank you for the glorious hope I have in Christ.

Sealed Forever

You were sealed with the Holy Spirit of promise.
EPHESIANS 1:13

When we want to say that something is totally completed, we say that it's signed, sealed, and delivered. The moment we came to Christ, we were signed, sealed with the Holy Spirit of promise, and delivered from death. We became his. We're no longer our own because we have been bought with a price. And that price was the precious blood of the Savior. Such is the value of the human soul to God. We were not worthy of salvation, but to God, we were worth the horror of the cross. Such is the love of God.

But notice that the Holy Spirit is called the Holy Spirit "of promise." In other places, the Bible calls him "Spirit of truth." These terms strengthen our faith because everything rests upon the integrity of God and the fact that it is impossible for him to lie. This is why we should never doubt his promises for a second. They are both sure and steadfast and an anchor for the soul. And the soul certainly does need an anchor in the storms of this life. Therefore, today, secure yourself to Jesus and determine never to let the poison of doubt come near your soul. God is the lover of your soul, and he will never let you go.

Father, today I determine to hold on to you with both of my hands and never let go.

By Grace Alone

By grace you have been saved through faith,
and that not of yourselves.
EPHESIANS 2:8

If you meet someone whom you think may be unsaved but you're not sure, simply ask if they think they're a good person. This is the most reliable litmus test to find out someone's state before God. Those who think they are good don't understand God's righteousness or their own sinful condition. And because they're ignorant of God's righteousness, they then go about establishing their own righteousness. These are then liable to get caught up in dead religions that deny that salvation is by grace alone.

How could we ever earn everlasting life by our religious works? How could we ever bribe the judge of the universe to dismiss our case? God will not be bribed by anything we offer him in the area of "good" works. The Scriptures say, "The sacrifice of the wicked is an abomination to the LORD" (Proverbs 15:8). The law puts salvation way out of reach of sinful humanity and makes us instead look to the mercy of the judge. And the Bible tells us that God is rich in mercy to all who call upon him. God's amazing grace brings that mercy down to the criminal, proclaims him not guilty, and then clothes him in the righteousness of Christ. Oh, what a Savior we have in Jesus!

Father, thank you for your amazing grace.

Our Advocate

If anyone sins, we have an Advocate with the Father,
Jesus Christ the righteous.

1 JOHN 2:1

The life of a Christian is one of sanctification. We work
to kill our sin and become holier and more righteous. We
want to imitate the examples of mature fellow Christians,
like Paul, and of course to imitate our Lord, Jesus. Paul
wrote, "Be imitators of me, just as I also am of Christ" (1
Corinthians 11:1 NASB95).

However, despite being born again, forgiven, and
washed in the blood of Christ, we are still sinful people. We
can fight our sin in ways that we couldn't before salvation,
but we still fail so many times. Whenever you do sin, repent
sincerely and ask God for forgiveness. And know that
you are forgiven. Jesus is at the right hand of the Father
advocating for you. "He Himself is the propitiation for our
sins" (1 John 2:2 NASB95). Jesus' righteousness is now yours.
In loving thankfulness, we are all the more motivated to live
righteously ourselves through his power.

*Father, when I'm tempted, let me remember Christ's sacrifice
and choose obedience instead.*

Water Divided from Water

"Let it divide the waters from the waters."
GENESIS 1:6

Genesis tells us that in the beginning, God created the firmament in the midst of the waters. The word *firmament* describes the heavens that dwell above the earth. God created the heavens and caused it to divide the two great waters. This is something that we often take for granted, and yet it is a great wonder. This earth is filled with water and so are the heavens. Above us are tons of water held in the sky until such a time as God releases it upon the earth to give it life. Think of the symmetry of a tiny drop of water as it falls down toward the earth, and then think of the explosive but still perfect symmetry as it hits the earth and disperses. That drop was just an infinitesimally small part of a cloud that mostly consisted of air, but the invisible air is made visible to us because of light striking each air molecule.

And so we look up to the heavens and see a massive white cloud that is forever moving and reshaping itself against the backdrop of the deep blue sky. And all this was set in motion when God divided the waters. How can we not fall down and worship the Creator of such things? The heavens truly declare the glory of God (see Psalm 19:1).

Father, I am overwhelmed with the greatness of your glory and power.

April

Sure and Steadfast Hope

This hope we have as an anchor of the soul, a hope both sure and steadfast and one which enters within the veil, where Jesus has entered as a forerunner for us, having become a high priest forever according to the order of Melchizedek.

HEBREWS 6:19–20 NASB95

The hope mentioned in this passage from Hebrews comes from a few verses earlier: "I will surely bless you and I will surely multiply you" (v. 14 NASB95). This was a promise to Abraham, but the author of Hebrews uses this promise as an example to show how sure all the promises of Scripture are for us. "God, desiring even more to show to the heirs of the promise the unchangeableness of His purpose, interposed with an oath, so that by two unchangeable things in which it is impossible for God to lie, we who have taken refuge would have strong encouragement to take hold of the hope set before us" (vv. 17–18 NASB95).

The surety of our salvation does not depend on our good deeds or even on how strong our faith is. Instead, it depends on God's faithfulness and his character. It is "sure and steadfast." We never need to doubt God's faithfulness or the hope he's given us.

Father, I am grateful that my salvation has nothing to do with my goodness and everything to do with yours.

Majestic Power

Who is a rock, except our God?—the God who equipped me
with strength and made my way blameless.
PSALM 18:31–32 ESV

The Bible is packed, start to finish, with descriptions of God's
power. It's so incredible that it's hard for us to even imagine.
That's why we are grateful that there are so many examples
of his power in the Bible, starting with the creation of the
world in Genesis. Then God delivers Israel through countless
miracles. He orchestrates nations to fulfill his purpose in
history, and he sent us his Son through the virgin birth.
In addition to these and other stories, the Bible has many
beautifully poetic descriptions of God's power. The book of
Psalms is a good place to look for them, and Psalm 18 is a
particularly good example.

In the beginning of the psalm, David was in trouble
and cried to God, and then God came with great power
to deliver him. "Then the earth reeled and rocked; the
foundations also of the mountains trembled and quaked,
because he was angry" (v. 7 ESV). God's majestic power
constantly inspires awe in God's people. We, too, should
praise him continually for it. Later, Psalm 18 says something
wonderful: God "equipped me with strength" (v. 32 ESV).
His power is incredible, and he supplies you and me with the
power we need.

*Father, open my blind eyes to the exceeding greatness of your
power.*

It Was Very Good

God saw everything that He had made,
and indeed it was very good.

GENESIS 1:31

No one from the human race was present to look upon what God created. He had already mentioned a number of times that what he had created was good. But here is a summation about everything that he had created, and indeed it was *very* good. God never exaggerates. We cannot begin to imagine what it was that he had created because when we look at the present creation, it is in a fallen and ruined state. The most beautiful sunrise, gorgeous flowers, birds, beautiful trees, the deep blue sky, white sandy beaches are nothing but a cursed and marred creation. But thanks to God and thanks to the cross of Calvary, we have the hope of seeing creation as it should be.

The Scriptures tell us that our eyes have not seen nor have our hearts imagined anything as wonderful as what God has prepared for those who love him. Notice it's not for those who are the most eloquent of preachers, the biggest, best, most successful, or the greatest of Bible teachers. It's prepared for those who love him. And we show that we love him by obeying his Word. May this world's fallen state never cloud our joy and excitement about the glorious coming kingdom.

Father, thank you for preparing a very good place for me.

The Tree in the Garden

The LORD God made…
the tree of the knowledge of good and evil.
GENESIS 2:9

The question that most of us have is, why did God put the tree of the knowledge of good and evil in the garden of Eden? Had that tree not been there, Adam and Eve would not have been tempted to eat its fruit. That would have meant that the human race would have lived in happy harmony forever. Instead, we are plagued with disease, pain, suffering, and death. Those who believe Scripture and yet don't fear the Lord may be tempted to point a finger at God and blame him for our moral discrepancies. However, we know that God is without sin and that all his judgments are righteous and true altogether (see Psalm 19:9).

He never does anything that is deceitful or morally wrong. Ever. Therefore, the problem is not with God. The problem is with us and our lack of understanding. That will bring us to an erroneous conclusion. We also don't fully understand why God allows suffering, but he does. But we do know that as high as the heavens are above the earth, so are his ways above our ways (see Isaiah 55:9). Therefore, in the meantime, we trust him with all our heart, and we lean not on our own fallen understanding because that will lead us astray.

Father, help me to keep my eyes on you and not on that which I don't understand.

The Promise to Israel

"I will…bring you into your own land."

Ezekiel 36:24

Here is stark evidence for any skeptic not only that God keeps his promises but also that the Bible is the inspired Word of God. He promised to gather the children of Israel from among the nations, out of all countries, and bring them back into their own land. It would be *their* land. Despite all the contention, according to the Scriptures, Israel belongs to the Jews. In AD 70, when Jerusalem was destroyed by the Roman general Titus, the Jews were scattered throughout the world, and yet over the last two thousand years, they retained their Jewish identity. They kept that unique identity as a scattered people.

Then, after the horror of the Holocaust of the Second World War in 1949, Jews from all around the world were drawn back to Israel. It became their own land, fulfilling the promise given in Ezekiel, written around twenty-five hundred years ago. In 1967, the Jewish people miraculously regained rule of Jerusalem, bringing into culmination the prophecy that Jesus spoke, saying that Jerusalem would be in non-Jewish hands "until the times of the Gentiles are fulfilled" (Luke 21:24). God is absolutely faithful to keep every promise he has made—both to the Jews as a nation and to every individual who has the good sense to put their trust in him and his promises.

Father, never let me doubt for a second any of the promises you have made.

No Longer Strangers

You are no longer strangers and foreigners.
EPHESIANS 2:19

Jesus said that he came "to seek and to save the lost" (Luke 19:10 ESV). Before we came to Christ, we were a displaced people, like sheep without a shepherd. We were just one among billions throughout the world. And yet in Christ, we are no longer strangers and foreigners. We now belong to the household of God. This verse tells us that we are fellow citizens with the Saints. When the father put the ring on the finger of the Prodigal Son, it was more than just a ring. When he returned to his father, the son only asked to be a hired servant. But with this ring, the father was distinguishing his son from the servants. He was giving him the power of attorney.

As Christians, we are members of the family of God. Our Father has given us a special ring in Christ that gives us great authority. The Most High God is now our Father. Knowing this should boost our faith in prayer and give us confidence to come before him and request what we will—knowing that we have his favor. And the Scriptures tell us that it is his good pleasure to give us the kingdom (see Luke 12:32).

Father, may I always come before you with confidence because of what you've given me in Christ.

Saved from Our Sins

"He will save His people from their sins."
MATTHEW 1:21

The world, the flesh, and the devil are a threefold cord that is not easily broken. This sinful world beckons us to indulge in its pleasure. That is a continuous battle because the carnal nature (the flesh) longs for its sinful pleasures…and the devil knows it. But Jesus came to save us from our sins. Through the cross, we have victory over its power. And now we have the task of reaching out to the lost world and telling them the good news that Jesus can save them from their sins. The irony is that we are telling them that they need to be saved from that which they love. We, therefore, need to tell them that he will save them from the consequences of their sins, which is death and hell. And we do this with the simplicity of the gospel.

Nothing can stress us like the thought of approaching a stranger with the gospel. The thought sparks fears of rejection, of not knowing how to answer a question, or of causing someone to become angry. The key is to be prepared—just as with anything else that we set our minds to do. Life is full of things that can cause stress, but if we prepare our hearts and think of the fate of the ungodly, we can overcome that fear and stress.

Father, help me never to be deceived into thinking that eloquence impresses you.

Handling Hand Grenades

"Blessed are the peacemakers,
for they shall be called sons of God."
MATTHEW 5:9 ESV

How do we handle it when someone gives us some juicy gossip about another Christian—or some rumor they heard about a pastor? We have been handed information that is potentially explosive. What do we do with it? Do we pass the hand grenade on to another person so that it will do greater damage, or do we bury it? Do we do the work of the enemy, or do we act like the sons and daughters of God? Many a unified church has been tragically divided and the pastor removed from the pulpit because the lies of the enemy have attacked his reputation. And others who forget that we are in a very real battle—fighting a very real enemy—believed those lies. And once the lies have done their damage, it is irreparable.

In several places in the book of Proverbs, we read that it's wise to be a person of few words. The person "who guards his mouth and his tongue, guards his soul from troubles" (Proverbs 21:23 NASB95). Instead of listening to or spreading gossip about others, we should instead use our time to meditate on the Scriptures. By meditating on the Word of God, we will find relief from the stress of daily living. See Psalm 1 for additional benefits of meditating on God's Word.

Father, remind me never to loan my tongue to the enemy.

Knowing This Truth

Count it all joy…knowing that the testing of your faith
produces patience.

JAMES 1:2–3

In the Bible, *knowing* is a powerful word that is often
directed toward the godly. It means that, as Christians, we
should be established in a particular fact. We should *know*
it. And the fact is that we need to be knowledgeable that the
trials that come our way should be producing patience in us.
Patience is the litmus test of our maturity in Christ.

How do we react when we get a blowout on the
freeway? What is our attitude when a loved one becomes
seriously ill? How do we respond when our finances
suddenly become depleted? Do we become impatient? Or do
we rest our head on the pillow of trust in God and say, "This
storm has only come to me by the permissive will of God,
and therefore, it has happened for my good" (see Romans
8:28). If I allow them to, the trials I face will cause my roots
to go deeper into the soil of God and his Word. I will then
rejoice in each trial, and I will be patient in it—with the
patience of Job—because I want to grow in godliness and my
faith in Christ. "Let patience have its perfect work, that you
may be perfect and complete, lacking nothing" (James 1:4).

*Father, please forgive me for all the times that I have
complained and become impatient during trials.*

The Virtue of Wisdom

If any of you lacks wisdom, let him ask God,
who gives generously to all.
JAMES 1:5 ESV

Here is an open promise from God. He gives this to "any of you." To any of us who lack wisdom. That automatically excludes those who are proud of heart because it takes humility to acknowledge that we lack wisdom. But a wise man or woman will always do that. As human beings with a fallen nature, we naturally lack the wisdom that is from above. How can we, therefore, not grab this promise with both hands? If we have godly wisdom, we will always think correctly and do and say the right thing.

Wisdom is a massive pain-saver. If we have wisdom we will have less suffering in our lives, less conflict in our marriage, less stress in our workplace, and less anxiety when we interact with people daily. This is because wisdom will ensure that we always do the right thing. And so he who thinks he is wise is a fool, and he who knows he lacks wisdom is wise. When we ask God for wisdom, we are to ask in faith with no wavering. So today, don't live in doubt. Step out in faith and believe this wonderful promise of God— who gives liberally to anyone who asks of him the most precious of virtues.

Father, make me wise this day. Help me to always do that which pleases you.

A Guide in the Dark

Do not be deceived,
my beloved brethren.
JAMES 1:16

Have you ever used a flashlight or a lantern to walk in the woods at night? If you've ever been deep enough in the country, maybe camping or at a cabin, you know what it's like to truly walk in darkness. Imagine walking on a rough path through the woods in the dark, one that's crossed with roots and spotted with rocks poking up from the dirt. You can't see anything apart from the pool of light shed by your flashlight. But that's okay because all you need to see is a few steps ahead of your feet.

That's how the Bible describes walking in the world. Darkness and deception surround us, but God's Word "is a lamp to my feet and a light to my path" (Psalm 119:105 NASB95). So many voices and opinions loudly demand our attention and compliance. It can be hard to choose what's right. How can we be sure that we're not walking in some sort of error? The answer is to walk in humility of heart, trusting the Lord to lead us into all truth. We must read and know God's Word. If the Bible teaches something, believe it with all your heart, trust it with all your soul, embrace it with all your mind, and live it out with all of your strength.

Father, keep me walking in the light of your Word.

Sin and Death

Sin, when it is full-grown,
brings forth death.
JAMES 1:15

There are good fears and bad fears. Bad fears are those that bring torment. They stop us from doing things we know that we should. They hold us captive. But there are good fears that we exercise every day. We fear being hit by a car. This makes us careful when crossing the road. We fear someone who could do us bodily harm, and so we avoid them. We fear poison, heights, dog bites, and fire. These are good fears that will keep us from placing ourselves in harm's way.

But there is one fear that we should cultivate and hold on to with all of our might. And that is the fear of sin. The world mocks such a puritanical thought. However, we know that sin, when it has its way, will bring forth death. It is a rose with deadly thorns. No matter how attractive to the eye, no matter how its fragrance stirs our senses, the word *sin* should never be separated from the word *death*. To avoid sin, busy yourself in God. Doing that will help to keep you from sin and the stress that often accompanies it. Fill your day with godly activities—read his Word daily, share your faith regularly, pray without ceasing, and walk in the fear of the Lord—knowing that you have an enemy that is waiting around every corner.

Father, help me to keep myself busy with godliness.

In Those Days

In those days John the Baptist came preaching
in the wilderness of Judea.
MATTHEW 3:1

John the Baptist came preaching the message of repentance.
He came because God had sent him. He was a forerunner
of Jesus, a voice in the wilderness calling all to prepare the
way of the Lord. John was chosen by God and filled with the
Holy Spirit from the womb of his mother. He came in a time
of darkness, between the last Old Testament book and the
birth of Jesus. After this long quiet stretch, God sent John to
prepare the hearts of the people for the coming of Jesus. He
was a small speck of light proclaiming that "the true light,
which gives light to everyone, was coming into the world"
(John 1:9 ESV).

God uses many means to give revelation and truth
to people on the earth. Although we were lost and in the
darkness, he didn't leave us there. He gave us his Word, and
he gives us people like John the Baptist and prophets and
pastors and teachers to guide us to a deeper knowledge of
the Lord. We thank him that "the people who were sitting
in darkness saw a great light, and those who were sitting in
the land and shadow of death, upon them a Light dawned"
(Matthew 4:16 NASB95).

Father, thank you for guiding me to your truth.

To the Jew First

It is the power of God for salvation to everyone who believes,
to the Jew first and also to the Greek.

ROMANS 1:16 ESV

Why should the Jews be first? We know that historically the
gospel went to them first (see Acts 1–10). But there's more
here than just chronological order. The Jews had the great
advantage of knowing the law of God. Because they had the
law, their hearts were prepared for the message of grace. The
law gave them the knowledge of sin and showed them their
need of the Savior. We see this happening in Acts 2 when
Peter preached the gospel to "devout" Jews (v. 5)—godly men
who were thoroughly versed in God's law. They had even
gathered on the day of Pentecost to celebrate the giving of
that law on Mount Sinai. Paul addresses this fact in Romans
3: "What advantage then has the Jew, or what is the profit of
circumcision? Much in every way! Chiefly because to them
were committed the oracles of God" (vv. 1–2).

The Jew is not better than the gentile. He is just better
off because of the knowledge of God's perfect standard. This
shows that a good knowledge of the law is a great advantage
for any one of us because it will shake our trust in our own
self-righteousness and throw us into the arms of Christ.
Charles Spurgeon said, "God be thanked when the Law
so works as to take off the sinner from all confidence in
himself!"

*Father, thank you for giving me your law. Help me to place my
confidence fully in Jesus.*

Swift to Hear

Let every person be quick to hear,
slow to speak, slow to anger.
JAMES 1:19 ESV

It's not uncommon for sinners to try to justify their sinful
lifestyle by saying that they pray every day. Statistics show
that most people pray regularly. They see God as their friend,
and they tell him what they want him to do. They want his
blessing and his protection. But he is not impressed with
what Jesus called "much speaking" (see Matthew 6:7 KJV).
An ancient proverb points out that we have two ears and one
mouth, so we should listen twice as much as we speak. Most
of us tend to avoid those who talk too much. We don't know
how to listen because we want to tell others about ourselves.
We are self-centered.

But when we come to Christ we should become
God-centered, and every one of us should strive to be swift
to hear. We should be good listeners. This takes discipline,
but it comes from the fountain of a loving heart. If I have the
love of Christ within me, I will be genuinely concerned for
those around me. Another way we can be swift to hear is to
read God's Word daily. That's because we are interested in
what God has to say, and the Scriptures give us his mind and
his will.

*Father, help me to be swift to hear and slow to speak, especially
with the unsaved.*

Give Thanks

In everything give thanks;
for this is the will of God in Christ Jesus for you.

1 THESSALONIANS 5:18

Picture a slow-moving line at a crowded bank. Most people in the line are grumbling and checking the time. But one man is patient and cheerful. Why is that? He's a retail employee waiting to make a deposit for his store. He's not in a hurry because he's on the clock. No matter how long the line takes, he still gets paid. Having a positive, optimistic attitude is an antidote to stress.

This verse gives us a good approach for the ups and downs of everyday stress. Inconvenient, frustrating, and stressful things happen, and it often feels like they occur at the worst times. It's natural to our sinful human natures to let outside occurrences dictate our emotions. We respond with anger at a mistake, anxiety at a delay, fear at a rumor. This reactive behavior throws us to and fro with what happens around us. But instead, if we give thanks in everything, it's better for our blood pressure, our hearts, and our minds. A heart inclined to thankfulness makes us stable and firm despite any chaos that surrounds us. Most importantly, it is glorifying to God, who has given us so much.

Father, today I choose to focus on the good things you've given me.

The Obedient Heart

Be doers of the word, and not hearers only,
deceiving yourselves.
JAMES 1:22

No one likes hypocrisy except the hypocrite. This is because (even though he doesn't think he's a hypocrite) he likes the fruit of his life choices. He has his cake, and he eats it too. He sins and believes he has the assurance of heaven. The hypocrite is a "Christian" in word only. He hears, but he doesn't do. He doesn't do because he chooses not to obey, and in doing so, he deceives himself. The following verses in James give us insight into the nature of his deception: "If anyone is a hearer of the word and not a doer, he is like a man observing his natural face in a mirror; for he observes himself, goes away, and immediately forgets what kind of man he was" (vv. 23–24).

But look at the contrast to the genuine convert: "He who looks into the perfect law of liberty and continues in it, and is not a forgetful hearer but a doer of the work, this one will be blessed in what he does" (v. 25). We all want God's blessing. We want to be blessed in our workplace, in our relationships, and in our marriages. Nothing helps us to live above the daily stresses of life like the knowledge that we have the blessing of our heavenly Father.

Father, help me to always be a doer of your Word and not a hearer only.

The Bridled Tongue

> If anyone thinks he is religious and does not bridle his tongue…this person's religion is worthless.
>
> JAMES 1:26 ESV

A wild horse is useless to man until its spirit is broken. It is then that a rider can put a bridle into its mouth and a saddle on its back. The horseman can then harness the horse's energy and safely ride it. In the same way, those whom the Bible calls "saved" have a broken spirit and a contrite heart. They do good works as evidence of their faith. A Christian is someone who has been sanctified—set apart from this evil world. But our tongue reveals the abundance of our heart, and those who continually speak thoughtless words show that they don't have a bridled tongue. That reveals a wild and unbroken spirit. What comes out of my mouth should be edifying and encouraging to those who are around me.

There are many aspects of rocky relationships that we can't control, but we can and must control our own responses and our own behavior. James calls us to control and sanctify our tongues. We must control our words and think before we speak. More than merely swallowing negative words, we should go further and speak positive, uplifting words to those around us.

Father, help me to keep a bridle on my tongue and to speak words that are pleasing to you.

The Foolishness of the Cross

The message of the cross is foolishness
to those who are perishing.

1 CORINTHIANS 1:18

There is a good reason why the preaching of the cross is
foolishness to this world. It has a simple explanation. If
someone has a terminal disease but refuses to listen to a
good doctor giving them a diagnosis, the patient is going to
reject any thought of treatment or of finding a cure. Why
should they want a cure when they believe that they are
completely healthy? A cure would be foolishness to them. In
the same way, when proud sinners refuse to listen to the law,
they are deceived into thinking that they are morally healthy.
Therefore, when they hear the gospel, it is nothing but water
off a duck's back. It goes over their heads, and they don't see
it is good news. Why should they when they think they are
morally healthy? They don't need God's mercy. They don't
see the cross as being good news because it's hidden from
them—because of their pride.

But when we embrace the cross, we have peace with
our heavenly Father. Nothing produces peace of mind and a
stress-free life like the knowledge that our debts have been
paid and our names are written in heaven. We are not as
those who have no hope. Thank God for his amazing grace.

*Father, I cry out for the millions who are deceived and blinded
by their own pride.*

The New Birth

If anyone is in Christ,
he is a new creation.

2 CORINTHIANS 5:17

In John chapter three, Jesus warned three times of the essential nature of being born again. Sadly, multitudes consider themselves to be born again simply because they have turned over a new leaf or shed some bad habit. They no longer have a drinking problem or drug problem, or they have suddenly adopted a new attitude to life. The new birth is not the turning over of a new leaf or a change of attitude. It is a completely new tree, and that tree will bring forth a good fruit.

Others think that they are born again because they were sprinkled with water as a toddler. But this is not the new birth because when the Bible speaks of water baptism, it speaks of the need of repentance and faith. A toddler cannot exercise repentance and faith until they are aware of their sins and their need of a savior. The new birth takes place when we are supernaturally placed "in Christ." It's then that we become a new creature. It is then that old things pass away and all things are made new and we cease from our labors. We enter into God's rest, knowing that we are saved not by our good works but by God's wonderful mercy. We trust in Jesus and need never worry about our eternal future.

Father, help me to trust in Jesus moment by moment.

Sin's Fearful Wages

"The soul who sins shall die."
EZEKIEL 18:20

One of the greatest tools that we can use in our endeavors to reach the lost is their will to live. The Scriptures tell us that God has placed eternity in our hearts (see Ecclesiastes 3:11). Every sane human being cries in the depths of the soul, *Oh, I don't want to die!* The book of Hebrews tells us that every sinner is haunted by the fear of death "all their lifetime" (Hebrews 2:14–15). I have found that the lost widen their eyes when I say that, in the Old Testament, God promised to destroy death, and the New Testament tells us how he did it. What sinner in his right mind would not want to open the pages of Scripture if that is true?

Another verse that I find touches the heart of the ungodly is, "The wages of sin is death" (Romans 6:23). It is good to explain that sin is so serious in the eyes of a holy God that he is paying them in death for their sins. For those of us who trust in Jesus, our debt has been paid in full. Nothing gives peace like the knowledge that we have peace with God. And whenever we count our blessings, that blessing is first and foremost because we have hope despite the certainty of death.

Father, help me to share the hope I have.

He Ought to Think

I say…to everyone who is among you,
not to think of himself more highly than he ought to think.

ROMANS 12:3

Ought is an interesting word. When we say we *ought* to do something, we're saying that we have an obligation to do it because it's the right thing to do. We are bound as Christians not to think more highly of ourselves than we ought to think. Scripture is saying that we should think right things of ourselves. This is because the human ego tends to inflate itself without a good reason and then to overlook our flaws. This is why we ought to read the Scriptures with such a humble heart that we allow every verse to read *us*. The Bible tells us that the entrance of God's Word gives us light (see Psalm 119:130), and if we have a humble heart, we will allow that light to enter our soul and search our inward parts. The psalmist said,

> Search me, O God, and know my heart;
> Try me, and know my anxieties;
> And see if there is any wicked way in me,
> And lead me in the way everlasting.
> (Psalm 139:23–24)

Thinking as we ought means thinking highly of others. This is the mind of a servant and the mind that Jesus had when he washed his disciples' feet.

Father, help me to think of myself as I ought to think and to consider others as better than myself.

He Ran and Worshiped Him

When he saw Jesus from afar,
he ran and worshiped Him.
MARK 5:6

This poor demon-possessed man saw Jesus from afar. I would dare say that Jesus was hard to miss since crowds almost always surrounded him. Jesus is hard for any sinner to miss in today's Western culture. We mark our time since his birth. Billions celebrate his birthday and his death and resurrection. Churches to his honor are built on almost every corner. He is the main character in the world's biggest selling book of all time. However, most of the world sees him from afar. They, and we, need to come close to truly see him.

And the man in this Gospel story didn't just run to Jesus out of curiosity. This man ran to Jesus and worshiped him. Though he was filled with demons, they couldn't stop him from coming to Christ. Remember to run to Jesus and worship him today because he is your only hope of salvation. Let nothing stand in your way.

Father, thank you for your Son, who loved me and gave himself for me.

Do You Not Know?

Do you not know that you
are the temple of God?
1 CORINTHIANS 3:16

As Christians, we are the temple of the living God. Christ dwells in us and causes us to be members of his church. The "church" is not a building with pews. It is made up of believers in whom the Spirit of God dwells. Ask many to define the church, and they will point to buildings or certain denominations, but God looks upon the hearts of those who truly love him. J. C. Ryle said,

> The one true Church is composed of all believers in the Lord Jesus. It is made up of all God's elect—of all converted men and women—of all true Christians… It is a Church of which all the members have the same marks. They are all born again of the Spirit; they all possess "repentance towards God, faith towards our Lord Jesus Christ," and holiness of life and conversation. They all hate sin, and they all love Christ. (…They all worship with one heart.) They are all led by one Spirit; they all build upon one foundation; they all draw their religion from one single book—that is the Bible.[1]

Father, today may I be continually aware of your immediate presence with me.

---

1   Bishop J. C. Ryle, "The True Church," Utah Lighthouse Ministry, accessed on December 30, 2022, http://www.utlm.org/onlineresources/truechurch_jcryle.htm.

Go Home to Your Friends

"Go home to your friends, and tell them what
great things the Lord has done for you."
MARK 5:19

Jesus had delivered this man from the demonic world. He
had been set free from his sins and wanted to follow Jesus.
Yet the Lord told him to go home to his friends and tell
them what great things Jesus has done "and how He has had
compassion on you" (v. 19). When you and I are delivered
from the powers of darkness and brought into the glorious
light, we want to be with Jesus. We want to be on the Mount
of Transfiguration, worshiping the Lord. And yet Jesus tells
us to go home to our friends and tell them what great things
the Lord has done and how he had compassion on us.

The cross is an expression of how much God had
compassion on us. Going home to friends may seem like a
limited sphere of influence, but our friends will be as many as
we make them. This is why we should make friends with the
ungodly—for the sake of the gospel. Any stranger we befriend
becomes a friend. That then opens up a whole new world for
us to tell sinners the great thing the Lord has done…that he
"abolished death and brought life and immortality to light
through the gospel" (2 Timothy 1:10 ESV).

Father, help me to have the love that befriends strangers.

Only Believe

"Do not fear, only believe."
MARK 5:36 ESV

Tragedy had suddenly struck the family of Jairus, one of the rulers of the local synagogue. He came in desperation to Jesus, "fell at his feet and implored him earnestly, saying, 'My little daughter is at the point of death. Come and lay your hands on her, so that she may be made well and live'" (vv. 22–23 ESV). This man had great faith that his daughter would be healed, but while Jesus was coming, some people told Jairus that his daughter had died, and all hope was gone. But Jesus said, "Only believe." He wasn't saying to ignore reality but to face it while trusting God. Jesus then went with Jairus, took the dead child by the hand, and look what happened: "Immediately the girl got up and began walking (for she was twelve years of age), and they were immediately overcome with amazement" (Mark 5:42 ESV).

Whatever our situation, we must keep trusting God, and the day will come (if not in this life, certainly in the next) when we will see that our trust was not misplaced.

Father, I long for the day when every tragedy that surrounds this sad world will be gone forever.

Not Self-willed

A bishop must be blameless…not self-willed, not quick-tempered, not given to wine, not violent.

TITUS 1:7

Someone who is high profile within the local church must have a spotless testimony. When a leader falls, it often becomes big news throughout the world because people know how a godly person should live. Notice one of the first qualifications Paul gives: bishops are not to be self-willed. No Christian should be self-willed. Everyone who comes to Christ lays their will on the altar. They should have a personal Gethsemane experience, where they cry, "Not my will but yours be done." It is self-will that lets the enemy have his way. It destroys marriages and friendships and brings to us "many foolish and hurtful lusts" (1 Timothy 6:9 KJV). Solomon described a person who lets the enemy in this way: "He that hath no rule over his own spirit is like a city that is broken down, and without walls" (Proverbs 25:28 KJV).

If we are yielded to the Lord, we will trust him in every area of our lives, and that will provide us with an anchor during the stresses in our life. Look at this promise: "You will keep in perfect and constant peace the one whose mind is steadfast [that is, committed and focused on You—in both inclination and character], because he trusts and takes refuge in You [with hope and confident expectation]" (Isaiah 26:3 AMP).

Father, help me to strive for these virtues in my own life.

Unclean Spirits

He…began to send them out two by two,
and gave them power over unclean spirits.
MARK 6:7

Jesus gave his disciples power over unclean spirits. How do you give somebody power over unseen spirits? As human beings, we are limited in what we can do, especially in the spiritual realm. But Jesus was God in human form and could give his disciples power over the supernatural. Most people in the world know that Jesus was the Son of God, and many believe that he had the ability to perform miracles. But they are not aware that the Scriptures tell us that Jesus was the express image of the invisible God—that the Creator prepared for himself a body and filled that one human body with himself. This is why Jesus had the ability to speak to the wind and have it obey him, to walk on water, and to multiply fish and bread to feed five thousand. This is why we need to hold on to every word he spoke in Scripture because his words are spirit and life.

The reason he came to this earth in human form was to destroy the power of the grave. Oh, what a wonderful message we have for the dying world! May God help us to use every day and all our energies to reach the lost while we still have time.

Father, help me to redeem the time because the days are evil.

Things That Matter

"The things which come out of him,
those are the things that defile a man."

MARK 7:15

We know that unhealthy eating habits and poor life choices can do serious damage to the human body. But when Jesus said, "There is nothing that enters a man from outside which can defile him" (v. 15), he wasn't speaking about these things. He was speaking of moral defilement.

Many people in the world are obsessed with what food they put into their temporal bodies, and they ignore what they put into their eternal souls. They live as though life consists only of the body. But Christians should know that human beings are much more than just a body. Jesus speaks further about the things that come out of the human heart: "Out of the heart proceed evil thoughts, murders, adulteries, fornications, thefts, false witness, blasphemies" (Matthew 15:19). These are the things that will matter on judgment day. These are the issues that concern the judge of the universe. So much of the stress that we carry has to do with things that don't matter nearly as much as this. Align your priorities with those of Jesus, and watch how he gives you the power to accomplish them.

Father, may I never be guilty of focusing on the wrong things. Help me to prioritize the things that matter.

Greatly Afraid

He did not know what to say,
for they were greatly afraid.
MARK 9:6

Three of the disciples followed Jesus onto the Mount of Transfiguration and witnessed the supernatural. Instead of being fascinated, they were terrified to the point where Peter didn't know what to say. The Amplified Bible renders the verse: "He did not [really] know what to say because they were terrified [and stunned by the miraculous sight]." This emphasizes for us the kindness of the Lord in appearing to us in human form, as a meek and humble servant, to save us.

Philippians says that Jesus, "although He existed in the form of God, did not regard equality with God a thing to be grasped, but emptied Himself, taking the form of a bond-servant, and being made in the likeness of men" (Philippians 2:6–7 NASB95). Jesus described himself in these words: "I am gentle and humble in heart, and you will find rest for your souls" (Matthew 11:29 NASB95). How wonderful that despite his majestic power and glory, too much for humans to endure, he put aside his full glory for a time to come among us, teach us, and show us his love. This gentle and loving Savior is with you today, by your side through whatever you face.

Father, thank you for the shed blood of Jesus, which washes away my sins and gives me the boldness to face you.

May

They Didn't Answer

They held their peace.
MARK 9:34 KJV

Jesus asked his disciples a question that they didn't answer. No doubt they had thought they were out of earshot as they argued with each other. His question was about their disputation as they walked together. They didn't answer because they were arguing about which of them was the greatest. Imagine that—human beings thinking that they were number one. How embarrassing.

As embarrassing as it is, that is the sad trait of our fallen nature. Most of us think that we are pretty terrific. Some think they're the best. We have an inflated view of ourselves. This is something we must not carry into our Christian walk. We instead need to sit at the feet of Jesus and learn to put others above ourselves. This takes a disciplined attitude because it is against our carnal nature. We naturally desire to have preeminence. We want people to look up to us. We dress ourselves while wondering how we will look to others. We want their praise and their acceptance. But the way to walk with humility of heart is to ignore conceited thoughts and to humbly serve others. And if we live this way, we need never be ashamed or embarrassed if Jesus asks us, "What have you been thinking about in the quietness of your heart?"

Father, let the words from my mouth and the meditations of my heart be acceptable in your sight.

Speaking to Grown Men

"Children, how hard it is for those who trust in riches
to enter the kingdom of God!"
MARK 10:24

The disciples were astonished that Jesus had just said that it was harder for a rich man to enter heaven than for a camel to go through the eye of a needle (see v. 25). This is clearly the eye of a literal needle, evidenced by the astonishment of the disciples. Then Jesus explained that those who are rich tend to put their trust in riches rather than in the integrity of God. Money becomes their God.

However, notice how Jesus began that sentence. He called his disciples "children." These were physically mature men, and yet he called them "children." Only Jesus could speak like this without offending his hearers. Imagine a president calling his political advisers or his opponents "children." They would immediately see such talk as condescension. But every human being is but a child in knowledge when it comes to the things of God. Our understanding is darkened, and we are alienated from the life of God through the ignorance that's in us (see Ephesians 4:18). We know as much about the kingdom of God as a man who is born blind does about light. But when we are born again, we enter a whole new realm. Everything becomes new. That's why we need to have humble and teachable hearts and to fully trust our Father.

You truly are my heavenly Father, and I'm your beloved child.

He Cried Out the More

He cried out all the more,
"Son of David, have mercy on me!"
MARK 10:48

When blind Bartimaeus heard that Jesus of Nazareth was coming his way, he began to cry out for Jesus to have mercy on him. He called him "Son of David," so he believed that Jesus was the promised Messiah. He also knew that only Jesus could give him his eyesight. But there is something more here than meets the eye, more than a blind man crying out for the healing of his eyes. He cried for "mercy." This shows what a humble, wise heart Bartimaeus had. His priorities were in the right place. He knew that the health of his soul was much more important than his eyesight.

This should cause us to examine our own priorities. Are they misplaced? Are we stressed about minor, temporary things, like a man begging for healing for a temporary body when his eternal soul remains sick? We should imitate Bartimaeus today. Our time and effort are best spent investing in our relationship with God and thanking him for his mercy. And then we should ask him to supply our physical requests as well, remembering that everything that we receive from God is mercy.

Father, help me to cry out in desperate, faith-filled prayer.

What Belongs to God?

"Render to Caesar the things that are Caesar's."
MARK 12:17 ESV

The religious leaders were furious because Jesus kept outsmarting them. This day, they sent certain Pharisees and Herodians to catch him in his words. They then formulated a trap by asking him if they should pay taxes to the occupying Romans. If Jesus answered, "No," he would be charged with treason against Rome. And if he said that Jews should pay taxes to the Romans, he would be accused of disloyalty to the Jewish nation, and that would turn the crowds against him. Yes or no…should they pay taxes or not pay taxes? But Jesus was aware of their deceit. He noted their hypocrisy, asked why they were testing him, and demanded to see a coin for the tax (see v. 15). Then he said the amazing words, "Render to Caesar the things that are Caesar's, and to God the things that are God's" (v. 17 ESV).

On hearing that, his enemies marveled and left. Their mouths were stopped, for Jesus had brilliantly answered their supposedly unanswerable question. Give to Caesar what was rightly his but give to God what God requires. That slammed the ball back into the Jews' court because that kept the tax question within the bounds of righteousness. If you owe the government taxes, pay them. And overarching that decision is our obligation to honor God in every way.

Father, may every decision I make in this life always honor you first.

Now Is the Time

Behold, now is the day of salvation.
2 CORINTHIANS 6:2

Those who dillydally at the door of salvation still belong to the kingdom of darkness. Like Agrippa the governor, they are almost a Christian (see Acts 26:28). When someone insists they need time to think on the issues, we need to come back at them with the insistence that now is the day of salvation. They're not promised tomorrow. If someone says that they need to think about whether they should put on a parachute, we must hang them out of the plane by their ankles. That will help them to understand the terrifying consequences that are before them.

We need to learn to hang sinners over eternity—to show them their terrible danger. God himself tells us when sinners should obey his command to repent and trust the Savior: "For He says: 'In an acceptable time I have heard you, and in the day of salvation I have helped you.' Behold, now is the accepted time" (2 Corinthians 6:2). Thinking about all that God has saved us from and all that he has given us has a way of bringing our problems into proportion.

Father, may I, like the apostle Paul, know the terror of the Lord and faithfully persuade men.

The Power of God

> "Is this not the reason you are wrong, because you know neither the Scriptures nor the power of God?"
>
> MARK 12:24 ESV

Once again, the deceitful religious leaders formulated a scenario to try to trap Jesus in his words. This time they created a script worthy of a Hollywood movie, in which a woman had seven husbands who died. In the resurrection, whose wife would she be because she had seven husbands? This was a jigsaw puzzle into which no piece could possibly fit. Their reasoning completely misinterpreted the resurrection. Jesus answered and said to them, "Is this not the reason you are wrong?" And their error was two-fold. They were ignorant both of Scripture and of the power of God.

When unbelievers come to us with the problems they have with God and the Scriptures, they are mistaken on both counts. Those who have problems with the Bible don't know the Bible. They don't know how to rightly divide the word of truth (see 2 Timothy 2:15). Every difficult passage is only difficult because of our ignorance. And every problem that sinners have with God exists because they don't understand the exceeding greatness of his power. With him nothing is impossible (see Luke 1:37). Every decision he makes is in absolute righteousness. All of his judgments are righteous and true altogether. This is an endless source of encouragement: no problem we encounter is unanswerable to our God, and no challenge is insurmountable.

Father, my faith in you changes every massive mountain into an insignificant molehill.

The Lord Knows

The LORD knows the way of the righteous.
PSALM 1:6 ESV

Psalm 1 tells us that God knows the way of the righteous. Those of us who are righteous in Christ can take comfort that God knows every thought that comes through our minds. That is because we have nothing to hide. Although we still sin, we are not trying to hide that sin. We know that it is forgiven. If we have any iniquity in our heart, we should immediately confess it and forsake it and be cleansed by the blood of Christ (see 1 John 1:9).

It's comforting to know that God, all-seeing, all-knowing, and all-powerful, takes the time and care to watch you and me. He knows us. He cares for each of us individually and personally. Jesus discussed this as well: "Are not two sparrows sold for a cent? And yet not one of them will fall to the ground apart from your Father. But the very hairs of your head are all numbered. So do not fear; you are more valuable than many sparrows" (Matthew 10:29–31 NASB95). The Lord sees everything that we are going through today. He knows what weighs on us. And he values us so much that he sent his Son to die for us.

Father, thank you for your loving care for me.

Stronger through Pressure

> "These things I have spoken to you,
> that in Me you may have peace."
> JOHN 16:33

Peter Marshall once said, "When we long for life without difficulties, remind us that oaks grow strong in contrary winds and diamonds are made under pressure." This is a good reminder. You might retort that you don't want to be a diamond or a big oak. You'd be content to remain a lump of coal or a weak sapling if only you could enjoy a stress-free life. But that is not your choice or mine to make. Jesus said that we will have "tribulation" in this life (John 16:33). Life isn't easy for anyone, and just because we are followers of Christ does not mean we won't have our difficulties. Therefore, we should be grateful that God strengthens us to face what is ahead of us. He gives us peace despite the tribulation.

The book of James discusses this topic. James wrote, "Consider it all joy, my brethren, when you encounter various trials, knowing that the testing of your faith produces endurance" (James 1:2–3 NASB95). We don't like trials, but we need to learn how to endure. Thank the Lord for growing you through hard things in the same way a parent trains a child. God prepares us for what we will need to endure later, just like parents make their children face their fears—like riding a bike or presenting a project in school—so they are prepared for their full life ahead.

Father, thank you for making me stronger.

Feeling Awful

Stand in awe, and sin not:
commune with your own heart.
PSALM 4:4 KJV

Unfortunately, the word *awful* has changed over the years. It's the word we now use to describe a terrible headache or how we feel when we are nauseous. However, it originally meant "worthy of respect or fear, striking with awe; causing dread."[2] Psalm 4 tells us to "stand in awe, and sin not." The two go hand in hand. If we have no respect for or fear of God that gives us a sense of dread, we will be given to sin. The Scriptures tell us that through the fear of the Lord, "men depart from evil" (Proverbs 16:6 KJV).

Today's verse continues by instructing us to commune with our own heart upon our bed and to be still. The inference is that when we are in the darkness and the stillness of our bedroom, we are free from daily distractions. That's when we should consider the greatness of God. That's when our conscience should speak to us and remind us of our obligations to consider God's kindness to us—not only in giving us the many blessings of life but also for what he did through the cross of Jesus Christ. Such thoughts can give us the necessary fear of God that will keep our hearts free from sin and help us to make our calling and election sure.

Father, help me to make my calling and my election sure.

---

2 *Online Etymology Dictionary*, s.v. "awful," accessed on December 21, 2022, https://www.etymonline.com/word/awful.

Greater Gladness

You have put gladness in my heart.
PSALM 4:7

God puts gladness in our hearts. It comes from him because he is the lover of our soul. But like any gift, it's up to us to receive it. David speaks of having a gladness in his heart, greater than the gladness of those who were prospering with an abundance of grain and wine. He said, "More than in the season that their grain and wine increased" (v. 7). It's natural to rejoice in abundance, and so we should. But it's easy to have gladness when all is well financially and there are no looming problems that tend to steal our joy. However, it takes faith to be glad about that which we do not see. When his disciples had a gladness in their hearts, Jesus said, "Nevertheless do not rejoice at this, that the spirits are subject to you, but rejoice that your names are recorded in heaven" (Luke 10:20 AMP).

The gladness that the Christian possesses comes because Jesus purchased eternal salvation for all those who trust in his shed blood. If we make heaven the object of our rejoicing, no one will steal our joy. Even though the fig tree fails to blossom and there are no cattle in the stalls, we will rejoice in the God of our salvation (see Habakkuk 3:17). If we do that, it should make our hearts glad.

Father, may I never forget that you are the God of my salvation.

The Consuming Fire

Our God is a consuming fire.
HEBREWS 12:29

Ask most people about the nature of God and they will say that he is love. And that's true—the Bible does say that "God is love" (1 John 4:8). But few will say he is a consuming fire even though the Old Testament also identifies him as a "consuming fire" in Deuteronomy 4:24 and 9:3. The Scriptures tell us God is holy, and it is his holiness that will devour anything that is evil:

> Now look, the name of the LORD
> comes from far away,
> Burning with His anger, and heavy with smoke;
> His lips are full of indignation,
> And His tongue is like a consuming fire.
> (Isaiah 30:27 AMP)

And yet this same God, who is a consuming fire of holiness that threatens to devour all evil, is also rich in mercy. When he manifested himself to Moses in the burning bush, the fire did not consume the bush (see Exodus 3:2). That is what amazed Moses. Equally amazing, in Christ, we will not be consumed because the fire of God's wrath fell on Jesus, and justice was once and for all satisfied. We are sheltered from the fire in the shadow of the cross.

Father, my future would be utterly hopeless and terribly fearful without your everlasting mercy.

Praise the Lord

I will recount all of your wonderful deeds.
<small>PSALM 9:1 ESV</small>

David began today's psalm by saying, "I will praise You, O LORD, with my whole heart" (v. 1). When God, by his grace, opens the eyes of our understanding, we cannot help but give our Creator praise. Those who look at a wonderful painting must praise the painter. They do so because it's the right thing to do. And when we look at the vast blue sky, the magnificence of the sun, the beauty of the snowcapped mountains, the sound of birds singing, the cuteness of a puppy or a kitten, we cannot but say, "Oh God, wonderful are your works! I joyfully praise you with all my heart."

But all these things fade into the background as a mere shadow when we catch a glimpse of the love of God expressed through the glorious cross of Jesus Christ. The apostle Paul said, "God forbid that I should glory, save in the cross of our Lord Jesus Christ, by whom the world is crucified unto me, and I unto the world" (Galatians 6:14 KJV). When we see the cross in truth, we will gladly yield our heart, mind, soul, and strength to the Lord, crucify our old sinful nature, and live to tell of all his wonderful deeds. Our life will be a reflection of the love of our wonderful God.

Father, I love you because you first loved me.

Too Busy

God is in none of his thoughts.

PSALM 10:4

Sinners are too busy with life to be concerned about God. Yet they owe their very existence to the kindness of their Creator. They can see because he gave them eyes. They can hear because he gave them ears. They are a living soul because God gave them life. But God is not in their thoughts. This is a great tragedy and a terrible sin. When David describes the state of the wicked one in Psalm 104 by saying that God is in none of his thoughts, the context is that they have no serious thoughts about pleasing God. Sinners don't seek him. This is because of their pride: "The wicked in his proud countenance does not seek God" (v. 4). They think that they have no need of him.

However, as Christians, we can also be guilty of devoting too few thoughts to our God and Savior. We, too, can become too busy with earthly concerns to remember God throughout the day. Instead, we should apply our knowledge of God and his power and love to every problem and event in our day. When God is in all of our thoughts, there is no room for stress or worry.

Father, please keep my mind on you today.

As for Me

As for me, I shall behold your face in righteousness.
PSALM 17:15 ESV

David had just spoken of evil men, saying, "deliver my soul from the wicked" (v. 13 ESV). These wicked were those who lived solely for this lawless world with all its sin and shame. The psalmist said that they have their portion in this life, that "they are satisfied with children, and they leave their abundance to their infants" (v. 14 ESV). Those could be said to have lived a full life. But David pulls back from such so-called success with an "as for me." Our reward, like David's, is much better than temporary earthly rewards: we have the incredible joy of dwelling with God himself.

James describes the end of the wicked who seemingly succeed in this life: "Do you not know that being the world's friend [that is, loving the things of the world] is being God's enemy?" (James 4:4 AMP). But as Christians, we are no longer enemies of God. The Bible says that we are his friends, and as such, we can approach him and cast all our cares upon him with no concern for an earthly reward.

Father, as for me, I will see your face because I have been given your perfect righteousness in Christ.

God's Ears

He came swiftly
on the wings of the wind.
PSALM 18:10 ESV

David had been in distress and cried out to the Lord, and his cry "reached his ears" (v. 6 ESV). Scripture uses anthropomorphic language for a reason:

> Then the earth reeled and rocked;
> the foundations also of the mountains trembled
> and quaked, because he was angry.
> Smoke went up from his nostrils,
> and devouring fire from his mouth.
> (vv. 7–8 ESV)

God doesn't have ears, nostrils, a mouth, or feet, but such language tells us that God hears, moves, and speaks. The psalm says that the earth shook and trembled and the foundations of the hills also quaked and were shaken *because he was angry*. It is easy to forget that "God is angry with the wicked every day" (Psalm 7:11), that his terrible wrath abides on sinners, and yet verse 10 of Psalm 18 says he "came swiftly on the wings of the wind." What a dramatic and majestic response to David's simple call for help! Though God is angry at sinners, his mercy sends him like a swirling wind to seek and save those who are lost and to rescue his children.

Father, I thank you for coming swiftly to my aid today.

If They Knew

"If you knew the gift of God…"
JOHN 4:10

Jesus had gone out of his way to pass through Samaria because he had a divine encounter to make with a lone woman at the well. He struck up a conversation by asking her for a drink. His agenda was to talk to her about her sin and her salvation because she had been living in adultery in violation of the seventh commandment and was on her way to hell because of it. After beginning in the natural (talking about water), he swung to the spiritual and said, "If you knew the gift of God, and who it is who says to you, 'Give Me a drink,' you would have asked Him, and He would have given you living water" (v. 10).

If only this blind and lost world knew what we have in Christ—that we have found the riches of immortality—they would ask and receive God's gift of eternal life. We have treasure in earthen vessels, what the apostle Paul called "his unspeakable gift" (2 Corinthians 9:15 KJV). Even as Christians, we can often forget the value of these treasures. Jesus himself speaks to us in the pages of our Bibles. And he speaks to offer us living water for all eternity with him.

Father, please make me treasure Jesus, the Living Water, and share him with everyone I meet.

The Food That Lasts

"Do not labor for the food which perishes."
JOHN 6:27

There are few foods that don't perish, and one of them is honey. The psalmist likens God's Word to honey: "How sweet are thy words unto my taste! yea, sweeter than honey to my mouth!" (Psalm 119:103 KJV). What percentage of each year do most of us spend laboring for food that perishes? More than likely, that portion of time is large. Of course, most of us are forced to labor to earn money to buy food to feed ourselves and our loved ones. But here, Jesus is telling us not to prioritize our energy for that which is temporal. Everything we can see in this world is transient. It is meaningless and vain.

And for us Christians, God has opened our understanding so that we don't only look at the things that are seen: "So we look not at the things which are seen, but at the things which are unseen; for the things which are visible are temporal [just brief and fleeting], but the things which are invisible are everlasting and imperishable" (2 Corinthians 4:18 AMP). Laboring for the food that never perishes has endless benefits for the godly. Not only do we develop a godly character, which includes the fruit of the Spirit, but we reap the reward of peace in the storm. Faith in God gives calmness to the soul.

Father, remind me to prioritize laboring for you.

The Declaration

The heavens declare the glory of God.
PSALM 19:1

The vastness of the heavens declares the glory of God. They state the undeniable fact that God is a reality. There is no argument against them. The brilliant painter has painted his painting. The great architect has built his building. The world is without excuse when it comes to having the knowledge of God: "Since the creation of the world His invisible attributes are clearly seen, being understood by the things that are made, even His eternal power and Godhead, so that they are without excuse" (Romans 1:20). In other words, nobody can say that there is no evidence that God exists. The immense heavens, with their glorious clouds, the deep blueness of the sky, and the amazing stars shining in the blackness of the night, all declare the glory of God. They blast a trumpet to our senses daily.

Through the Scriptures, God has given light to every man. But also, "day unto day utters speech" (Psalm 19:2). They speak to us. Every time the sun rises, it shouts to the glory of God, and night after night does the same. The Scriptures say that there is no speech and no language where their voice is not heard. Their line has gone out through the whole earth and their words to the end of the world (vv. 3–4).

Father, let me use every moment of every day to think of your great kindness and declare it to this world.

The Perfect Law

The law of the LORD is perfect,
converting the soul.
PSALM 19:7

Jesus told his disciples to be perfect (see Matthew 5:48). They were to be perfect as their Father in heaven is perfect. That's more than spiritual maturity because God has never been immature and then matured. It rather means for us to be morally perfect. This is because God is morally perfect, his law is perfect, his way is perfect (see Psalm 18:30), and he demands moral perfection in our thoughts, words, and deeds.

Before declaring the law of God to be perfect, the psalm begins with talk of the magnificence of the sun, how it rises and moves across the sky like a strong man running a race—from one end of heaven to the other end—saying that nothing is hidden from its heat (19:5–6). Just as the sun sends burning heat upon the earth, so the perfect law of God sends its burning rays upon every sinner. It stores up its wrath minute by minute. Nothing is hidden from its heat (see Romans 2:5–7). However, God, in his great mercy, made a way for us to be hidden from the burning wrath of God's judgment. We are safe from its fury in the shadow of the cross. The perfect law acts as a schoolmaster to bring us to Christ, converting the soul.

Father, keep me in the shadow of the cross, safe from the heat of your wrath.

The Merciful Attitude

With the merciful You will show Yourself merciful.
PSALM 18:25

The Bible highlights the mercy of God, telling those who have been forgiven to show mercy toward those who are around them, warning that if we don't have a merciful attitude, God will not have mercy toward us. Jesus told a story about a man who refused to show mercy upon his servant when he himself had been forgiven: "His lord was wroth, and delivered him to the tormentors, till he should pay all that was due unto him. So likewise shall my heavenly Father do also unto you, if ye from your hearts forgive not every one his brother their trespasses" (Matthew 18:34–35 KJV).

Then Scripture tells us that God will show himself upright to the upright and pure to those who are pure. However, he resists those who are proud and arrogant. He gives grace to the humble, saves the afflicted people, and brings down high looks (see Psalm 18:27).

In obedience to this Scripture, we thank God for the undeserved mercy he shows us and learn to treat others as he has treated us. Every person who crosses our path should experience the mercy of God through us.

Father, never let me forget that I have been forgiven for a multitude of sins.

The Simple Made Wise

The testimony of the LORD is sure,
making wise the simple.
PSALM 19:7

God has given testimony to all of humanity. We have the testimony of creation. It is utterly impossible for that which is created to have no creator. Every building has a builder, and every painting has a painter, so the creation surrounding us testifies to the genius of the Creator. God has also given us the testimony of his law. He gave it to Moses on Mount Sinai, and he gave it so that the whole world might have their mouth stopped and that they would be left guilty before God (see Romans 3:19).

That same law is written upon the heart of humanity, referred to as "the work of the law" (see Romans 2:15). Every human being intuitively knows that it's wrong to lie, to steal, to kill, and to commit adultery. We all know that God should be first in our lives. And then there is the wonderfully sure testimony of Jesus Christ. From his birth until he was taken up into heaven, his teachings were the Word of God, making wise the simple. Those who are proud and think themselves wise never stoop to sit at the feet of Jesus and learn from him. But those who are simple find the wonderful wisdom of God in the testimony of Jesus Christ.

Father, thank you for making your great wisdom available to all those who believe your Word.

The Rightness of the Law

The statutes of the LORD are right,
rejoicing the heart.
PSALM 19:8

How good it is to know that God's statutes are not only right but that they are also the best foundation upon which we can build our lives. They are a moral measuring rod by which we might know right from wrong. We live in a world that is a ship without a rudder. Unbelievers have no compass for their conscience; they drift around however their darkened desires and the pressures of the world draw them. The world commends and even celebrates the wickedness of abortion, adultery, fornication, lying, theft, and covetousness—actions that can only hurt those who pursue them.

However, we have moral direction. The statutes of the Lord are right, and they never change. They are written in stone. And they will be the standard by which God will judge this wicked world on judgment day. This is the reason we warn them—because God "has appointed a day on which He will judge the world in righteousness" (Acts 17:31). But our message is not one of condemnation; it is one of mercy. It is one motivated by love and kindness. We don't point at this world with a holier-than-thou finger. Instead we point to the cross and tell them that they can find peace with God and be saved from the wrath to come.

Father, thank you for giving me a moral rudder in your law.

Eye-Opening

The commandment of the LORD is pure,
enlightening the eyes.

PSALM 19:8

When the Bible speaks of the commandment of the Lord, it is speaking of the moral law. These commandments are unadulterated righteousness that shines from heaven itself into the darkness of this world, enlightening us as to the requirements of almighty God. He "is light and in Him is no darkness at all" (1 John 1:5). When we begin to understand the requirements of God's law, it opens the eyes of our understanding. We begin to realize our own sinfulness and thus the wrath we deserve. It enlightens our eyes not only to the wrath of God but also to his mercy. When Jesus opened up the moral law in the Sermon on the Mount, he was giving us light—that God requires truth in the inward parts, that he considers lust to be adultery, and that anger without cause will put us in danger of judgment.

The better we understand the depths of our sin, the more we value the sacrifice that made us right with God. Seeing God's justice is a necessity for understanding his wonderful mercy and grace. Dear Christian, if you are downcast about your sins today, allow that sorrow to push you all the more passionately into the loving arms of Jesus. Thank God for allowing you to see your sin humbly. Let your sorrow over your sin fuel grateful love for Christ.

Father, thank you for saving me from my sin. Make me more like Jesus every day.

Who Can Understand?

Who can understand his errors?
Cleanse me from secret faults.
PSALM 19:12

Most of us have a problem with seeing our own faults. And it's easy for us to judge others and difficult for us to judge ourselves. The psalmist asks the rhetorical question about who of us can understand his errors. To do so, we need an outward source to tell us. This is why the world needs to look into the mirror of God's law to see their sin and understand the need for the Savior.

However, this doesn't stop at conversion. The godly need the mirror of God's Word to continually guide us into righteousness. This is because, even as Christians, we can make mistakes when dealing with others. Sometimes we lack mercy or lack love, or we don't understand that we've done something wrong until we reflect on how we could have done it differently. This is the right use of a good conscience before God. It is a still and small voice, a light in the darkness, an inner mirror that reflects what we are in truth. One of the greatest mirrors we can ever look into is the life of Christ. He is our example of how we should live in the present world.

Father, help me to think about Christ today and follow his example.

His Amazing Grace

"Have you not even read this,
what David did when he was hungry?"
LUKE 6:3

The above verse is taken from an incident in Scripture where the disciples walk through the grainfields on the Sabbath and pluck ears of grain and eat them, rubbing them in their hands. The Pharisees see the incident and tell Jesus that he and his disciples were doing that which was not lawful on the Sabbath. Jesus answers them by saying that David did a similar thing in the Old Testament when he was hungry. He went into the house of God and ate the showbread and gave it to those who were with him. He was doing that which was unlawful, and yet God did not hold him guilty. This is what is known as "the spirit of the law."

Sometimes we can violate certain laws without guilt because of mitigating circumstances. A good judge will often take these circumstances into account when judging someone charged with a crime. For example, someone may be caught driving well over the speed limit. He is breaking the law, but the mitigating circumstance is that his wife was giving birth to their child in the car and needed to get to the hospital quickly. And yet, the love of God went even further. We violated the law willfully, without mitigating circumstances, but in Christ, God showed us mercy. This is why the words of the old hymn "Amazing Grace" are so meaningful. Christ died for us while we were yet sinners.

Father, your grace overwhelms me.

He Gave Us Light

For God, who commanded the light to shine out of darkness,
hath shined in our hearts.

2 CORINTHIANS 4:6 KJV

What do you have that everybody else sees but you've never
seen? The answer is your face. We have seen images of our
face through photography. We may have seen paintings
of our face. We regularly see our face in the mirror as a
reflection, but even then, it is backward. But we've never
actually seen our own face.

Moses had a face-to-face relationship with God:
"The LORD spoke to Moses face to face, as a man speaks to
his friend. And he would return to the camp, but his servant
Joshua the son of Nun, a young man, did not depart from
the tabernacle" (Exodus 33:11). But just a little later, we see
what seems to be a contradiction when God spoke to Moses:
"He said, 'You cannot see My face; for no man shall see Me,
and live'" (v. 20). It simply means that God had an intimate
relationship with Moses, but no one can see God's presence.
This is the God who commanded the light to shine out of the
darkness in the beginning. But he also "hath shined in our
hearts, to give the light of the knowledge of the glory of God
in the face of Jesus Christ" (2 Corinthians 4:6 KJV).

Father, thank you for entering into a relationship with me.
Help me to know you more.

The Way Out

God…will also make the way of escape,
that you may be able to bear it.
1 CORINTHIANS 10:13

This is the go-to verse when it comes to temptation to sin. It tells us that there is no need for anybody to fall into sin. This is because God makes a way of escape. For Joseph in Genesis 39, the way of escape from temptation was to run. However, some sin is far more subtle than a temptation to commit adultery. We can be tempted when someone compliments us, and we secretly become engrossed in conceited thoughts. We can be tempted to be jealous when we hear somebody being praised. These are the subtle sins that grow like weeds in the human heart, and if we don't nip them in the bud, they will grow into great hedges that are so deep-rooted they're almost impossible to pull out.

So be careful of the whispers of the devil. Shouts are easy to recognize, but the whispers separate the best of friends (see Proverbs 16:28), and they can separate us from God if we take notice of them. Always remember "God is faithful, who will not allow you to be tempted beyond what you are able, but with the temptation will also make the way of escape, that you may be able to bear it" (1 Corinthians 10:13).

Father, help me to be aware of subtle sins. Thank you for always providing an escape from temptation.

What Abraham Found

What then shall we say that Abraham
our father has found?

ROMANS 4:1

Abraham found something that was without price. He didn't
find a massive diamond or clump of nugget gold. What
he found was so simple, but it is the key to immortality.
Abraham found that he could be made righteous with God
and, because of that righteousness, be granted everlasting
life. Romans 4 tells us that he discovered that simple, childlike faith in God opened the door to heaven. Multitudes
throughout the world (and down through the ages) have
vainly thought that they could achieve righteousness by
their own deeds. This was because they were ignorant of the
righteousness of God.

That's why we preach the perfect requirements of the
moral law to this dying world. It results in the revelation that
salvation can only come by God's grace through the medium
of faith. God imputed righteousness to Abraham because of
his simple faith. The reason this is a stumbling block for many
is that it is humbling to know that we cannot save ourselves.
God helps those who cannot help themselves: "It was not
written for his sake alone that it was imputed to him, but
also for us. It shall be imputed to us who believe in Him who
raised up Jesus our Lord from the dead" (Romans 4:23–24).

Father, I trust you alone for my eternal salvation.

We Will Rise Again

Jesus said to her,
"Your brother will rise again."
JOHN 11:23

It was a hopeless situation. Martha's brother Lazarus was dead. He'd been dead for four days, and Jesus had shown up too late to save him. And so Martha said an "If only." If only Jesus had shown up and healed her brother, she wouldn't be mourning his death. It would seem that Jesus then tried to console her by saying that her brother would rise again. She made the mistake of thinking that he was talking about the resurrection of the just and the unjust—when the whole world will rise and stand before God on judgment day. But he wasn't. He was telling her that he was about to raise her brother from the dead right then. But before he did so, he said an utterly amazing statement! "Jesus said to her, 'I am the resurrection and the life. He who believes in Me, though he may die, he shall live. And whoever lives and believes in Me shall never die. Do you believe this?'" (vv. 25–26).

When each of us dies, the invisible life force that inhabits our bodies passes on, leaving a dead shell. Jesus was saying that he is that invisible life source itself, who had become flesh, and whoever believes in him would not perish but have everlasting life. Then he backed up his words with power by raising Lazarus from the dead.

Father, what a glorious hope we have in Christ.

In a Moment of Time

We shall all be changed—
in a moment.
1 CORINTHIANS 15:51–52

When we say we are "blessed" as Christians, we are saying that God has especially favored us. We are blessed because we have an inner joy and blessed because we have God's care in this life. However, the Bible says that the biggest blessing is still to come. We shall be "changed." In a moment, in the twinkling of an eye. In one five-hundredth of a second, we are going be transformed from this lowly body of death that is subject to suffering. In a split second, it will all be gone, and we will have a body like Jesus had when he rose from the dead. This is a glorified body that isn't subject to disease, death, and decay. And as evidence, we have been specially sealed by the Holy Spirit for this purpose.

Never let sin seriously tempt you for a second from trusting the amazing promises of God. Hold fast with both hands to what you have in Christ. Walk in the fear of the Lord, soak your soul in his Word, and plead with God to make sure you have an obedient heart that listens to his voice and that lives by a conscience that is void of offense toward God and man.

Father, help me to prioritize my walk with you and to let everything else be second.

Be Confident

Being confident of this very thing,
that He who has begun a good work in you
will complete it until the day of Jesus Christ.
PHILIPPIANS 1:6

We have been created to excel best when we achieve an attitude of confidence. Confidence will help us make a speech, drive a car, ride a bike, or play a sport. *Confidence* is another word for *faith*. When a football team begins to score points, the team plays better because the possibility of winning gives them more confidence. They begin to take risks and push themselves further.

Today's verse tells us to be confident of this very thing—that God has begun a good work in us the moment we began to serve and that he will complete it. He will cause us to win this game we call life. Philippians uses the phrase, "until the day of Jesus Christ." The day of Jesus Christ is the day of his appearing in glory, when we shall be changed from this vile body and be given a glorious body like his glorified resurrected body. That is the goal of God as he works in us and for us: "It is God which worketh in you both to will and to do of his good pleasure" (Philippians 2:13 KJV).

Father, I have complete confidence in you to do what you have promised.

June

The Tempter

Jesus was led up by the Spirit
into the wilderness.
MATTHEW 4:1

When Jesus began his ministry, he was led by the Spirit into the wilderness to be tempted by the devil. The first temptation came when Jesus was hungry. Second, Satan tried to tempt God by commanding Jesus to cast himself off the top of the temple. And the third temptation was for Jesus to become a Satan worshiper in exchange for worldly glory. It would have been easy for Jesus to turn inanimate stones into fresh bread to feed his hunger. But he didn't listen to the Enemy. Neither should we listen to the devil, no matter how attractive his whispering may seem, if we know that it isn't in God's perfect will. Neither will we listen to thoughts of suicide that can come with depression. Nor will we bow the knee to evil, no matter what promises of pleasure come with it.

Instead we do what Jesus did. We go to the Word of God and stand on its immutable promises. Nor will we forget that the greatest foothold of the devil is a proud heart. A proud person won't submit to God. A humble one will: "He giveth more grace. Wherefore he saith, God resisteth the proud, but giveth grace unto the humble. Submit yourselves therefore to God. Resist the devil, and he will flee from you" (James 4:6–7 KJV).

Father, keep my eyes open to the subtleties of the devil. Thank you for giving me more grace.

You Shall Receive Power

"Ye shall receive power,
after that the Holy Ghost is come upon you."
ACTS 1:8 KJV

Everything we see is subject to the second law of thermodynamics. This law (often called "entropy") says that everything is running down. Everything around us will, in time, turn back into dust, including all the planets, all the trees, the mountains, all the animals, and every person. The whole of creation is subject to this law in different ways. Boiling water will eventually lose its heat and become cold, energy dissipates, and the batteries go dead in your flashlight. However, the Bible says this about what happens when we are born again: "Though our outer self is [progressively] wasting away, yet our inner self is being [progressively] renewed day by day" (2 Corinthians 4:16 AMP).

This is because what we see is temporal, but the unseen is eternal. There was another energy that is not from this world. Jesus said, "Ye shall receive power, after that the Holy Ghost is come upon you: and ye shall be witnesses unto me" (Acts 1:8 KJV). The word *power* in the original Greek is *dynamin*. That's the word from which we derive the word "dynamite." That invisible explosive power is not from this world. It is not, therefore, subject to the second law of thermodynamics. It won't run down. So you need never lose your zeal to be a witness of Christ.

Father, please keep the dynamite power flowing through me to reach this lost world.

Stubborn Beasts

Do not be like the horse
or like the mule.
PSALM 32:9

Horses are wild and free, and mules are stubborn. The horse will run from a man until it is captured and its spirit is broken. But mules often refuse to obey the voice of their owners. The Scriptures tell us not to be like either of these. We are not to be like them because they have no understanding. We do. They are beasts, and we are not. We are made in the image of God. They have to be harnessed with bit and bridle and directed by their owners. We have been created with understanding and know that we're no longer our own, but we are bought with a price.

We don't need to be harnessed with a bit and bridle like a beast, but rather we willingly run to do the will of the one who gave us life. The Scriptures say that when we are born again, God takes his law and writes it upon our heart and causes us to walk in his statutes (see Ezekiel 36:27). A paraphrase of this verse in the Bible says that God causes us to do the things that he wants us to do without him even telling us. That's why we run to seek and save those who are lost. We know that's his will and that it's the right thing to do.

Father, cause me to walk in your statutes today.

By the Word of God

By the word of the LORD
the heavens were made.
PSALM 33:6 ESV

Even though God has opened our eyes to his glory, as human beings in this fallen state, we are limited in our perception of the magnificence of his power. Breathtaking beauty surrounds us, and we can't even absorb it all. As the darkness of each night recedes, the curtains are pulled back to reveal wonderful color and light from the sun that becomes so radiant we can't even look upon it. All this was made by the word of the Lord. He spoke it from nothing into something. That which didn't exist now does because God told it to exist.

And the Scriptures further say that all the host of heaven were made by the breath of God's mouth. God said let there be light and there was light. Then, this Word of the Lord that brought the universe into existence became flesh and dwelt among us. What a glorious truth we have in the incarnation. Thank God he gave us the Gospels and four perspectives of the life of Jesus as he walked upon the earth that God created. May we never tire of reading about the glorious Son of God, who told us that "Man shall not live on bread alone, but on every word that proceeds out of the mouth of God" (Matthew 4:4 NASB95).

Father, you are glorious beyond words.

Do Not Neglect This

Do not neglect to extend
hospitality to strangers.
HEBREWS 13:2 AMP

One of the reasons we are not to neglect being hospitable to strangers is because there is a possibility that we have the opportunity to show kindness to angels—without knowing it. That was Abraham's experience (see Genesis 18:1–15). Hospitality is an expression of servant-love. It is putting the Golden Rule into practice by treating others as we would like to be treated. Inviting people into your home may be an inconvenience, but the Scriptures admonish us to do so without complaining: "Show hospitality to one another without grumbling" (1 Peter 4:9 ESV). And the Bible doesn't confine being hospitable to our Christian brethren: "As we have opportunity, let us do good to all, especially to those who are of the household of faith" (Galatians 6:10).

The famous entrepreneur J. C. Penney said, "Courteous treatment will make a customer a walking advertisement." And it's true. When an employee treats us with courtesy and kindness, we will tell others about that business. And it's the same when we are about our Father's business. Those unsaved to whom we show kindness in the form of hospitality will be impressed with our witness for Christ. Sometimes one act of kindness can speak louder than a thousand sermons because others can see our faith by our works.

Father, today show me ways that I can show your love in the form of hospitality to others.

Always Be Ready

Always be ready to give
a defense to everyone.
1 PETER 3:15

This is a challenging verse. We are to *always* be ready. That means we should study God's Word diligently so that we have an answer for why we believe what we believe. Look at today's verse and notice the motivation of godly fear: "Sanctify the Lord God in your hearts, and always be ready to give a defense to everyone who asks you a reason for the hope that is in you, with meekness and fear" (v. 15). The preceding verse speaks of persecution and threats: "Even if you should suffer for righteousness' sake, you are blessed. 'And do not be afraid of their threats, nor be troubled'" (v. 14).

We have a greater fear than the fear of man. It's the fear of God. God has entrusted us with his gospel. It is the greatest news this world could ever hope to hear, but at the same time, it is a warning that if sinners don't repent, they will perish. This is not a message that we should confine to the church just because we are fearful of the unsaved and their reaction. Instead, our fear of God frees us from any stress regarding what other people think. When we care first and foremost about pleasing him, we can run to do his will without fear.

Father, may I always fear you more than I fear man.

He Subjected Himself

Jesus said to her,
"Give me a drink."
JOHN 4:7 ESV

Jesus sat on the well in Samaria and said to the woman who was drawing water, "Give me a drink." This was God manifest in the flesh asking a woman he created for a drink of the water he created. He is the one who created the sun, the moon, the stars, all the oceans and rivers in the world—and yet he humbled himself, became a human being, and relied on other human beings. He subjected himself to being born as a tiny baby in a manger. He grew up in a small town and ate food he had created. The Scriptures say that "Jesus… was made a little lower than the angels, for the suffering of death" (Hebrews 2:9).

When the devil tempted him, Jesus could have turned the stones into bread, but he didn't. When he was to be nailed to a cross, he could have called upon legions of angels to deliver him from the hands of evil men, but he didn't. And he did all this so that rebellious sinners could have forgiveness of sins and receive the gift of everlasting life. We, therefore, should be eager to follow his example and become servants to this world. It is in serving others that we will find both our calling and perfect peace in a world of stress.

Father, may I never exult in myself but have a lowly Christlike mind toward others.

This Is a Warning

Be kind to one another, tenderhearted, forgiving one another.
EPHESIANS 4:32

Sometimes a dog that has a skin irritation will begin licking where he is irritated and will keep licking until the spot becomes a horrible sore. It is of his own causing. Then the only effective way to break this habit is to put a cone over the dog's head so he can't reach the wound.

There is a good reason Scripture encourages Christians to be tenderhearted and to be forgiving toward one another. We can irritate each other. The pastor can irritate us if he goes on too long in a sermon. Others may say things that lack discretion, and that can irritate us. And these irritations can fester and cause serious problems if we dwell on them. Look at where these minor irritations can lead:

> Let all bitterness and wrath and anger and clamor [perpetual animosity, resentment, strife, fault-finding] and slander be put away from you, along with every kind of malice [all spitefulness, verbal abuse, malevolence]. Be kind and helpful to one another, tender-hearted [compassionate, understanding], forgiving one another [readily and freely], just as God in Christ also forgave you. (Ephesians 4:31–32 AMP)

Dwelling on irritations can lead to bitterness, wrath, anger, and a lot of stress. The key is to put a cone of tenderheartedness over our heads and be forgiving because God forgave us when we more than irritated him.

Father, help me today not to be irritated by anyone around me.

The Reason for Gentleness

Be kind to everyone.
2 TIMOTHY 2:24 ESV

There is no place for impatient anger in a Christian. We are to instead be "kind to everyone, able to teach, patiently enduring evil" (v. 24 ESV). This command is something we need to remind ourselves of, particularly when we are in seasons of anxiety. We've all seen the stereotypes on TV of the stressed-out businessman who takes it out on the people working below him or on his family and the waiters in restaurants. But that's often true of all of us to a certain extent. Stress can tempt us to snap at those around us, taking out our anxiety on those we should be treating with kindness and gentleness. The circumstances we are facing can be gigantic and daunting, but that is no excuse for treating others badly.

Have I been imitating Jesus? Have I been patient and kind to all or focused on my own problems? We never want to use harsh tones or impatient words. In fact, we should go out of our way to show gentleness and kindness to our families, the coffee shop cashiers, our coworkers, and everyone else we see.

Father, help me to be meek, lowly of heart, and gentle of soul.

He Comforts Us

Blessed be…the Father of mercies and God of all comfort.

2 CORINTHIANS 1:3

We would have no hope in our death if God were not the Father of mercies. The Bible tells us that his mercy endures forever. Mercy is part of his eternal nature, evidenced by the fact that he has "no pleasure in the death of the wicked" (Ezekiel 33:11). He's like a judge who looks at a criminal, longing for the accused to be sorry for his crime so he can show mercy.

But the Scriptures tell us that God is also the God of all comfort: "As a father shows compassion to his children, so the LORD shows compassion to those who fear him" (Psalm 103:13 ESV). God, like the Prodigal Son's father in Luke 15, longs to fall upon sinners, embrace them, and rejoice when they get up out of the pigsty of sin and return to him. The Scriptures also tell us that because God is the Father of mercies and the God of all comfort, he comforts us in our tribulation. And he does this so that we may be able to comfort others who are in trouble with the same consoling mercy that God shows us in the darkness of our trials. So rejoice in tribulation because God is working in you and equipping you to minister life to others.

Father, help me to be a comfort to those around me with the comfort you have shown me.

Loaded with Benefits

Blessed be the Lord,
who daily loads us with benefits.
PSALM 68:19

We were once blind and loaded down with the weight of our own sins. But Jesus relieved us of that unbearable burden. Now we understand the goodness of God as he "daily loads us with benefits." If you have been born again, your name is written in heaven. You are saved from wrath, have the gift of eternal life, and consequently have hope in your passing. But if you further count your blessings and name them one by one, you will see even more God-given benefits, from your eyesight, hearing, health, friendships, and loved ones to the ability to work, to speak, to walk, and to hear. Then there are amazing fruits, a smorgasbord of different food, your complex tastebuds, music, humor, love, laughter, sports, massive snowcapped mountains, blue skies, the sunrise, birds, the love of your pet, and the ability to appreciate what only human beings can appreciate. Dogs, horses, cats, and cows don't have an awareness of these things because they aren't made in the image of God.

But all these benefits pale in the light of the cross. The cross of Christ opened up the door to joy forevermore. That, in comparison to the pleasures of this life, is like the light of the noonday sun compared to a single flame of a flickering candle.

Father, thank you for loading me daily with a multitude of amazing benefits.

He Must Be Delivered

"The Son of Man must be delivered."

LUKE 24:7

Must is such a wonderfully consoling word in this Scripture verse. It speaks of the love of God who was determined to see our redemption as something that was nonnegotiable. The fact is that Jesus' being delivered into the hands of evil men, being nailed to a cross, and rising from the dead had to happen. It was as sure as creation had to happen in the beginning when God said, "Let there be light," and it had no choice. There was no question of Jesus pulling back from invading this earth in the form of a man and paying our debt to the insatiable law of God.

Jesus knew this as he wrestled in the garden of Gethsemane, where fear gripped his heart and pushed drops of sweat and blood through his terrified flesh. But his eye was on the will of the Father and on those for whom he died. They were the trophies to which he gazed during that terrible nightmare. Love caused him to push aside fear and say, "Not My will, but Yours, be done" (Luke 22:42). And so we must also be resolute as we ignore our own fears regarding whatever our situation is today and say, "Not my will but yours be done." He has ordained it, and we will run to follow him. We must.

Father, give me total submission to your will today.

The Fear of God

There is no fear (dread) of God before his eyes.

PSALM 36:1 AMP

Here is the deep-rooted problem with the wicked one. He doesn't fear God. It is because of his wrong image of God that he has a wrong image of himself. Almost every ungodly person thinks he or she is morally good: "For he flatters and deceives himself in his own eyes thinking that his sinfulness will not be discovered and hated [by God]" (v. 2 AMP). This is why we must hold up the mirror of God's law to the world. This is what Jesus did with the rich young ruler in Mark 10:17–20. He focused the man's eyes on five of the Ten Commandments to bring him the knowledge of sin and show him his true moral state before God.

Someone once said, "Just when the caterpillar thought the world was ending, he turned into a butterfly." That is a good thought for stress-free living today. It is a picture of the very real hope we have in Christ. Even as we gaze into the mirror of the law ourselves and see our failures, we must never forget that the Christian life is but a cocoon in which God is working a miracle. Keep your eyes on that living hope.

Father, never let me sweat the small stuff.

The Shadow of His Wings

The children of mankind take refuge
in the shadow of your wings.
PSALM 36:7 ESV

A dejected farmer was once walking through the remains of his barn that had burned down the night before. His heart broke as he looked at the devastation, which included a dead hen that had been caught in the flames lying on the ground. He nudged it gently with his foot and found that underneath its wings were a number of squirming little chicks that had been sheltered and spared from the terrible flames by their mother. What a wonderful picture of what God did for us in Christ. He came to this earth and spread his loving wings over sinners so they might be sheltered from the fire of his wrath.

The Bible says that God revealed his great love for us "in that while we were still sinners, Christ died for us" (Romans 5:8). That cross is a brilliant light of the love of God in a world of terrible tragedy. Just as what the mother hen did for her chicks was hidden from the farmer, the good news is hidden from the lost until they respond with an honest and humble heart and acknowledge their sins. It's only then that they get a glimpse of the love that God showed in Christ. "How precious is your steadfast love, O God! The children of mankind take refuge in the shadow of your wings" (Psalm 36:7 ESV).

Father, thank you for revealing your love to me.

They Recognized Him

The men of that place
had knowledge of Him.
MATTHEW 14:35 KJV

The men of that place knew who Jesus was, and because of that knowledge, "they sent out into all that country round about, and brought unto him all that were diseased; And besought him that they might only touch the hem of his garment: and as many as touched were made perfectly whole" (vv. 35–36 KJV).

These were compassionate men, and that compassion caused them to send word to all the surrounding region to bring to Jesus those who were sick. Then the sick begged Jesus that they might only touch the hem of his garment. And those who touched the hem were made perfectly well. These people brought their sicknesses to Jesus and trusted him to heal them. Consider this thought if you are having a stressful day: "Not everything that weighs you down is yours to carry." Worry, fear, and stress are no longer yours if you give them to the Lord. Do you know and recognize who Jesus is? Let him carry them, and you, through the day. Trust him to heal, to oversee, and to manage your burdens.

Father, let me bring all my cares to you and be like these men who were driven by compassion, urging others to come to Jesus for healing.

Wait Patiently

I waited patiently for the LORD.
PSALM 40:1

The Scriptures give us the mind of God, and they are filled with exceedingly great and precious promises—of provision and consolation. The book of Psalms is one place in particular to which we should run when we find ourselves in the many frightening storms of life. It is a God-given oasis. There we find special comfort and encouragement for the downcast and weary traveler. Psalm 40 is a testimony of the Christian who has waited patiently for the Lord, knowing that he has already inclined his ear to hear us. Our testimony is that he lifted us up out of the horrible and hopeless pit of sin, set our feet upon the rock of his Word, and established our comings and goings. And so we sing, "Rock of Ages cleft for me; let me hide myself in thee."

It is true that stress can steal our joy. However, faith looks past the trouble. It looks to Jesus, who carries our fears. Let him do that for you today. Wait patiently for him.

Father, use my life as a signpost to point sinners to the cross.

The Example the Disciples Gave

"Why do Your disciples transgress
the tradition of the elders?"
MATTHEW 15:2

The religious leaders didn't like the fact that the disciples didn't go through the ritual of washing their hands before they ate bread. They accused the disciples of sinning against God for failing to keep this tradition. However, instead of defending his disciples, Jesus used the law to show the religious leaders that *they* were sinning against God. He said, "Why do you also transgress the commandment of God because of your tradition?" (v. 3).

The disciples are good examples for us in this passage. They followed Jesus even though it went against the surrounding culture and even the religious traditions. They cared more about what Jesus commanded and what he thought than about what their society and religious leaders thought. This is important for us to remember today. When we have God's opinion of our actions at the forefront of our thoughts, we don't worry about what other people think. Having God's will as our priority can provide a level of peace and calm that is incredible.

Father, help me to care first and foremost about pleasing you with what I do today.

The Continuous Battle

[Pray] always with all prayer and supplication in the Spirit.
EPHESIANS 6:18

Every Christian finds himself in a constant battle with the world, the flesh, and the devil. Our fleshly mind is forever tempted by the sinful pleasures of this world. And the one the Bible calls "the tempter" (Matthew 4:3) pours gasoline onto the fire, often making us feel burned and battle weary. Here is the weapon the Scriptures give when speaking of fighting off the enemy: "Praying always with all prayer and supplication in the Spirit."

Prayer is, of course, the answer. Therefore, formulate a positive prayer that is everything the enemy wouldn't like you to pray. And when those unwanted thoughts come, they will act as an alarm-bell for you to pray your super positive prayer. For example, if a jealous thought enters your mind, that negative thought will remind you to pray your positive prayer. Pray that you will get so much love in your heart that there will be no room left for jealousy. A positive prayer turns a nasty negative into a powerful thought that is pleasing to God. In the face of the enemy, you will then become strong where the enemy wanted to make you weak. Instead of turning you toward sin, Satan will be turning you toward God.

Father, thank you for the Spirit's help in my battles.

That Which Was Lost

"The Son of Man has come
to seek and to save that which was lost."
LUKE 19:10

It took the pigsty to show the Prodigal Son that he was lost. He wasn't physically lost. He was lost spiritually. Jesus spoke of sinners as being sheep without a shepherd. Sheep without a shepherd are vulnerable to wolves that will devour them. The problem with this world is that sinners don't realize that they are lost. Many have homes, families, and jobs, and they would never consider themselves to be "lost" until they realize that without God, they have no idea where they came from. Neither do they have any real purpose for existence other than to live life and die. And they don't know where they are going. They have no idea what's going to happen to them after they die. They are lost.

We were once also lost, but now we're found. We have returned to the shepherd of our souls. And now we lie down in green pastures, knowing that Jesus is our shepherd. Those green pastures speak to us of perfect peace. He also leads us by still waters, free from the tumultuous storms of daily life (see Psalm 23). Jesus said, "These things I have spoken unto you, that in me ye might have peace. In the world ye shall have tribulation: but be of good cheer; I have overcome the world" (John 16:33 KJV).

Father, words to express my gratitude fail me.

Ultimate Justice

Fear him which is able to destroy
both soul and body in hell.
MATTHEW 10:28 KJV

The thought of hell should be bittersweet for the Christian. It's sweet because it means that mass murderers, like Hitler, who have taken the lives of multitudes of innocent people, will one day receive ultimate justice. But the existence of hell should also make us tremble in fear at the holiness of God. Its reality should cause us to keep ourselves close to the Savior and continually deny ourselves the pleasures of sin, knowing that God sees everything we think and do and will hold us accountable. Look at these sobering words of Jesus: "Fear not them which kill the body, but are not able to kill the soul: but rather fear him which is able to destroy both soul and body in hell" (v. 28 KJV).

When we count our blessings, we can often overlook the greatest blessing of all. The greatest blessing for any of us may not be clear today, especially if we have many stresses and contradictions in life. But the day will come when we stand before God and are separated into everlasting life—all because of what Jesus did on the cross. On the day when we are saved from a very real hell, it will be evident to us how blessed we are. Such thoughts should help us not to sweat the small things or let stress have its way.

Father, thank you for your everlasting mercy.

The Necessary Letter

I found it necessary to write to you.
JUDE 1:3 AMP

Jude wrote this letter to his beloved brethren to exhort them to contend earnestly for the faith. He reminded them to fight for the truth of the gospel. Ungodly men had crept in and turned the grace of God into an opportunity to sin. Jude wrote his letter in earnest because the message of these men was subtle. They didn't deny the forgiveness offered in Christ, but they distorted that grace by saying that it gave the believer freedom to live any way he wished—without yielding to Christ: "They distort the grace of our God into decadence and immoral freedom [viewing it as an opportunity to do whatever they want], and deny and disown our only Master and Lord, Jesus Christ" (Jude 1:4 AMP).

Instead of making us careless, the precious forgiveness of God should make us more careful than ever to obey. We should strive to please him ever more because of his great mercy to us. And we should diligently guard against anyone tempting us or others to do otherwise.

Father, keep me aware of doctrines that are contrary to your Word.

Stir It Up

I remind you to stir up the gift of God.
2 TIMOTHY 1:6

The apostle Paul reminded Timothy to stir up the gift that he received through the laying on of his hands. This was in reference to the subject of fear. Paul said, "God has not given us a spirit of fear, but of power and of love and of a sound mind" (v. 7). That's all we need to overcome our fears—the dynamic power of God (see Acts 1:8), the love of God within us, and a sound mind that will run to do the will of God. Then Paul said, "Therefore do not be ashamed of the testimony of our Lord" (v. 8). We must stir up the gift.

We are living in an age where stress is a part of life to the point where the Scriptures say of the ungodly that their hearts will fail them for fear of what is coming upon the earth (see Luke 21:26). It should break our hearts that so many in the world live in a hopeless fear of the future. They are stressed to a breaking point for fear of the future. We don't have that tormenting fear because we know him who knows the future. Knowing what we have—treasure in earthen vessels—should help us to reach out and share that treasure with others.

Father, never let me be ashamed of the testimony of Jesus.

All Things Were Made by Him

…through whom also He made the worlds.
HEBREWS 1:2

How fortunate we are to have the Scriptures. They're so precious. They tell us our origins, and they tell us of our purpose and our future. In the beginning, God created the heavens and the earth, and he did this by his Word. He spoke and it came to pass. And the Word became flesh and dwelt amongst us (see John 1:14). All things were made by him. That includes your cat, dog, horse, house, car, cow, the plants in your yard, and the light that shines in your room. He created your hands, your feet, your eyes, and your hair, as well as the materials that make up many things in your home. Jesus Christ made everything. Plus, God has spoken to us through his Son, whom he has appointed heir of all things. The Scriptures tell us that he is the brightness of the glory of God and the express image of his person and that he upholds all things by the word of power (see Hebrews 1:3).

Author and entrepreneur Adam Braun said, "We all have those things that even in the midst of stress and disarray, they energize us and give us renewed strength and purpose. These are our passions." When the Bible is our passion, it is the light in the darkness. When God is our passion, he is our peace in the storm and strength in our weakness.

Father, your wonderful Word is a lamp to my feet and a light to my path.

Fleeing Temptation

Flee sexual immorality.
1 CORINTHIANS 6:18

The Bible doesn't say to "resist" sexual immorality. It says to *flee*. Run away as you would if you knew someone was going to try to kill you and you had no weapon to defend yourself. And when it comes to sexual sin, we have little to no resistance outside of the fear of God. How different it would've been for King David if he had run away from Bathsheba instead of running to her. How many marriages would be saved if men and women who are tempted to sin resisted the temptation and ran from immorality? When Joseph was tempted to commit adultery with Potiphar's wife, he knew how vulnerable he was and wisely fled from the scene. He is our example of what to do when tempted.

Other temptations are more subtle, but we must flee those sins just as earnestly. We must flee temptations to doubt the promises of God. We must reject thoughts dishonoring to him.

Father, lead me not into temptation but deliver me from all evil.

Learning from the Ant

Go to the ant, you sluggard!
Consider her ways and be wise.
PROVERBS 6:6

Every Christian is a disciple of Christ. The moment we put our trust in Jesus, we begin the process of being discipled, and the essence of discipleship is discipline. We're no longer ruled by the desires of our flesh, but we are motivated to do the will of God, and that will is clearly laid out in his Word. The ant doesn't need to be told what to do. The Bible says of the tiny insect, "Which, having no captain, overseer or ruler, provides her supplies in the summer, and gathers her food in the harvest" (vv. 7–8).

When we are lazy, we must "go to the ant" and imitate the creature's diligence. And we must do the same when we are feeling stressed. We must be proactive about addressing the source of our worry and anxiety, and we must be diligent in abounding in the work the Lord has laid out for us.

Father, help me to be disciplined each day to do your will.

Those Precious Eyes

"If your right eye causes you to sin,
pluck it out."
MATTHEW 5:29

We often take eyesight for granted. How many of us have humbly bowed our heads and thanked God for the fact that we can see? We get to see the amazing spectrum of colors that fill our lives every day. We get to see the awesome spectacle of the sun coming over the horizon and spreading its array of colors across the sky as it makes its entrance into another day. And yet Jesus said if that precious eye with which we see causes us to sin, we should pluck it out and cast it from us rather than end up with eyesight in hell. This should remind us of the terrible nature of sin.

But when we bring faith in Jesus into our lives, everything changes. We have the power to fight sinful desires and achieve true victory. We also get to see the invisible because God has opened the eyes of our understanding. Seeing God's blessing means the end of stressing. We can now give God the glory for such kindness in creating us and lavishing his goodness upon us.

Father, help me to set my eyes on that which is pleasing in your sight.

Woe unto You

"Woe to you when all men
speak well of you."
Luke 6:26

These words of Jesus should make us very nervous because it's natural to want people to speak well of us. None of us enjoys rejection, let alone being hated for our faith. The desire to have all people think and speak well of us can cause us a lot of anxiety from day to day. It can have a huge impact on our decisions. But Jesus says this desire should not be our motivation. In fact, the Scriptures warn that all who live godly in Christ Jesus shall suffer persecution (see 2 Timothy 3:12). If we are not being persecuted in some way, it's possible that we're not living godly in Christ Jesus. We have to live with the fact that the world is offended by certain major doctrines of Christianity. It is also offended by our lives; often, people persisting in sin feel shame when they see the lives of Christians who walk in obedience to Christ.

If we are not living for the praise of humanity, whose praise should we be striving for? There's only one opinion that truly matters: God's. Live for his approval, and the stress of trying to please everyone else will cease.

Father, may I never betray the truths of your Word simply because I want the approval of this evil world.

Glorified by All

He taught in their synagogues,
being glorified by all.
LUKE 4:15

When Jesus first began his ministry in Galilee and the surrounding region, he gained a stellar reputation. However, when he came to Nazareth, where he had been brought up, something happened that changed everything. He went into the synagogue on the Sabbath day and read a Messianic passage from Isaiah. Every eye in the synagogue was fixed on him. Then he said, "Today this Scripture is fulfilled in your hearing" (v. 21). Everybody then marveled at the gracious words he spoke. But Jesus then shared the reality that God's grace wasn't confined to the Jews. It also reached the gentiles. Suddenly, every one of those who had been marveling at his words was filled with wrath, and they took him to a cliff and tried to kill him (see v. 29).

Everyone listening that day had a choice: to believe and glorify Jesus or to reject him. Even if we have already believed in Jesus, we still encounter choices daily and must continually choose to follow Jesus and glorify him in our thoughts and our actions. We tend to complicate the issue when the cure is simple. When temptation comes to the door, love and faith in Jesus bar its entrance.

Father, help me glorify Jesus every moment through my thoughts and actions.

Keep Curiosity

The sun was setting.
LUKE 4:40

Curiosity is the catalyst of learning. It is a hunger of the soul. We must never forget that the Bible is supernatural in origin, and we should never hesitate to ask questions of it. And as with everything else in creation, there is more to it than meets the eye.

Why would the Bible tell us that the sun sets? It happens every night. However, the rest of the verse tells us what was happening when the sun was setting. "When the sun was setting, all those who had any that were sick with various diseases brought them to Him; and He laid His hands on every one of them and healed them" (v. 40).

The Sabbath began when the sun went down. Right from the beginning, Jesus did not keep the traditions of the Jews. He healed the sick on the Sabbath. Oh, what joy it is to see Jesus do the will of God without being restricted by the traditions of dead religion! What a thrill it is to hear him rebuke those who pretended to love God and to see him flex his muscle by clearing the temple of hypocrites. And the day will come when this same Jesus will burst through the heavens and bring justice to this evil world. What a glorious day that will be!

Father, thank you for what I read of Jesus in your Word.

Emboldened in Sin

The goodness of God endures continually.
PSALM 52:1

God continues his kindness "on the just and on the unjust" (Matthew 5:45) for a reason: "Do you have no regard for the wealth of His kindness and tolerance and patience [in withholding His wrath]? Are you [actually] unaware or ignorant [of the fact] that God's kindness leads you to repentance [that is, to change your inner self, your old way of thinking—seek His purpose for your life]?" (Romans 2:4 AMP). Divine kindness is meant to lead us to repentance, not to be emboldened in our sin.

We should be driven by the gratefulness and peace that God's continual goodness inspires in us. Despite what we have done, God shows goodness to us. He showed goodness to us in saving us even before we had turned to him in faith. In response, we should show similar goodness to those around us. No matter what they have done, we should show them undeserved kindness because that is what we have received.

Father, thank you for your kindness to me before I came to faith in Jesus and for your care for me now.

July

They Worshiped Jesus

They came and held him by the feet,
and worshipped him.
MATTHEW 28:9 KJV

When the disciples worshiped Jesus, he didn't reprove them and say that we are to worship the Lord our God and him only shall we serve. Rather, he said, "Be not afraid: go tell my brethren that they go into Galilee, and there shall they see me" (v. 10 KJV). Some angels refused worship (see Revelation 22:8–9). But Jesus accepted the disciples' worship because he was "God…manifest in the flesh" (1 Timothy 3:16 KJV). Jesus was the express image of the invisible God (see Colossians 1:15). This was the Word that created the world, walking among humanity (see John 1:14). Incredibly, God condescended to become flesh so that he could pass through death and deliver us from its power (see Hebrews 2:9, 14–15).

The disciples recognized Jesus' true identity, but not everyone did. Matthew tells us why that is. People had many different theories about who Jesus was, but Jesus asked his disciples what they thought. Peter said, "Thou art the Christ, the Son of the living God" (Matthew 16:16 KJV). Jesus told him that "flesh and blood hath not revealed it unto thee, but my Father which is in heaven" (16:17 KJV). God the Father is the one who reveals his Son to you, me, and anyone who will be saved through Jesus. As we share the good news with our friends and neighbors, we need to be in prayer that God will work and bring revelation.

Father, thank you for my salvation because of your incarnation.

The Brilliant Savior

Again He began to teach by the sea.
MARK 4:1

This wasn't a small group of people who had gathered to hear Jesus. It was a "great multitude" (v. 1). Nowadays, teachers use a microphone to amplify their voice so their students can hear them. We are told Jesus "got into a boat and sat in it on the sea; and the whole multitude was on the land facing the sea" (v. 1). This was not only to control the crowd so that they wouldn't press in on Jesus, but it also amplified his voice so that he could be heard: "If you are sitting in a boat, a sound coming from the shore will seem louder than the same sound heard by a person on land. Sound seems to be amplified when it travels over water. The reason is that the water cools the air above its surface, which then slows down the sound waves near the surface."[3]

The disciples must have been in awe at how Jesus so brilliantly used the ocean, but later on, he spoke to it and it obeyed him. That caused them to say, "Who can this be, that even the wind and the sea obey Him!" (v. 41). Then he walked on the sea (see 6:45–52). He used it, spoke to it, walked on it.

Father, thank you that you put all things under the feet of Jesus (see 1 Corinthians 15:27).

---

3   Ron Kurtus, "Sound Seems Amplified Over Water," School for Champions, accessed on August 15, 2022, https://www.school-for-champions.com/science/sound_amplified_over_water.htm.

A Good Man

He was a good man,
and a just.
LUKE 23:50 KJV

The Bible seems to have many contradictions. But the humble search the Scriptures for understanding. For example, we are told of Joseph of Arimathea: "Behold, there was a man named Joseph, a counsellor; and he was a good man, and a just." He was a good man. But look what another verse says: "There came one running…and asked him, Good Master, what shall I do that I may inherit eternal life? And Jesus said unto him, Why callest thou me good? there is none good but one, that is, God" (Mark 10:17–18 KJV).

Joseph is described as a man of good character, but in the Gospel of Mark, "good" refers to the moral perfection of God. Joseph was not fully righteous; he was a sinner saved by grace. We strive to grow from being good like Joseph—as redeemed Christians with the Holy Spirit in us—to being more and more truly good as Christ is: becoming holy like him (see 1 Peter 1:16). This lifelong effort can be overwhelming. But God gives us the power.

Father, only you are morally perfect.

Why We Should Pray

The end of all things is at hand.

1 PETER 4:7

Biblically, we have been in the last days for the last two thousand years. Peter said that it was the last days when he preached on the day of Pentecost (see Acts 2:17), and here in his epistle he is saying that the end of all things is at hand. This is because a day to the Lord is a thousand years to us (see 2 Peter 3:8). To God, the last two thousand years have only been a couple of days. Peter then gives us an admonition to "therefore be serious and watchful in your prayers" (1 Peter 4:7). As we are much closer to the second coming of Christ, we should be serious and watchful in our prayers. Prayer is visible evidence that we believe the words of Jesus: "Apart from me you can do nothing" (John 15:5 ESV).

Preacher Charles Spurgeon said, "As well could you expect a plant to grow without air and water as to expect your heart to grow without prayer and faith." We must pray with a heart of thanksgiving, in faith, nothing wavering. We must pray for those who are in authority—that the gospel will continue to go forth with freedom. We must pray for everything that we may be tempted to stress about and ask God to fulfill his many promises to us.

Father, stir me to pray in a way that will move your mighty hand.

The Status of Man

> Let them thank the LORD
> for his steadfast love.
> PSALM 107:31 ESV

If all the nations before God are but a drop in a bucket (see Isaiah 40:15), how much less are we as individuals? Yet we tend to place great importance on the status of people. We esteem them for their wealth, for their athletic ability, for their physical beauty, or for the political power they wield. But to God, their abilities, power, wealth, and appearance are less than nothing. Look how the Bible puts in place those who carry some sort of self-importance:

> Surely men of low degree are a vapor,
> Men of high degree are a lie;
> If they are weighed on the scales,
> They are altogether lighter than vapor. (Psalm 62:9)

And yet, at the same time, among the billions of individuals, almighty God thinks of you and me. He is the lover of our soul. He made the earth for us. It is for you and me that we have fruits, the sunrise and sunset, the ocean, blue skies and rain, dogs and cats, horses and cows, love and laughter. He created all of this for our pleasure. And it was that same unmerited kindness that led the Savior to the cross and thrust open the door to everlasting life. It was for us that he did that.

Father, help me to continually praise you for your great kindness.

They Carried the Sick

Straightway they knew him.

MARK 6:54 KJV

The Scriptures tell us when Jesus came to the land of Gennesaret, his fame had gone before him. They knew him. As in many other places, the residents then began to run through the region to carry to Jesus those who were sick. They had a feeling of excitement and a sense of urgency. They ran because they cared. Love does that. When they saw where he was going, "they laid the sick in the streets, and besought him that they might touch if it were but the border of his garment: and as many as touched him were made whole" (Mark 6:56 KJV).

Dear Christian, we only have a short time until the door of grace closes. We must run to this world with a sense of urgency and carry sinners to the Savior. They won't come of their own volition. The Bible says, "There is none who seeks after God" (Romans 3:11). We have to go into the world to reach them (see Mark 16:15).

Father, help me to carry sinners to the Savior.

The Handle of Faith

"Do not worry then, saying, 'What will we eat?' or 'What will we drink?' or 'What will we wear for clothing?' For the Gentiles eagerly seek all these things; for your heavenly Father knows that you need all these things."

MATTHEW 6:31–32 NASB95

Henry Ward Beecher said, "Every tomorrow has two handles. We can take hold of it with the handle of anxiety or the handle of faith." They are the choices we have set before us: trust in God or unbelief. On this day, what will you and I take hold of? The words of Jesus in this passage of Matthew are so simple but so powerful. He told us, "Do not be worried about your life" (v. 25 NASB95). Jesus promised us that God would feed and clothe us. Those without faith wear themselves out trying to attain things for themselves. But Jesus said, "Your heavenly Father knows that you need all these things." He knows that we need money for food, clothes, and rent or mortgage. He knows because he made us. He knows because he has a plan for us.

Believe Jesus. Take hold of him today by the handle of faith. And encourage others to grasp that handle with you.

Father, help me grasp today by the handle of faith.

Insight into the Divine

God spoke to our fathers by the prophets.
HEBREWS 1:1 ESV

The book of Hebrews opens by pulling back the curtains to reveal heaven. It gives us a remarkable insight into the Old Testament, telling us that God, at various times and in differing ways, spoke to us through the prophets—from the moral law God gave to Moses on the Mount, where Israel trembled in fear, to the fearsome judgments Jeremiah gave them (see 2 Chronicles 36:22–23), to the reproofs they received through the minor prophets. But "in these last days he has spoken to us by his Son" (Hebrews 1:2 ESV).

In the opening verses of the book of Hebrews, look at the five breath-taking revelations: 1. God made Jesus the heir of all things. Everything is his. 2. He made the entire universe (the worlds) through Jesus. 3. Jesus was the brightness of God's glory and the express image of his person, the Creator come to us in human form. 4. The word of his power upholds everything; it continues to exist because of him. 5. After Jesus had purged our sins, he sat down at the right hand of God (see Hebrews 1:2–3). How can we then not read with wide-eyed awe the words that Jesus spoke in the Gospels and fall before him who is the King of kings and the Lord of lords!

Father, thank you for these revelations of your power and majesty. Help these truths to comfort my heart and mind today.

Hear Him

He was transfigured before them.
MARK 9:2 ESV

Today's verse is from a strange and wonderful portion of Scripture (see Mark 9:1–8). Jesus took James, Peter, and John up into a high mountain, and there he was transfigured in front of them. His clothes became brilliantly white, and suddenly two men who had died hundreds of years before were talking with Jesus. It seems that Moses and Elijah were somehow introduced to the disciples because the disciples knew their identities. Impetuous Peter, as usual, suggested something that was a little thoughtless. He wanted to start a mountaintop building program. His idea was to erect three structures—one in honor of Jesus, one for Moses, and one for Elijah. The Scriptures say that he said this because he was both fearful and dumbfounded (see v. 6).

Then things became even scarier for the disciples because God himself spoke from a cloud, saying that Jesus was his beloved Son and that they were to listen to him. And that's our message to this world: listen to Jesus. Hear him. His words are the words of eternal life. He is the only one who really matters in this entire universe because, without him, we will perish.

Father, help me to listen to all you have to tell me.

Drifting Away

Give the more earnest heed…
lest we drift away.
HEBREWS 2:1

Scripture uses the analogy of marriage for the Christian life—that the true church is the bride of Christ, and Jesus is the groom. In marriage, couples sometimes drift apart because they lose their passion for each other, and their eyes then wander. The grass seems greener on the other side of the fence. Spouses can drift apart because they don't communicate. They don't work at their relationship. And so it is with our relationship with the Lord.

We must never lose our passion for God. The way to keep it is to understand what God saved us from. We must look at the cross and see wondrous love so evidently displayed. And just like in a marriage, we are to keep the lines of communication open. Prayer is the oxygen of the Christian life. When we communicate with the Lord and listen to him through his Word, we will certainly draw closer to him. Both marriage and our walk with the Lord are held together with love. If we lose our first love, we won't want to communicate. The key to a good marriage and our walk with God is to prioritize that which makes them healthy. "We must pay much closer attention than ever to the things that we have heard, so that we do not [in any way] drift away from truth" (Hebrews 2:1 AMP).

Father, may I always love you with all my heart, mind, soul, and strength.

Looking to Jesus

We also are compassed about
with so great a cloud of witnesses.
HEBREWS 12:1 KJV

There are a number of ways to improve your chances of winning a race. The number one priority is to be fit and reduce excess body fat. Without fitness, we go nowhere. Wearing light clothing and shoes is also essential. Then, having a crowd cheering us on can be a great source of encouragement. But another key is to set our eyes on our goal of breaking the tape and winning the race. Scripture says of our spiritual race that God has made us fit for the kingdom—through the cross. We are surrounded by a great cloud of witnesses who are, in a sense, cheering us on as we run the course.

We are also told to lay aside every weight and the sin which so easily ensnares us and to run with endurance the race that is set before us: "Wherefore seeing we also are compassed about with so great a cloud of witnesses, let us lay aside every weight, and the sin which doth so easily beset us, and let us run with patience the race that is set before us" (v. 1 KJV). And here is the winning tape: Look "unto Jesus, the author and finisher of our faith; who for the joy that was set before him endured the cross, despising the shame, and is set down at the right hand of the throne of God" (v. 2 KJV).

Father, help me to keep my eyes on Jesus.

Worthy of Note

He called His disciples to Himself.
MARK 12:43

Jesus sat down and watched people give money to the temple treasury. This was a visible collection plate. Then he saw something worthy of calling his disciples over and explaining to them what he had witnessed. The wealthy were giving out of their excess, but a poor woman had given all the money she had. She had given to God out of her poverty. In other words, the sacrifice of the rich had been little, but the widow's had been great. While the chief lesson for us is to give sacrificially and trust God to supply our needs, we can take even more from this wonderful lesson. The apostle Paul instructed new Christians in this way: "I beseech you therefore, brethren, by the mercies of God, that ye present your bodies a living sacrifice, holy, acceptable unto God, which is your reasonable service" (Romans 12:1 KJV).

We can and should give of our money. But in addition to that, we are commanded to give everything that we are to God. We are to give of our time and our energy. We are to devote all of our faculties to the Lord: our minds, sight, speech, and hearing. We are to go where he leads and do what he commands. The life of a living sacrifice is worthy of our pursuit.

Father, may I live sacrificially.

Loose the Donkey

"The Lord has need of it."
MARK 11:3

As Jesus approached Jerusalem, he told two of his disciples to go to a village and find a young donkey that no one had ever ridden. They were to untie it and bring it to him. It was for Jesus to ride into the city. He said that if anyone questioned why they were letting the donkey loose, they were to simply say that "'the Lord has need of it,' and immediately he will send it here" (vv. 1–3). The disciples went to the village and found the colt tied by a door where two ways met, and they released it. Some of the people there asked them why they were loosing the colt, and when the disciples said what Jesus told them to say, the people let them go.

We were once tied to sin, but we were loosed from its grip for the purposes of God. We entered the door of the Savior (see John 10:9), by a place where two ways met—righteousness and peace kissed each other at the cross (see Psalm 85:10). Like a donkey, we are lowly and stubborn creatures, but God wants to use us. We are to carry Jesus to this world, and if man or demon questions us, they will have to let us go because we have a divine commission (see Mark 16:15).

Father, no one can stop you from doing your will.

Make a Difference

Of some have compassion,
making a difference.
JUDE 22 KJV

Times of stress and anxiety can make us very selfish. We can be consumed with our own discomfort and turn inward, forgetting to think about others. Let this not be true of you! Foster compassion in your heart for those who don't know our Savior. Seek to save them with fear, "pulling them out of the fire" (v. 22 KJV). You are like a firefighter: you give a blanket to comfort some while others need you to pick them up and carry them to safety. Charles Spurgeon said,

> Reckon then that to acquire soul-winning power, you will have to go through mental torment and soul distress. You must go into the fire if you are going to pull others out of it, and you will have to dive into the floods if you are going to draw others out of the water. You cannot work a fire escape without feeling the scorch of the conflagration, nor man a lifeboat without being covered with the waves.

The best way for us to acquire the necessary biblical skills to reach the lost is to study Scripture and then put our knowledge into practice by speaking with the unsaved. A dive is a full commitment. Do it. Turn toward others and be compassionate to all you meet.

Father, make me a 24/7 soul winner to your glory.

Effective Prayer

Confess your faults one to another, and pray one for another, that ye may be healed. The effectual fervent prayer of a righteous man availeth much.

JAMES 5:16 KJV

It is deeply consoling to know that our Christian brothers and sisters go through the same battle against sin that we go through. Each of us is incessantly tempted by this sinful world, the carnality of our own flesh, and the subtle wiles of the devil, and knowing that other Christians possess the same weaknesses gives us a good reason to keep them in prayer. And prayer prayed with a passion cuts through the heavens. It stops the mouths of demons.

The word *effectual* in the Greek language is *energeo*, from which we derive the word *energy*. The energy we put into our intercession is very real evidence of our love, of our concern, and of our faith. It is a sad fact that we pray most fervently when we are going through fiery trials. Lions' dens and Red Seas tend to cause us to look to God when the alternative is hungry lions or deep waters. The Prince of Preachers, Charles Spurgeon, said, "I know of no better thermometer to your spiritual temperature than this, the measure of the intensity of your prayer." Thank God that his ear is always open and he acts on our behalf if we merely ask with faith!

Father, remind me to keep my prayers full of believing energy.

Count It a Great Joy

Count it all joy when you fall into various trials.
JAMES 1:2

When we fall, we tend to hurt ourselves. We bruise our flesh and even break our bones, and with that comes pain. However, the Scriptures tell us to count it all joy when we fall. This is not easy without a living faith. Faith in God immediately gives us comfort because we know that the trying of our faith works patience. God is well pleased when we are patient in tribulation because a lack of panic is evidence of our trust in him. When Daniel was in the lion's den, it could not have been easy for him to look at the lions and have patience. It's natural to want to quickly get out of the lion's den if we fall into it. That makes sense. But after the fact, no doubt Daniel counted it all joy—after seeing that God worked on his behalf so miraculously.

It is said that our eyesight is 20/20 after the fact. But Scripture gives us 20/20 eyesight *before* the fact. So next time a trial comes our way and throws us into a fearful lion's den, let's be quick to be patient and joyfully thank God that he allowed that circumstance, knowing that all things are working together for our good because we love him (see Romans 8:28).

Father, help me to handle my next trial with spiritual maturity.

The Angry Man

Let everyone be quick to hear.
JAMES 1:19 AMP

The wisdom of Solomon tells us to stay away from those who are angry: "Make no friendship with an angry man, and with a furious man do not go" (Proverbs 22:24). Angry people aren't "swift to hear." They are poor listeners. They lack the wisdom that's from above—wisdom that is open to reason and logic. Angry people aren't slow to speak. Their anger produces fire from their lips, so they are not slow to wrath.

But Scripture tells us that there is a God in heaven who is considered with every human emotion. We must be swift to hear. That is, we must be careful, thoughtful listeners. We must be open to reason and logic because we possess the wisdom that's from above. We must be speakers of carefully chosen words. It is because we fear God that we set aside that which makes others angry. Such thoughts will help us in our daily interactions with others, both off and on the freeway. Such thoughts will put a halt to the violence and the murder that is so prevalent in today's society. Look at what Scripture says, "the [resentful, deep-seated] anger of man does not produce the righteousness of God [that standard of behavior which He requires from us]" (James 1:20 AMP).

Father, put a watch on my tongue. Help me to always be swift to hear.

That Noble Name

Do they not blaspheme?
JAMES 2:7 AMP

The Scriptures are specific about blasphemy: "Do they not blaspheme the precious name [of Christ] by which you are called?" (James 2:7 AMP). How horrifying to think that the name of Jesus Christ was being blasphemed when this was written nearly two thousand years ago. That precious name is still blasphemed across this evil world. It is the only name in all of human history that's ever been used as a cuss word. Such is the hatred the children of darkness have for the light. And yet Scripture goes from the condemnation of blasphemy to telling us how we should love sinners:

> If, however, you are [really] fulfilling the royal law according to the Scripture, "You shall love your neighbor as yourself [that is, if you have an unselfish concern for others and do things for their benefit]" you are doing well. But if you show partiality [prejudice, favoritism], you are committing sin and are convicted by the Law as offenders. (James 2:8–9 AMP)

Do we have an unselfish concern for others? That is a key that will increase our joy. It truly is more blessed to give than to receive. And bedfellows of love and joy are two other fruits of the Spirit—peace and faith. Both of these fruits will help us to trust God and be free from worry.

Father, help me to always look beyond the wickedness of a blaspheming world.

Always Ask Questions

He is a perfect man.
JAMES 3:2

A wise person once said, "Never accuse. Ask questions." Instead of accusing an employee of being slack because he was late for work, it's wise to ask, "Is there any reason why you were late this morning?" If he tells you that a family member died, you'll be glad you asked a question rather than angrily accusing him. The Bible says that if we're able to control our tongue and not cause some sort of offense, we are a perfect person (see James 3:2). There are not many people in that category. Those who are in that category, more than likely, are slow to speak, walk in the fear of the Lord, and have a heart soaked in the Word of God.

The Scriptures liken the tongue to a rudder that turns a great ship. That tiny tongue can cause massive shipwrecks. And then Scripture moves from ships, rudders, and wind to describing the tongue as a terrible fire: "The tongue is a fire, a world of iniquity. The tongue is so set among our members that it defiles the whole body, and sets on fire the course of nature; and it is set on fire by hell" (v. 6). So let's be careful to use our tongues as peacemakers rather than lending it to the devil and becoming fire-starters.

Father, help me to use my tongue to edify and encourage those who are around me.

Eternal Perspective

He has put eternity in their hearts.
ECCLESIASTES 3:11

Do you ever think about eternity? Some subjects are big. Perhaps this is the biggest of all. It's a dimension we can't imagine, one where there's no time. We think back to before we were born, where time existed but we didn't. It's hard to grapple with that thought. Someone said that we should have eternity tattooed on the inside of our eyelids. If we did that, every time we blinked, it would be a reminder that eternity is looming.

At the moment, it seems to be on the horizon, but time will bring eternity to us one day. We must, therefore, bring that same vision before the multitudes who can't see past tomorrow. Many of them can't even see past the day. They make no provision for their eternal salvation. So we must put eternity in their thoughts by telling them that their salvation is infinitely more important than deciding whom they marry or what they will do for a job. Those decisions are just temporal.

In the meantime, we do ourselves a great favor by remembering that everything in this life is temporal. Having an eternal worldview lifts us above the problems and pains that life brings. Having, metaphorically, "eternity stamped on our eyes" lifts us above the daily causes of stress because it helps us to see things from the divine perspective.

Father, help me to be eternally minded.

What to Do

Zacharias said to the angel, "How shall I know this?"
LUKE 1:18

The opening of Luke is one of the most amazing portions of Scripture in that it establishes the credibility of the inspirational Gospel. Luke had first-hand knowledge of Jesus. He begins the gospel by telling the story of Zacharias, to whom the angel of the Lord appeared and told him of things that would certainly come to pass. The angel used the word *shall* many times to establish the credibility of his prophetic word. It was going to happen. And what was Zacharias's response to this wonderful prophecy? He said, "How shall I know this?" He doubted the angel's word and was instantly struck dumb for his unbelief.

It's easy to forget that the Bible says that unbelief is a sin. When we get stressed and worry about problems in the future, we are reaping the fruit of unbelief (see Romans 14:23). This is because stress and worry would not be there if we fully trusted God and his promises. It's a gross insult to any human being to not trust them. Try saying to a friend that you don't trust them, and you can be certain it will damage your friendship. Tell your boss you don't trust him, and it may be the end of your job. So how much more should we trust God, believe his promises, and in doing so, live a life free of stress.

Father, forgive me for my lack of trust in you.

We Can Question

"How can this be,
since I do not know a man?"
LUKE 1:34

The Scriptures tell us in the first chapter of Luke that the angel Gabriel appeared to Mary, told her that she was blessed among women, and said that she had found favor in the sight of God. Then he said that she would bring forth a son and that his name would be Jesus. He was to be called the Son of the highest, and of his kingdom there would be no end (see vv. 28–33). Then Mary said to the angel, "How can this be, since I do not know a man?"

As he did with Zacharias, Gabriel had said that these things would surely come to pass—using the word *shall* many times to establish the credibility of his prophecy. And like Zacharias, Mary had questioned this. How could this happen since she was a virgin? However, she was not struck dumb for her unbelief. This is because her question was not provoked by doubt. How do we know this? Because Scripture tells us so: "Blessed is she who believed, for there will be a fulfillment of those things which were told her from the Lord" (v. 45). This is a wonderful source of encouragement in that we can question God as long as we trust in him and don't doubt his promises.

Father, thank you for the encouragement of your Word and its exceedingly great and precious promises.

Faith and Fear Motivate

Noah…moved with fear.
HEBREWS 11:7 KJV

Noah believed God's warning of things to come. The great flood would destroy all of humanity. No doubt, he feared God, and he feared for those who were going to come under his wrath. But he didn't just tremble in fear. The fear motivated him; it moved him to prepare the ark. "By faith Noah, being warned of God of things not seen as yet, moved with fear, prepared an ark to the saving of his house" (Hebrews 11:7 KJV).

This chapter in the book of Hebrews is a list of the heroes of the faith. These heroes are men and women who trusted in God despite the hatred of this world, and that trust produced courage in them to do his will. Abel, Enoch, Noah, Abraham, Isaac, Joseph, and Jacob were all moved by fear. There were also women of faith who received their dead raised to life again. Others were tortured, not accepting deliverance, so they might obtain a better resurrection. Today, be moved by faith and fear to warn the ungodly of what's to come. Be a hero of the faith. You need not be tall, strong, or gifted. Anyone can exercise faith. And when you do so, by trusting in God (no matter what is happening around you), you will lift yourself above the troubles of this world. True faith does that.

Father, let me be one of your heroes of faith.

The Antidote

…so that you will not grow weary and lose heart.
HEBREWS 12:3 AMP

It's easy to become discouraged, and discouragement often comes to us when we are weary. Every day brings new trials. Some are small, and some are breathtakingly big. The daily news is also often discouraging. There are horror stories every day. People die in floods, in fires, from falls, and from disease. Others are assaulted, murdered, and kidnapped. If we're not careful, we can feel overwhelmed with the onslaught of negativity and evil. But here the Scriptures give us an antidote to discouragement: "Just consider and meditate on Him who endured from sinners such bitter hostility against Himself [consider it all in comparison with your trials], so that you will not grow weary and lose heart" (Hebrews 12:3 AMP).

We're told to think of Jesus, especially what happened to him when he fell into the hands of evil men. The light shone in the darkness and exposed their sin. Consider how a crowd moved from crying, "Hosanna!" to shouting, "Crucify him!" They united and called for his innocent blood, and then they shed it. Think of how he suffered in an agony we can't begin to imagine all so that we could be saved from death and damnation. Meditating on his great love that drove him to the cross will stave off depression and keep us energized in our labors.

Father, I love you because you first loved me.

In the Way of Righteousness

"Seek first the kingdom of God and His righteousness."
MATTHEW 6:33

Living in modern times has some great advantages. Air conditioning is one of them—a big one, in hot weather. So is electricity and the convenience of iPhones and iPads. But the greatest advantage we have is that we can look back and see God's redemptive plan unfold. Imagine living thousands of years ago and seeing a Bible verse that seems to promise hope in your death: "In the way of righteousness is life: and in the pathway thereof there is no death" (Proverbs 12:28 KJV). Imagine seeing its absolute promise but not knowing the way of righteousness.

But we're not living thousands of years ago. We can easily flip through the pages of Scripture and see Thomas ask Jesus, "How can we know the way?" (John 14:5 KJV). And we can see him answer, "I am the way, the truth, and the life: no man cometh unto the Father, but by me" (v. 6 KJV). Then we can flip over to the book of Philippians and see, "Be found in him, not having mine own righteousness, which is of the law, but that which is through the faith of Christ, the righteousness which is of God by faith" (Philippians 3:9 KJV). You've found the righteousness in which there's no death. It comes by simple faith in Jesus. It is the gift of God, yours for the asking.

Father, your grace is amazing.

Natural Consequences

Fools…because of their iniquities, were afflicted.
PSALM 107:17

How foolish it is to ignore God. It's the same as building a house on sand, and when the storm comes, the house will certainly collapse. When we refuse to obey the gospel, we stay in the kingdom of darkness, serving sin and the devil. Jesus called a man a fool who did just that. The man built bigger barns in which to store his goods. He forgot about his Creator, and he forgot about death, and the grim reaper seized him unawares one dark night. The thoughtless man reaped what he sowed.

This foolish world doesn't realize that if it serves sin, it will reap affliction and death. We know that there are unseen laws that are unforgiving. These are laws of morality that will crush those who transgress them. Sinners become slaves to tobacco, alcohol, and drugs and often die untimely deaths. But there is also self-inflicted pain that comes with adultery. A spouse caught in adultery will likely face divorce, anger, hatred, bitterness, and jealousy. Those given to greed often leave a trail of pain by being consumed by the love of money. How thankful we should be that God has shown us through his Word how to avoid many of these afflictions, how to live above them, how to have peace in times of trouble and faith in place of stress.

Father, thank you for turning me away from the path of destruction.

Go Tell That Fox

"Leave and go away from here."
LUKE 13:31 AMP

Jesus had healed a woman who had been afflicted by the devil for eighteen years. She had been bent double and couldn't stand up. One sentence from Jesus and she was miraculously made perfectly well. But instead of rejoicing at the power of God, the religious leaders complained that Jesus had healed the woman on the Sabbath day. That's when Jesus called the spokesperson a hypocrite, and when he explained why, everybody was ashamed. That was the reason the religious leaders hated Jesus. He humiliated them for their hypocrisy. And so they tried to use fear to get Jesus to leave: "At that very hour some Pharisees came up and said to Him, 'Leave and go away from here, because Herod [Antipas] wants to kill You.' And He said to them, 'Go and tell that fox [that sly, cowardly man], "Listen carefully: I cast out demons and perform healings today and tomorrow, and on the third day I reach My goal"'" (Luke 13:31–32 AMP).

We also have goals: to obey the Lord, reach the lost, and honor God in our daily work. In all this, we should take note of the example of Jesus by letting nothing deter us from our noble tasks. When the enemy tries to use fear to discourage us, we will not listen to that sly fox.

Father, let nothing deter me from doing your will today.

A Friend of Sinners

"This Man receives sinners."

LUKE 15:2

The religious leaders complained because Jesus not only welcomed despised tax collectors and the immoral, but he also ate with them. But they may have been provoked by jealousy. The Bible tells us that "all the tax collectors and the sinners drew near to Him to hear Him" (v. 1). They drew near to Jesus to hear him. They wanted to know what he had to say. In another portion of Scripture, where he was asked why he received sinners, Jesus said, "Those who are healthy have no need of a physician, but [only] those who are sick; I did not come to call the righteous, but sinners [who recognize their sin and humbly seek forgiveness]" (Mark 2:17 AMP).

Before any of us comes to a place of genuine repentance, we have to catch a glimpse of our own sins. Doing that should forever stop us from being like the accusing religious leaders. When we see ourselves in truth, we will never look at another human being with condescension. Neither will we look at them with fear or annoyance. Rather our heart will go out to them with empathy, and we will want to be like Jesus and be a friend of sinners. We will not only receive them, but we will also desire to have fellowship over a meal with them because we truly love them and want to see them in heaven.

Father, help me to be like Jesus.

Infinitely Higher

"Ye are they which justify yourselves."
LUKE 16:15 KJV

Jesus had just spoken about loving money more than loving God. He said that we cannot serve God and money. Then the Scriptures tell us that the Pharisees were lovers of money, and when they heard him say these things, they derided him. Now watch Jesus use the law to bring the knowledge of sin. Firstly he said, "That which is highly esteemed among men is abomination in the sight of God" (v. 15 KJV). God's standard of morality is infinitely higher than ours. Then Jesus said, "The law and the prophets were until John: since that time the kingdom of God is preached, and every man presseth into it" (v. 16 KJV).

In other words, the law was doing its job in Israel—in showing the nature of sin. Israel knew God's holy requirements, and as soon as the kingdom of God was preached, they pressed into it. The law put salt on their tongue. Thankfully, Jesus did more than bring the law and knowledge of sin. He also offered himself as a way of deliverance from the law. We have no need of hopelessly attempting to justify ourselves. Rather, we trust in Jesus and in his perfect righteousness.

Father, may I always honor and uphold your law.

Where Is God?

Has God forgotten to be gracious?

PSALM 77:9 AMP

If we lack simple trust in God, life can seem full of unanswered prayers. Grandma gets sick, and she tragically dies. We don't get the new job we needed and for which we prayed earnestly. The Red Sea didn't open as we hoped it would, and now we can't pay bills after constantly pleading with God for financial relief. It's in times of stress that we can wonder, *Has God forgotten to be kind to me? Where is his lovingkindness?* This was David's question in his times of darkness. He even wondered if God was angry at him because of his sins (v. 9). But his victory came when, by an act of his will, he delved into his memory:

> "I will [solemnly] remember the deeds of the LORD;
> Yes, I will [wholeheartedly] remember Your wonders of old.
> I will meditate on all Your works
> And thoughtfully consider all Your [great and wondrous] deeds." (vv. 11–12 AMP)

Then David considered God's amazing power, his greatness, and his magnificent works. Never forget what the Lord has done. Think of his kindness in giving us life and then lavishing us with many blessings—especially with the "indescribable gift" of the cross (2 Corinthians 9:15). That's evidence of trust in him. It is the key to lifting us above the many trials that can steal our joy.

Father, please help me to trust you in difficult times.

The Sin of Ingratitude

"Jesus, Master, have mercy on us!"
LUKE 17:13 AMP

When Jesus passed through Samaria and Galilee, ten men with leprosy, who stood far off, isolated from the rest of the world, called out to Jesus to have mercy on them. And Jesus did. He healed them all of their plague. But only one returned to give Jesus thanks for cleansing him of the deadly disease:

> One of them, when he saw that he was healed, turned back, glorifying and praising and honoring God with a loud voice; and he lay face downward at Jesus' feet, thanking Him [over and over]. He was a Samaritan. Then Jesus asked, "Were not ten [of you] cleansed? Where are the [other] nine? Was there no one found to return and to give thanks and praise to God, except this foreigner?" (vv. 15–18 AMP)

When the ten lepers first cried out, they said the right thing. They showed respect by calling Jesus by name. They called him "Master." And they cried out for mercy. We tend to be respectful when we want something, but true respect is revealed in a response of gratitude. The final reaction of the other nine was one of sinful ingratitude. How are we responding today, knowing that Jesus cleansed us of our sins? Do our lives glorify God daily with a loud voice? Think on his mercy to you today, praise him for it, and watch how gratitude brings you joy and peace.

Father, may my life glorify you with a loud voice.

August

Don't Give Up

They ought always to pray
and not lose heart.
LUKE 18:1 ESV

Many people who take Bible promises out of context no doubt become disillusioned with God's seeming inaction. However, it is healthy to take careful note of the requirements to have a successful prayer life. Jesus told us that we should constantly pray, but in doing so, we should never lose heart. This is because the God who made lightning also made the snail. Sometimes he is slow to react to our requests. It's then that we need to consider the story that Jesus told about a certain judge who had no fear of God and didn't care what people thought of him (see Luke 18:2). But this man's will was bent by a persistent widow. She kept hounding him until she got what she wanted.

That's the attitude that Jesus said we must have when we pray. Never give up. Pray without ceasing. Rather than becoming desperate, we should be filled with faith that God hears and will respond in his own time and in his great wisdom. This is the sort of faith that pleases God. Let's say with Jacob, "I will not let You go unless You bless me" (Genesis 32:26). Hold on, be strong, trust him with all your heart, and never depend on your own understanding (see Proverbs 3:5–6).

Father, I trust you because I know that you hear me and will answer in your own good time.

Take Heed to the Law

Give ear, O my people,
to my law.
PSALM 78:1

It is God himself who says to give ear to his law. That's why we should take notice. The Scriptures tell us that he appointed that law in Israel. He gave it to Moses, and Moses gave it to the children of Israel. And then the Scriptures say that fathers should make the law known to their children so that they might set their hope in God and not forget his works "but keep His commandments" (v. 7). Any generation that is left without the law is left without a moral rudder, and in time, they will become shipwrecked.

God gave us the law, but he also gave us his Son. While on earth, Jesus heeded the law perfectly and died to atone for our deafness to the law. Faith is the opposite of fear. Trusting in God means that we never have to worry about our standing in God's righteous sight because he is faithful to keep his Word and forgive our sins when we are covered with Jesus' blood. And out of gratitude, we strive to obey him and follow him every minute of the day.

Father, may my spirit always be steadfast with you, trusting you alone for my eternal salvation.

Vengeance Is Mine

Alexander the coppersmith did me much evil:
the Lord reward him according to his works.

2 TIMOTHY 4:14 KJV

The apostle Paul gives us no details of who Alexander was
or what he did that caused Paul so much evil. Perhaps as a
coppersmith, he was a maker of idols, and Paul's preaching
against idolatry took away his income. Or maybe he was
simply a wicked man who loved the darkness and hated the
light that Paul preached. Christianity has many opposers
because it is against everything this world loves. It speaks
against the pleasures of sin that so delight an evil world, and
so those who love the darkness are often passionate about
putting out the light of the gospel.

But Paul's reaction to the evil that the coppersmith had
personally done to him is the biblical reaction. The Bible says
of Jesus that "when He suffered, He...committed Himself to
Him who judges righteously" (1 Peter 2:23). We don't take the
law into our own hands or seek personal vengeance. Instead,
we trust ourselves to the omniscient God, who sees all and
therefore judges righteously. The day will come when his
righteous judgment will fall upon all those who have opposed
the most wonderful message this world could ever hope to
hear. God protects his children and fights our battles for us.

Father, I trust you to handle my opposers.

Gaining Jews

To the Jews I became as a Jew.
1 CORINTHIANS 9:20

The apostle Paul had a burning passion for reaching his own people. He said, "I could wish that I myself were accursed and cut off from Christ for the sake of my brothers, my kinsmen according to the flesh" (Romans 9:3 ESV). As Christians, we long to reach all people, but we can feel a little intimidated when we find out that somebody is Jewish.

How do we witness to a Jew? The key is to set aside our fears of the person's reaction and instead focus on our love and care for the person in front of us. Paul's passion for his brothers should be our guide. Therefore, we treat Jews as we would anyone else. We open up the divine law and appeal to the conscience, trusting that the work of the law will do its God-given duty. We are driven by love and have continual hope in God's power to save through any means—even through you and me.

Father, help me to become all things to all people that I might by any means save some.

The Standard of Men

I am not as other men are.
LUKE 18:11 KJV

It seems like the less we know about something, the better we think we are at it. That's why we yell at athletes when they drop the ball. This prevalence of thinking of ourselves as better than we are is never more evident than when we morally judge others and especially when we judge ourselves. We are hard on others and soft on ourselves. In the story Jesus told of two men who went to pray, he said, "The Pharisee stood and prayed thus with himself, God, I thank thee, that I am not as other men are, extortioners, unjust, adulterers, or even as this publican" (v. 11 KJV). The Pharisee's error was that he judged himself by human standards. He said, "I'm not as other men are."

But other people are not our standard. Our standard is Jesus. We should not be worrying about others and stewing on their actions, but rather focusing on growing more Christlike ourselves. That is what God calls us to do.

Father, help me to be free from judging the sins of others.

Death Has Been Destroyed

Our Savior Jesus Christ…has abolished death and brought
life and immortality to light through the gospel.

2 TIMOTHY 1:10

Today's verse is fantastic in the true sense of the word. It
sounds like fantasy because people still die. How could Jesus
have abolished death? To answer that question, we have to
find the cause of death. The Bible tells us that the "wages of
sin is death" (Romans 6:23). In other words, God pays us in
death for our sins. Our death is evidence that he is deadly
serious about sin.

Through the cross, Jesus paid the fine for the law
that we violated. That means God can dismiss our case. He
can legally take the death sentence off us. That happens the
moment we're born again. Death has no dominion over those
who trust in Jesus Christ. Death has been abolished. At the
same time, God gives us his Holy Spirit—which is life itself.
He seals us with his Spirit. That means that not only has he
destroyed death, but he has also given us everlasting life as a
free gift. That's why Jesus could say, "I am he that liveth, and
was dead; and, behold, I am alive for evermore, Amen; and
have the keys of hell and of death" (Revelation 1:18 KJV).

Father, thank you for destroying our greatest enemy.

Heart Humility

"I am gentle and lowly in heart."
MATTHEW 11:29 ESV

The proud person has the attention of God. But in a negative sense. The Bible tells us that "God opposes the proud" (James 4:6 ESV). There is a battle between the proud and God. The proud man is an enemy of God in his mind because of wicked works (see Colossians 1:21). The only way any human being can get the attention of God in a positive sense is to have a humble heart. This is foreign to many human beings.

There are those who can feign humility on the outside and impress other human beings with public foot washings and helping the poor. However, the Bible speaks of humility of the heart. God's not impressed with outward humility. He sees the motive and the thought-life (see Hebrews 4:12). There was only one who always did that which pleased God. And that was Jesus: "He who sent Me is [always] with Me; He has not left Me alone, because I always do what pleases Him" (John 8:29 AMP). In Christ, we are forgiven, washed, and given a robe of righteousness, but we strive to always do that which pleases God. And so, with the psalmist, we say, "Let the words of my mouth and the meditation of my heart be acceptable in Your sight, O LORD" (Psalm 19:14).

Father, help me to always strive to see your smile by having a humble heart.

Our Wages

"The soul who sins shall die."
ᴇᴢᴇᴋɪᴇʟ 18:20

There are two things the world tends to soften. One is sin, and the other is death. It softens sin with substitutionary words. Lies are called "fibs." Adultery is called "having an affair." But despite the softening, the wages that sin pays is still death (see Romans 6:23). Which brings us to how the world softens the horror of death. When someone dies, we say they "pass." We call a corpse "the deceased." However, substituting other words doesn't lessen the terrible consequences of sin. Jesus didn't dress down sin, nor did he dress up death. And neither should we.

Our guilt is real, and the just penalty is brutally real. But so is the redemption Jesus offers. We have lied; Jesus told only the truth. Jesus truly died, and he truly rose. Our sin is stark and concrete, but so is the perfect life of Jesus that he gives to us if we only believe. We must wake up the world to the reality of their sin and the resulting death. And we must wake them up to the reality of the hope and redemption the Father freely offers as well.

Father, help me to share the hope you've given me.

Bearing False Witness

Lying lips are an abomination to the LORD.
PROVERBS 12:22

Scripture tells us that lying is one of the prevalent signs of the last days (see Matthew 24). We read that one sign in the world would be "Speaking lies in hypocrisy, having their own conscience seared with a hot iron" (1 Timothy 4:2). There are at least four ways to spot a liar. When confronted about lying, sinners will often:

Repeat the question, stalling for time to think of how they can avoid the subject.

Try to spread the blame. "Everyone lies." In other words, it's no big deal.

Give a mass of insignificant details in an attempt to lose the original question.

Have physical reactions. For example, when someone lies, their heart might beat faster, and that produces pupil dilation.

What we call "lie detectors" aren't really "lie" detectors. They are conscience detectors. The conscience produces guilt, which speeds up the heartbeat. Romans 2:15 gives us insight as to what's happening when someone tells a lie. It says that even those who are not Christian "show the work of the law written in their hearts, their conscience also bearing witness," and then it speaks of "their thoughts accusing or else excusing them." In other words, when we lie, the conscience speaks up (like an impartial judge in the courtroom of the mind), and its voice accuses us of sinning.

Father, help me to always speak the truth, the whole truth, and nothing but the truth.

Selfish Desire

Where do wars and fights
come from among you?
JAMES 4:1

There are not only wars among nations and kingdoms, but
there are even wars within homes, such as when husbands
and wives war in front of their kids. Then there's the never-
ending war going on within the human heart, where evil
thoughts seek to conquer the good. The Scriptures address
all these wars by saying, "Where do wars and fights come
from among you? Do they not come from your desires for
pleasure that war in your members?" (v. 1).

Every war, whether in the home or among nations, is
sparked by selfish desire. We, of course, look forward to the
day when the nations lay down their weapons and choose
peace: "He shall judge between the nations, and rebuke
many people; they shall beat their swords into plowshares,
and their spears into pruning hooks; Nation shall not lift up
sword against nation, neither shall they learn war anymore"
(Isaiah 2:4). Until that time we can beat our swords (our
cutting tongues) into tools for sowing good seed, not bad,
because the antidote to every war is love.

*Father, give me a loving tongue and make me an instrument of
peace in every situation today.*

Eternal Love

"For the mountains shall depart and the hills be removed, but My kindness shall not depart from you, nor shall My covenant of peace be removed," says the LORD, who has mercy on you.

ISAIAH 54:10

This promise is truly beautiful and comforting. God promises to always love us. Such steadfast, pure love may be hard for us to understand. We live among changeable humans like ourselves, and even the strongest love we've experienced is subject to temptation and self-interest and anger. But God's love isn't like that. That's why the metaphor he gives is so helpful. It shows how incredible and dependable his love is. His love is stronger and more stable than the mountains. Have you ever seen a mountain move a few feet to the side? The thought is ridiculous, but such an event is more likely than God's love ever departing from you and me.

We must trust in this love and emulate it in our own lives. Our love for others should grow ever stronger and steadier. Our kindness should never depart from those we live with, those we encounter at our work or school, or the unsaved we meet every day. We must be loving as our heavenly Father is loving.

Father, thank you for your everlasting love.

Liar, Liar

"All will be Yours."
LUKE 4:7

Jesus said just four words that hold the key to totally overcoming sin and the devil. He said them without any human witnesses while in the heat of a bloodless but epic battle. He said them privately, but the words were made public so that we could know exactly what Jesus said. The devil took Jesus onto a high mountain and showed him all the kingdoms of the world in a moment of time. Then the devil said, "If You will worship before me, all will be Yours." In other words, Satan was trying to tempt Jesus to become a devil-worshiper. That's when Jesus said those four very powerful words: "Get behind Me, Satan!" (v. 8).

What do these words mean? And just as important, how can we also use that phrase when the devil promises us a world of sin? The key is to understand that the saying comes packed with dynamite because it carries explosive connotations. When we even whisper, "Get behind me, Satan," we are saying, "Satan, I once served you. But I've stopped following you. So get behind me, Satan. Get out of my sight. I don't want to look at you because I'm now looking to Jesus, the author and finisher of my faith. He is the reservoir of absolute truth."

Father, I am yours forever. Thank you for giving me power to overcome any temptation.

The Specifics

You may be partakers
of the divine nature.
2 PETER 1:4

We are partakers of the divine nature. While Peter doesn't give us the specifics of what that means, Paul does: "The fruit of the Spirit [the result of His presence within us] is love [unselfish concern for others], joy, [inner] peace, patience [not the ability to wait, but how we act while waiting], kindness, goodness, faithfulness, gentleness, self-control. Against such things there is no law" (Galatians 5:22–23 AMP).

As Christians, we are no longer partakers of the carnal nature of Adam. The light of God invaded the darkness of our sinful hearts the moment we trusted in Jesus. We were immediately transferred from the kingdom of darkness into the glorious light, delivered from the power of death to life, given citizenship in a world without end. Before us in his Word are "exceedingly great and precious promises" (2 Peter 1:4) upon which we firmly stand. Thank God for what he's already done in making you more like himself, and commit to furthering that sanctification even more with his help and the help of his Holy Spirit.

Father, thank you for making me more like yourself.

I Trust in Your Word

So shall I have an answer
for him who reproaches me.
PSALM 119:42

The world hates us for the same reason it hates Jesus, and he said that they hated him because he testified of their evil deeds (see John 7:7). And so the world reproaches those who belong to Jesus. They look on us condescendingly. They mock us and taunt us for our childlike faith in Jesus. What we believe is not only an offense to them, but it is also a threat. They, therefore, war against our stand for righteousness. They fight to normalize every kind of sin and ridicule those who don't agree.

But we have an answer for those who reproach us—an answer that comes from the authority of God's Word. We trust that the Bible is the Word of the Creator because it is axiomatic. It proves itself to be true through its amazing prophecy, its commonsense teachings, the utter uniqueness and power of the words of Jesus, and many other reasons. The inspiration of the Scriptures is the reason we can live a stress-free life. Being a Christian and having access to the Bible is like watching a sporting event being replayed on television and already knowing the final score. You never have to get stressed because you know your side wins. We need never stress because we know our side wins. God wins over the devil, and righteousness wins over sin.

Father, I reiterate your Word. How will the world escape if they neglect so great a salvation?

Times of Affliction

Before I was afflicted
I went astray.
PSALM 119:67 ESV

Our sinful heart points us toward sin as a compass needle points toward the north. We can't help but sin until God transforms us through new birth and gives us a love for that which is good and right. And now we have a battle of our two natures. We still have the propensity to sin and, at times, go astray in our walk. And so our Father, in his great love, afflicts us. The book of Hebrews says:

> "My son, do not make light of the discipline of the LORD,
> And do not lose heart and give up when you are corrected by Him;
> For the LORD disciplines and corrects those whom He loves,
> And He punishes every son whom He receives
> and welcomes [to His heart]" (Hebrews 12:5–6 AMP).

It is true that when we as Christians are prospering and there are no problems, we tend to lack any urgency in prayer. We don't draw near to God with a whole heart. But when affliction comes, it causes us to seek God with a deep, earnest cry. When the storm lashes out, it's then that we seek shelter in him. Therefore, it is good that affliction comes because it keeps us on our knees. And that is the safest place for any Christian.

Father, I give you thanks in all things.

My Choice

My life is continually in my hand.
PSALM 119:109

The Psalms are filled with "I will." This is because our walk with God is *our* walk. We have free will to walk in any direction we desire. My life is continually in my hand to do as I please. I can walk directly into temptation. I can willfully sin if I so desire. My independent freedom to choose is God's gift to me. I didn't have anything to do with my initial salvation; that was completely a work of grace, but I have everything to do with my everyday choices.

To sin or not to sin. That is the question. To take up the cross daily and deny myself the pleasures of sin is my choice and my choice alone. Such a thought is frightening because of the fearful consequences of a wrong choice. So the psalmist adds a little: "My life is continually in my hand, yet I do not forget Your law" (Psalm 119:109). I do not forget the divine law that threatens me if I dare to serve sin and the devil. The law was a schoolmaster that brought me to Christ (see Galatians 3:24), and it is my keeper in driving me close to him. For that I am eternally grateful.

Father, how I love your law for what it has done for me and for what it continues to do for me.

The Christian Life

I cried unto thee; save me,
and I shall keep thy testimonies.
PSALM 119:146 KJV

In this short verse, we have the entire life of the Christian. It encompasses our testimony of God's saving power and of our godly walk. I cried out to God, and he heard me. I cried out because I became aware that I had sinned against heaven and needed his mercy. I cried out because death was waiting for me, and I was helpless and hopeless before its terrible power. I called upon the Lord because there was no other name under heaven, whereby I must be saved. He alone has the words of eternal life. And God saved me from death because of his great love and because of his kindness. He was able to forgive me because he had already invaded this earth in the person of Jesus of Nazareth and suffered and died on a cruel cross to satisfy the demands of eternal justice. Such was his love for guilty sinners.

And now I gladly keep his testimonies. I keep his testimonies because he has given me a new heart that loves righteousness. I once loved the darkness and hated the light, but because I'm a new creature in Christ, I now love light and hate the darkness. I keep his testimonies not to be saved but because I'm saved. My motivation is one of unspeakable gratitude for such amazing grace.

Father, your love for me amazes me.

Reproduction of Our Own Kind

Entrust [as a treasure]
to reliable and faithful men.
2 TIMOTHY 2:2 AMP

Rabbits have a reputation for breeding to the point of becoming a plague very quickly. If only godly Christians who are on fire for the Lord would become a plague that would reach the world for Jesus Christ. This is the biblical key to successful reproduction: "The things [the doctrine, the precepts, the admonitions, the sum of my ministry] which you have heard me teach in the presence of many witnesses, entrust [as a treasure] to reliable and faithful men who will also be capable and qualified to teach others" (2 Timothy 2:2 AMP).

It is very wise (if you want to see this world reached with the gospel) to use your local church as a training ground for soldiers of Christ. Teach them how to reach the lost, how to answer atheists, how to rightly divide the Word of Truth, how to go through the law to bring others to the knowledge of sin, as Jesus did. Teach them how to preach Christ and him crucified. This is the right way to reach this dying world with a glorious gospel. This is the right way to encourage your soul daily as well. When you are fighting the good fight with your fellow believers, studying the Word and sharpening each other, your faith will grow, and you will have a faithful support system to encourage you in the storms.

Father, help me to train others to reach the lost as Jesus did.

Dividing the Word

Remind them…
not to strive about words to no profit.
2 TIMOTHY 2:14

One way to reduce some of the stress in our life is to reject any urge to behave argumentatively. It's easy to strive about words without profit. The problem is that we often don't realize that it was a waste of time until after the event. This can happen when we argue about secondary issues or about important issues with people who don't have a receptive heart.

We want to make sure our conversational time and energy "profit." Jesus spoke about this as well: "Do not give what is holy to dogs, and do not throw your pearls before swine, or they will trample them under their feet, and turn and tear you to pieces" (Matthew 7:6 NASB95). We are called to speak to the lost, and we should always stand for truth. But we should not continue to engage in fruitless arguing. We should be willing to drop a discussion if we see that the Word of God is getting trampled in an unreceptive heart. In the same way, we should be willing to drop less holy discussions or arguments when we realize they're going nowhere.

Father, please give me wisdom on how to redeem the time.

The Common Salvation

Ye should earnestly contend for the faith.

JUDE 3 KJV

Jude was writing with a very serious tone. He said he gave "all diligence" to write to them of the salvation that they had in common. He added that there was a great need for him to write on a particular subject—that they should earnestly contend for the faith. Being "earnest" results from a sincere and intense conviction. Earnestness drives the world to reach their goals, whether it be fame or fortune or temporal happiness. These desires are often legitimate, but of all the things the Christian should desire, the most important is to contend for the faith.

We must earnestly stand up for truth and for righteousness. This can require courage if it means contradicting the majority view of the culture around us. But God promises that he "is with you wherever you go" (Joshua 1:9 NASB95). He spoke those words to Joshua before a military campaign, and he is with you today as well. Step out in faith today for the gospel, and watch as your dependence on the Lord grows.

Father, help me to fight for the defense of the faith.

Eternal Righteousness

Your righteousness is an everlasting righteousness.
PSALM 119:142

The righteousness of God is eternal. His law was not something he created. It is part of his eternal nature. And just as a criminal finds himself in trouble because the law he violated demands retribution, so righteousness is the enemy of sinners. The Scriptures warn that riches won't profit us on the day of wrath but that "righteousness delivers from death" (Proverbs 11:4). The very thing that will condemn sinners to hell is the very thing that can save them and send them to heaven.

Righteousness issues from the throne of God like lightning, and it will burn up all those who have transgressed the moral law. However, it was righteousness that came in Jesus. He came to give that same righteousness to lost sinners. When the Prodigal Son returned, his father clothed him in a robe (see Luke 15:22). That's a picture of what happens when someone comes to Christ. We are clothed in a robe of righteousness—not just covering our sins but also blotting them out—so that we can stand in the presence of perfect righteousness on that great and terrible day. "This Good News tells us that God makes us ready for heaven— makes us right in God's sight—when we put our faith and trust in Christ to save us" (Romans 1:17 TLB).

Father, your righteousness made sure you made me righteous in Christ.

The Heavenly Party

"When he has found it,
he lays it on his shoulders, rejoicing."
LUKE 15:5

Luke chapter 15 is a great tonic for the Christian. It shows us how much God loves us. In it, Jesus tells a very similar story three times. Each one is about something that was lost and how finding it caused great rejoicing. The first story is about a woman who lost a coin. When she found it, she called friends together to rejoice. The second story is about a lost sheep. The shepherd left the flock of ninety-nine to find that one lost sheep, and when he found it, he came back rejoicing, carrying the sheep on his shoulders. The third story is about a wayward son who left his father and spent his money on prostitutes and partying. When he came to his senses, he went back to his father and apologized. That produced tremendous joy in the heart of his father, who then had a great barbecue, celebrating that his son had returned.

Each one of these stories is a wonderful picture of how heaven rejoices at the repentance of a lost sinner. We were once lost, but the moment Jesus found us, our repentance and faith in the Savior caused great rejoicing in heaven. How can you not explode with joy at such a wonderful thought—that God and the angels rejoiced when you came to Christ.

Father, what a joy to know that I am your prodigal child.

A Rock of Stumbling and Refuge

The LORD is my rock and my fortress and my deliverer,
My God, my rock, in whom I take refuge.
PSALM 18:2 NASB95

Jesus warned in Matthew: "Whoever falls on this stone will be broken; but on whomever it falls, it will grind him to powder" (21:44). Jesus had just referred to himself as the stone of stumbling. Whoever falls upon him shall be broken. We cannot remain proud when we come to Christ. "The sacrifices of God are a broken spirit...and a contrite heart" (Psalm 51:17). It is in our broken weakness that we come to God for help and find the divine help we need to take us through each day.

The Scriptures also describe God the Father as a stone. Our verse today describes him as "my rock and my fortress." As our fortress, he is a strong, secure place in which to hide. Although we cannot always see his hand, we know he is sheltering us from life's storms. Look at this wonderful promise: "God is our refuge and strength [mighty and impenetrable], a very present and well-proved help in trouble" (Psalm 46:1, AMP). Our great God is indeed a strong and mighty fortress, well-proved and ready to help us.

Father, help me to run to you for shelter and help no matter what I face today.

Godly Wisdom

The wisdom that is from above is…
without partiality, and without hypocrisy.
JAMES 3:17 KJV

The Scriptures use very strong language to describe what is often called "worldly wisdom." Some evil people have a measure of wisdom, but the Bible separates this from the wisdom that's "from above"—from God. The wisdom that comes from him is "pure [morally and spiritually undefiled], then peace-loving [courteous, considerate], gentle, reasonable [and willing to listen], full of compassion and good fruits. It is unwavering, without [self-righteous] hypocrisy [and self-serving guile]" (James 3:17 AMP). Compare this wisdom with the wisdom of this world: "If you have bitter jealousy and selfish ambition in your hearts, do not be arrogant, and [as a result] be in defiance of the truth. This [superficial] wisdom is not that which comes down from above, but is earthly (secular), natural (unspiritual), even demonic" (vv. 14–15 AMP).

It is God's will for your life that you live and grow in godly wisdom. What wisdom are you allowing to guide you? Pursue God's wisdom from above. Grow in the peace-loving, unwavering wisdom he commands and provides.

Father, let your wisdom from above grow in me and help me to live by it.

Walking in Light

God is light and in Him
is no darkness at all.

1 JOHN 1:5

The apostle John summarized the message of the gospel in one sentence. The Bible repeatedly compares God to light: "His brightness was as the light; he had horns coming out of his hand: and there was the hiding of his power" (Habakkuk 3:4 KJV). In the verse in 1 John, the meaning is that God is pure righteousness. The Bible often likens righteousness to light and evil to darkness. Jesus spoke of this when he talked with Nicodemus: "This is the condemnation, that light is come into the world, and men loved darkness rather than light, because their deeds were evil" (John 3:19 KJV).

The Bible tells the whole story of the battle of darkness versus the true Light. It starts with the Fall in Genesis and continues through the incarnation of Jesus, the Light of the world. It tells us in advance of the ultimate consummation of his triumph over darkness in Revelation. Sometimes watching the news and seeing the pain and suffering everywhere around us tempts us to forget the big picture. We can worry about the end of the world or fear worst-case scenarios. But victory is already assured. Light has triumphed, and this darkness is only temporary. We must continue to walk with God in the light and never fear the darkness.

Father, help me to always walk in the light.

Clever Talk

Your minds may be corrupted
from the simplicity that is in Christ.
2 CORINTHIANS 11:3

Eloquent speech can be fuel for the ego. It's tempting to impress hearers with big words. But in doing so, we can leave them confused regarding our message. When it comes to the issue of salvation, it is wise to keep the message very clear and simple. If someone's house is on fire, you shouldn't warn them with eloquent words. "Your house is on fire. Get out now!" is appropriate. The world is on fire, so we must make the warning of the gospel very clear.

In the same way, it can be tempting for us to give more heed to people who complicate the Bible and its message. It sounds impressive when people pile on requirements and add to the law of God. They might sound holier or more committed. But the message of the Bible for us is simple too. When you feel overwhelmed or discouraged, remember the basics: "Believe in the Lord Jesus, and you will be saved" (Acts 16:31 NASB95). Trust that Jesus fully delivered you from your sins. Love him for it. Remember that the Holy Spirit lives in you and guides you.

Father, help me to stay with the simplicity of the message of the gospel.

The Sweetest of Foods

"With honey from the rock I would satisfy you."
PSALM 81:16 ESV

Honey is unique because it doesn't spoil. Archaeologists have found honey that's thousands of years old that you could still spread on your toast and enjoy.[4] Honey is also unique in the way that it's gathered. Bees visit flowers, collect the nectar, and somehow produce this wonderful substance that is sweet to the human taste. But this verse from Psalm 81 speaks of honey being taken from the rock. Not a rock, but *the* Rock. This is speaking prophetically of the Son of God, the Rock of ages, the foundation of the church of the living God, giving us the sweetest gift of all. From the Rock of Jesus Christ comes the honey of the glorious gospel.

We remember the sweet moment when we had the revelation of who Jesus was and what he did and what we now have in Christ. It truly is the unspeakable gift that continues to give throughout eternity. One great gift of honey is that it produces energy within the human body. And it is the raw essence of the gospel that gives us energy to face any situation with peace and strength. As we think of what Jesus did on the cross, we cannot help but be energized and say with the apostle Paul that we will always be steadfast and immovable in the work of the Lord (see 1 Corinthians 15:58).

Father, Jesus is the sweetest name I know.

---

4   Natasha Geiling, "The Science behind Honey's Eternal Shelf Life," *Smithsonian Magazine*, August 22, 2013, https://www.smithsonianmag.com/science-nature/the-science-behind-honeys-eternal-shelf-life-1218690/.

Shining for Jesus

You also are the called of Jesus Christ.
ROMANS 1:6

We are the "called" of Jesus Christ. God has called us out of this sinful world to be a special people. Paul said that we are to "shine as lights in the world" (Philippians 2:15). The reason we are to shine as lights is so sinners are reminded of the Creator and the moral responsibility that he requires— so that they will then respond to the gospel. Peter said, "You are a chosen generation, a royal priesthood, a holy nation, His own special people, that you may proclaim the praises of Him who called you out of darkness into His marvelous light" (1 Peter 2:9).

The apostle Paul said that we are "called to be saints" (Romans 1:7). That means we live differently than the sinful world. Then he says, "First, I thank my God through Jesus Christ for you all, that your faith is spoken of throughout the whole world" (v. 8). Paul speaks of the most important aspect of their faith. Their faith was spreading throughout the whole world. The light was shining—the world was speaking about the gospel because of their witness. May that be our testimony also. Each day we should ask ourselves who in this world is seeing our light and to whom will we take that light today.

Father, cause me to shine.

Ready to Preach

I am ready to preach the gospel.
ROMANS 1:15

It is a lost battle indeed if soldiers are confused about the purpose of their fight. They must be clear about what they are trying to achieve and always be ready to achieve that goal. And it is a lost cause for the church if we lose sight of that for which we are fighting. We are in a battle for the souls of men and women who are sitting in darkness, in the shadow of death. The apostle Paul told the Romans that he did not want to have them ignorant and that he wanted to see fruit among them (see v.13). And he added that he was a debtor to this world—that as much as was in him, he was ready to preach the gospel to those who were in Rome also.

The question we need to ask ourselves is, are we ready today to preach the gospel? Have we prepared ourselves? Have we studied to show ourselves approved, a workman who needs not be ashamed? And then Paul said, "I am not ashamed of the gospel of Christ, for it is the power of God to salvation" (Romans 1:16). We mustn't be ashamed because we have within our hands the gospel—and it can snatch dying sinners from death and give them everlasting life.

Father, may I always be ready to be a true and faithful witness for you.

Sun and Shield

The LORD God is a sun and shield.
PSALM 84:11 KJV

Once God had changed our hearts so that we could see that which is invisible, our desires for this world quickly changed. So says the psalmist: "A day in thy courts is better than a thousand" (v. 10 KJV). We would "rather be a doorkeeper in the house of my God" than dwell "in the tents of wickedness" (v. 10 KJV). This is because the Lord is not only the giver of life, but he's also the lover of our soul—who demonstrated his great love for us by sending Christ to die for us. "The LORD God is a sun and shield; the LORD will give grace and glory; no good thing will he withhold from those that walk uprightly" (v. 11 KJV).

Our God is both a sun and a shield from the sun. He is burning righteousness, but he has provided a shield to protect us from the righteousness that demands death for sin. And because we now have peace with God, he can continue to express his love for us by showering his kindness upon us, like a father who longs to give good gifts to his child. "O LORD of hosts, blessed is the man that trusteth in thee" (v. 12 KJV).

Father, you are my sun and shield.

Beware of Covetousness

"Ananias, why has Satan filled your heart?"
ACTS 5:3

When Judas gave in to a desire to betray Jesus, Satan entered his heart. So the same tempter came to Ananias and whispered a covetous thought to his heart, and that temptation, like a viper's egg, hatched into sin (see Acts 5:1–11). The incident began with a covetous thought in the mind of Ananias and ended with his tragic death and the death of his wife, who was privy to his deceit. The Scriptures say that they conspired to lie to God. They sold their own possession and then lied about how much money they received from the sale.

We don't know exactly why Ananias wanted extra money, but he was clearly trying to take things into his own hands. The poet Kahlil Gibran said, "Our anxiety does not come from thinking about the future, but from wanting to control it." As believers, we know that God is truly in control. When we give that control over to God, we will no longer have a reason to stress. Instead of having a grasping attitude like Ananias, we should be trusting God to supply our financial needs. When we rely on God for these things, we are content with what we have. We don't feel the need to grab what we can or lie to protect ourselves. We are at peace and can contemplate the future, happy that God is in control of every detail.

Father, help me to be free from the slightest covetousness.

September

When to Take No Notice

They did not cease teaching
and preaching Jesus as the Christ.

ACTS 5:42

Revival broke out and caused great indignation among
the leaders of Israel (see Acts 5:12–42). They forbade the
disciples from speaking further in the name of Jesus and
put them in prison. The angel of the Lord then opened the
prison doors and told the disciples that they should take no
notice of the leaders: "Go, stand in the temple and speak to
the people all the words of this life" (v. 20).

When they were again arrested and reminded that
they were forbidden to speak of Jesus, the disciples said, "We
ought to obey God rather than men" (v. 29). That's when
Gamaliel, a Pharisee, a doctor of the law, who had a good
reputation among all the people, stepped up and told the
council that they should leave the disciples alone in case they
found themselves fighting against God. The council agreed
with him but took no notice of his advice: "They agreed with
him, and when they had called for the apostles and beaten
them, they commanded that they should not speak in the
name of Jesus, and let them go" (v. 40). But the disciples took
no notice: "And daily in the temple, and in every house, they
did not cease teaching and preaching Jesus Christ" (v. 42).

*Father, may I take no notice of an offended world and continue
to preach the gospel.*

Stubborn Pride

Resist the devil and he will flee from you.

JAMES 4:7

The Scriptures tell us that Satan fell because of pride, and pride is still the number one stumbling block for sinners seeking after God. The Bible says: "The wicked, through the pride of his countenance, will not seek after God: God is not in all his thoughts" (Psalm 10:4 KJV). And so Satan has a stronghold over the lives of the unsaved because of their stubborn pride. It is appropriate that the letter *i* is in the middle of *pride*. Isaiah 14:13–14 is believed by many respected scholars to describe the fall of Satan. Look for how many times he says "I": "Thou hast said in thine heart, I will ascend into heaven, I will exalt my throne above the stars of God: I will sit also upon the mount of the congregation, in the sides of the north: I will ascend above the heights of the clouds; I will be like the most High" (KJV).

"Pride of life," in addition to being a grievous sin, is a recipe for stress as we constantly agonize about making ourselves look good in the sight of others. We tend to want to impress with our house, our car, our clothes, our hairstyle, our intellect, and so on. If we worried less about what others think, we would worry less.

Father, I renounce pride, humble myself, and joyfully submit to your divine authority.

The Better Way

"Am I not better to thee
than ten sons?"
1 SAMUEL 1:8 KJV

Hannah was desperate to have children, but the Lord had shut up her womb. Scripture tells us that "her adversary also provoked her sore, for to make her fret, because the LORD had shut up her womb. And as he did so year by year, when she went up to the house of the LORD, so she provoked her; therefore she wept, and did not eat" (1 Samuel 1:6–7 KJV). Then her husband was grieved that she wept and asked, "Am I not better to thee than ten sons?"

Dear Christian, what are you desperate for today? What taunts are you facing continually from those around you? What is causing you stress? I have found from many years of experience that our faith grows the more we concern ourselves with the will of God. It's a matter of seeking first the Kingdom of God and his righteousness and having all other things added to us (see Matthew 6:33). When our faith becomes strong, that's when stress has little effect on us because we are fully convinced that God is in control of every part of our lives. Faith does that. That is the better way.

Father, I am desperate to do your will. Please grow my faith and guide me in your will.

No Longer Rare

The boy Samuel ministered to the LORD.
1 SAMUEL 3:1

The Bible tells us that the word of the Lord was rare around the time that the child Samuel ministered to the Lord: "there was no widespread revelation" (v. 1). Heaven was silent. But God was about to raise up a new prophet for Israel. How blessed we are that heaven broke that silence. God has spoken to us through the prophets, and now he has spoken to us through the words of Jesus. We have these preserved in the Scriptures.

The Bible is everything we need for a revelation of the will of God. It is a lamp to our feet and a light to our path: "God, having spoken to the fathers long ago in [the voices and writings of] the prophets in many separate revelations [each of which set forth a portion of the truth], and in many ways, has in these last days spoken [with finality] to us in [the person of One who is by His character and nature] His Son [namely Jesus]" (Hebrews 1:1–2 AMP). This is why we should soak our souls in the Word of God. We should memorize it and discipline ourselves to read it daily— because it is his love letter to us. Do you read it daily, without fail? Put your Bible before your breakfast and you will never be the same.

Father, thank you for your wonderful gift of your Word.

Little Did He Know

And so he did.
ACTS 12:8 KJV

When Herod put Peter in prison, little did he know that he gave us a wonderful picture of our salvation: "Behold, the angel of the Lord came upon him, and a light shined in the prison: and he smote Peter on the side, and raised him up, saying, Arise up quickly. And his chains fell off from his hands. And the angel said unto him, Gird thyself, and bind on thy sandals. And so he did. And he saith unto him, Cast thy garment about thee, and follow me" (vv. 7–8 KJV).

We were in the prison of sin when the light of the gospel came to us. After the law woke us, our chains fell off. As the angel told Peter to "bind" on his sandals and we are told "And so he did," so we tie on our gospel shoes. We need to bind them on with great resolve because the enemy will insist that we remove them. He wants us to do anything other than obey the Great Commission—to "proclaim the gospel to the whole creation" (Mark 16:15 ESV). According to Ephesians 6, a vital part of our armor is the helmet of salvation. When we are assured that our salvation is secure and that our names are written in heaven, nothing really matters compared to that truth. So when the enemy tries to whisper negative thoughts, make sure your helmet is on firmly.

Father, help me to be secure in my salvation and ready to obey your commands.

His Lovingkindness Is Everlasting

Give thanks to the LORD, for He is good,
for His lovingkindness is everlasting.
PSALM 136:1 NASB95

Psalm 136 is truly unique. Twenty-six times, once for each verse, the psalm repeats, "for His lovingkindness is everlasting." This repetition occurs every other line and gives the psalm a catchy quality that's fun to read aloud. That's probably intentional on the part of the psalmist, because this psalm is a call to proclaim God's great actions together and praise him. Many of his wonderful characteristics are conveniently listed for just this purpose.

The psalmist shows God's power and creativity as displayed in creation, inviting us to give thanks "to Him who made the heavens with skill, for His lovingkindness is everlasting" (v. 5 NASB95). It lists his miracles during the exodus and the conquest of Canaan: "to Him who led His people through the wilderness, for His lovingkindness is everlasting" (v. 16 NASB95). Praise the Lord for his wonderful works in history and creation! Do we thank God daily for the kindness and power he's displayed in our own lives?

Father, I praise you because your lovingkindness is everlasting.

Manaen's Testimony

There were in the church that was at Antioch certain prophets and teachers; as Barnabas…and Manaen, which had been brought up with Herod the tetrarch, and Saul.

ACTS 13:1 KJV

Manaen was one of the church leaders at Antioch, and Scripture says that he was brought up with Herod the tetrarch. This was the same Herod who beheaded John the Baptist. Respected Bible scholars believe that Manean was perhaps Herod's foster brother. Most of us look at a local church and think to ourselves that it is made up of a group of people who were raised in the shelter of a Christian home. But this is not always so. This is why it is good (and God-glorifying) for a church to have its members give public testimony within the church.

It is both illuminating and encouraging to hear of the backgrounds of those we now consider to be wholesome brethren. We know that much of the early church was made up of the idolatrous, adulterers, thieves, the greedy, drunkards, revilers, and extortioners. We know this because Scripture gives that list in 1 Corinthians 6:9–10 and then says of them, "Such were some of you: but ye are washed, but ye are sanctified, but ye are justified in the name of the Lord Jesus" (v. 11 KJV).

Father, thank you for saving a wretch like me.

The God of All Comfort

God...comforts us in all our affliction so that we may be able
to comfort those who are in any affliction.

2 CORINTHIANS 1:3–4 NASB95

When you're in the middle of a trial, it can be hard to believe
that good will come out of the hard things you're going
through. But it is true. Paul discusses that promise here in
the opening chapter of 2 Corinthians. He wrote, "Blessed be
the God and Father of our Lord Jesus Christ, the Father of
mercies and God of all comfort, who comforts us in all our
affliction so that we will be able to comfort those who are in
any affliction with the comfort with which we ourselves are
comforted by God. For just as the sufferings of Christ are
ours in abundance, so also our comfort is abundant through
Christ" (2 Corinthians 1:3–5 NASB95).

One of the benefits of the stress and tribulation you
are enduring is that you are learning how to comfort others
who will experience similar affliction. The first step of this
is to be on the lookout for God's comfort to you. Don't lose
sight of that promise in the middle of this passage: "who
comforts us in all our affliction." God will comfort you. Be
ready to recognize and receive it—and remember it to share
with others.

Father, thank you for being a God of comfort.

They So Spoke

There they continued
to preach the gospel.
ACTS 14:7 ESV

When the disciples went to Iconium, they went into the synagogue and "spoke in such a way that a great number of both Jews and Greeks believed" (Acts 14:1 ESV). We need not wonder what they said because they had been commissioned to preach the gospel to every person (see Mark 16:15). You and I can speak in such a way that sinners will come to Christ. God's Word does not return void. Our labor is never in vain. After such victory it was no wonder that the enemy stirred up hatred against the disciples. But they continued to speak boldly in the Lord.

We should never become discouraged by resistance. Resistance builds muscle. That's the principle of a workout at a gym. If there's no pain, there's no gain, and resistance builds character in the Christian. As the disciples continued to preach, again there was great victory, and predictably, the city was divided. When both Jews and gentiles, with their rulers, planned to stone them, the disciples fled. There is nothing wrong with walking away from violence. But we should remain encouraged. No matter what resistance you may encounter today, remember that God's Word can be working even when it doesn't appear to be advancing. Remember that even the disciples experienced persecution so strong they had to flee. But God was with them, and God is with us.

Father, make me continually stubborn to preach the gospel.

Many Tribulations

They stoned Paul and dragged him out of the city,
thinking he was dead.
ACTS 14:19 AMP

Once again, a revival broke out after the preaching of Paul
and Barnabas. However, the enemies of the gospel arrived
from Antioch and Iconium, and having won over the crowds
to a point where they stoned the apostle Paul, they left him
for dead. But he was still alive, and when the disciples stood
around him, he rose up and left for another city—where he
and the other disciples preached the gospel and taught many
(see v. 21). What a wonderful testimony to their courage, to
their faith in God, and to their love for the lost.

Instead of being discouraged, the disciples continued
to preach. And look at what they then did: "They returned
to Lystra and to Iconium and to Antioch, strengthening
and establishing the hearts of the disciples; encouraging
them to remain firm in the faith, saying, 'It is through many
tribulations and hardships that we must enter the kingdom
of God'" (vv. 21–22 AMP). We must never be discouraged
because of many tribulations and hardships. Praise God
that the antagonism of his enemies will never stop his
kingdom purposes. He preserves his people through trials.
He supports us to continue being fruitful and effective for
the kingdom even in the midst of persecution. Persecution is
never too much to prevent God's will from prevailing.

Father, I need your continual help to fulfill your will.

He Gives Rain

"He did good…
filling our hearts with food and gladness."
ACTS 14:17 KJV

When Paul and Barnabas were in Lystra, the apostle Paul noticed the man had a disease in his feet and that he had faith to be healed. So he told him to stand up and walk—and he did. This sent the men of Lystra into a frenzy, thinking that the gods had become human. To the disciples' horror, the people of Lystra then decided to sacrifice to them. The Scriptures give us insight as to how the disciples responded to idolatry: "they…ran in among the people, crying out" (v. 14 KJV). There was a sense of urgency that caused them to *run* in among the people and *cry out* not to pay them homage.

We, too, must have a sense of urgency and run in among those who have their own image of God, crying out that while there are many false gods, there is only one Creator—who "left not himself without witness, in that he did good, and gave us rain from heaven, and fruitful seasons, filling our hearts with food and gladness" (v. 17 KJV). We can see evidence of both God's existence and his kindness in how he lavishes his goodness upon us—in giving us the many blessings of life, including rain, without which we wouldn't exist. It gives us all of our food. Every drop falls with divine kindness.

Father, thank you for giving me the blessings of life.

Saved by Grace

By grace you have been saved
through faith.
EPHESIANS 2:8

Ephesians reminds us that we are involved in a continual battle with demonic forces (see 6:12–20). If they can't discourage us from preaching the gospel, they will invade our ranks with poisonous doctrine to break down our unity of spirit. This is what happened in Acts 15. Certain men came into the midst of the disciples and began to teach that believers had to be circumcised to be saved, and this caused no small dissension and disputation from Paul and Barnabas. And they stood on the truth that we are saved by grace alone (see Ephesians 2:8–9).

When the apostles and the elders came together to discuss the situation, that caused more arguments (see Acts 15:6–7). Peter then said to the disciples that when he preached to the gentiles, they were saved by the grace of God. Water baptism didn't save them (evidenced by the fact that they received the gift of the Holy Spirit before they were water baptized). Peter said that there was no difference between Jew or gentile in how they were saved: "We believe that we are saved through the [precious, undeserved] grace of the Lord Jesus [which makes us free of the guilt of sin and grants us eternal life], in just the same way as they are" (v. 11 AMP).

Father, I am saved by your grace alone.

Sudden Hope

He called for a light.
ACTS 16:29

Paul and Silas had been beaten many times. Paul had stirred up demons after casting the demon out of a woman (see vv. 18–19). Then they were thrown in jail and put in chains. Life was certainly a roller coaster for Paul and Silas. One moment they were up, and the next moment they were down. And they certainly were down this time. They were in great pain, in chains, in the darkness of a dungeon. But they sang hymns to God because they knew that whatever came their way came only by divine permission. God had allowed this terrible incident because he had a divine purpose.

Suddenly, around midnight, there was a great earthquake, the chains fell off Paul and Silas, and the doors were opened. The jailer was about to kill himself because Roman law demanded he be put to death for losing his prisoners. But Paul said something that suddenly brought hope to his ears: "'Do yourself no harm, for we are all here.' Then he called for a light, ran in, and fell down trembling before Paul and Silas" (vv. 28–29). When God gives condemned sinners light, they suddenly see that the gospel gives them a living hope in the face of certain death.

Father, thank you for giving me such glorious light and hope in the dark hopelessness of impending death.

Preaching Jesus

Paul...reasoned with them out of the scriptures, Opening and alleging, that Christ must needs have suffered, and risen again from the dead; and that this Jesus, whom I preach unto you, is Christ.

ACTS 17:2–3 KJV

Paul regularly reasoned with people out of Scripture by pointing to the cross and the resurrection. The focal point of his message was to preach Jesus to them. We are to do the same with those around us two thousand years later. In fact, we should do the same with ourselves. We need to remind ourselves how fully and freely God has forgiven us. We had no hope in ourselves of escaping the punishment for our sin, but God, in his great kindness, provided a Savior in Jesus.

We need to meditate on the perfect life that Jesus lived in our place. We preach to our fellow man and to our own hearts the cross of Jesus Christ and his glorious resurrection. Rehearse the gospel to yourself. Read gospel-filled passages of the Bible. Do this for the health of your own soul and so you're ready to preach to anybody in need of Jesus.

Father, thank you for your Son. Make me meditate on the gospel, the wonderful good news, every moment of the day.

They Searched the Scriptures

These people were more noble and open-minded.

ACTS 17:11 AMP

The following verse is like an oasis in a desert: "Now these people were more noble and open-minded than those in Thessalonica, so they received the message [of salvation through faith in the Christ] with great eagerness, examining the Scriptures daily to see if these things were so" (v. 11 AMP).

While some of the Thessalonians had received the Word, others had been contentious to a point where the Christians in Thessalonica whisked Paul and Silas away during the night to Berea (see v. 10). As was their custom, Paul and Silas went to the synagogue to share the gospel. We are then told that their hearers were more noble than those who had so poorly treated them in Thessalonica in that they listened with open hearts. How encouraging it must have been for Paul and Silas to have hearers who were open to what they had to say and were wise enough to make sure that what they were saying was based on holy Scripture. Such a reverence for the Scriptures goes hand in hand with the belief that every word is God-inspired. And knowing that Scripture is filled with precious promises helps us to overcome daily worries. Search the Scriptures today, find a promise, and believe it today with "great eagerness."

Father, make me a noble hearer of your Word.

The Example

Apollos…an eloquent man,
and mighty in the scriptures, came to Ephesus.
ACTS 18:24 KJV

Apollos almost sounds too good to be true. He was Jewish, born at Alexandria, Egypt—"an eloquent man and mighty in the Scriptures." He was well-versed in the Old Testament, zealous, and able to accurately teach his hearers about Jesus, though his knowledge was confined to what he had heard of Jesus from John the Baptist (see v. 25). He perhaps preached repentance and faith in Jesus and may not have been fully versed in his death and resurrection. When Apollos began to speak boldly in the synagogue, friends of Paul (Aquila and Priscilla) heard him, took him aside, and "expounded unto him the way of God more perfectly" (v. 26 KJV). They shared with him the fullness of the gospel. We're also told that when Apollos went to Achaia, the brethren gave him a letter of commendation and exhorted the disciples to receive him. When Apollos arrived, he was extremely helpful and "he mightily convinced the Jews, and that publicly, shewing by the scriptures that Jesus was Christ" (v. 28 KJV).

What an amazing example for us to imitate! May God make us mighty in the Scriptures and continue to provide us with what we need to share the gospel even as we are growing in knowledge ourselves.

Father, make me mighty in the Scriptures and guide me to those who can strengthen me further in the Word.

Prisons

"Paul has persuaded
and turned away many people."
ACTS 19:26

The disciples in the book of Acts were a magnet for trouble. Wherever they went, they caused contention. This is because their message was offensive. They preached that this world was evil and that sinners needed to repent and trust Jesus Christ. It was no different when they arrived at Ephesus. The Scriptures tell us "and about that time there arose a great commotion about the Way" (v. 23). This time the message threatened the lucrative idol business (see v. 24) so much so that the industry heads called a special meeting and said, "Men, you know that we have our prosperity by this trade. Moreover you see and hear that not only at Ephesus, but throughout almost all Asia, this Paul has persuaded and turned away many people, saying that they are not gods which are made with hands" (vv. 25–26).

Paul was a wonderful example of godliness. His refusal to compromise his divine commission to preach the gospel to the unsaved continually attracted persecution. At one time he was thrown into prison with a companion in Christ, and instead of becoming stressed, they sang hymns to God (see 16:25–40). Life is full of "prisons"—situations that can either imprison us or have us singing hymns to God.

Father, make me a godly troublemaker.

The Pulpit Lesson

Paul…continued his message until midnight.
ACTS 20:7

Charles Spurgeon was aware that long-winded preachers sometimes bore congregations. In reference to these, he said, "No human being, unless gifted with infinite patience, could long endure to listen to them, and nature does well to give the victim deliverance through sleep." The apostle Paul wasn't a boring preacher. But listen to what happened in Acts 20:7–12. The disciples were gathered together in an upper room, along with a young man who was extremely sleepy. He fell asleep while Paul was speaking, fell out the window from the third story, and was tragically killed. But as he lay dead, Paul embraced him and said, "'Do not trouble yourselves, for his life is in him'…And they brought the young man in alive, and they were not a little comforted" (vv. 10, 12).

The young man was not condemned for falling asleep during a sermon. Instead, his life was given back to him, and those around were comforted. God has compassion on us. And we know that Jesus himself was human. Although he was fully God, he also felt the full range of human struggles. He felt hunger and exhaustion and temptation. "For we do not have a high priest who cannot sympathize with our weaknesses, but One who has been tempted in all things as we are, yet without sin. Therefore let us draw near with confidence to the throne of grace, so that we may receive mercy and find grace to help in time of need" (Hebrews 4:15–16 NASB95).

Father, let me come to your throne confident in your grace.

Clearly Seen

The invisible things of him from the creation of the world are clearly seen, being understood by the things that are made, even his eternal power and Godhead.

ROMANS 1:20 KJV

God is not willing that anyone should perish. To that end, he gave us his written Word that explicitly states his will, his commands, his love, and the good news of how to be reconciled to him. He also emblazons his character and attributes across the world. He reveals himself through his creativity in color and scent and sound and sensation. This is the general "book" or revelation of nature. Unbelievers can clearly see God's moral requirements and his very existence if they stop and think about the world around them. People innately know the general lines of right and wrong behavior. They can look around them and know that there has to be a Creator.

Nature is helpful for us as believers too. Many passages in the Bible reference nature when discussing God's attributes. We can feel his love in a gentle summer breeze and see his majesty in a glorious sunset. We can worship him for his power and creativity.

Father, teach me about yourself today.

The Covered Head

O GOD the Lord, the strength of my salvation,
You have covered my head in the day of battle.
PSALM 140:7

The psalmist called God "the Lord, the strength of my salvation." When God is our Lord, we know that our salvation is of the Lord. It isn't dependent on us; it is dependent on him because we are saved by his grace alone. He's the beginning and the end of our faith. God covered the psalmist's head in the fury of battle. We are also in the midst of a terrible battle, but ours isn't against flesh and blood but against wicked demonic forces. Look at how God has covered us in the day of our war: "Taking the shield of faith, wherewith ye shall be able to quench all the fiery darts of the wicked. And take the helmet of salvation, and the sword of the Spirit, which is the word of God" (Ephesians 6:16–17 KJV).

The shield covers our heart, and the helmet covers our head. But it's up to us to protect both. Scripture says, "*Taking* the shield of faith…*take* the helmet and sword." If we don't deliberately take hold of the protection of faith and use it to guard our hearts, fiery darts will wound our soul.

Father, thank you for furnishing me with the armor that I need to finish the battle.

October

Holiness and Love

All Israel stoned him with stones.

JOSHUA 7:25

When Israel retreated in the face of its enemies, Joshua fell on his face before the Lord. Then God told him the problem (see Joshua 7:1–26). Achan had taken forbidden treasure and buried it in his tent. When God revealed this great sin, the people stoned Achan to death. That story should make us shudder at the thought of sinning against God because it reveals that our Creator is holy and, therefore, demands retribution against sin. We should shudder at the thought of treasuring sin in the secret place of our own hearts.

Some maintain that the God of the Old Testament is wrathful and the God of the New Testament is loving. Such talk reveals an ignorance of the Bible. A quick read of the books of Hebrews and Revelation reminds us that we are still dealing with a holy Creator who will demand retribution for every transgression. In the same way, the Old Testament reveals brilliantly beautiful stories of the grace and love the Father has shown throughout all of history. Even as far back as the third chapter of Genesis (Genesis 3:15), he promises a hero to defeat evil. Reiterations of that promise continually point to Jesus throughout the Old Testament. Thank God for providing the Savior.

Father, never let me forget your holiness or your love.

Seek First the Kingdom

All these things will be added to you.
MATTHEW 6:33 ESV

The Bible speaks of a fatness that is good: "The liberal soul shall be made fat: and he that watereth shall be watered also himself" (Proverbs 11:25 KJV). A liberal person is someone who is kind to others. They have an open hand when it comes to money. They think of others and not of themselves. Someone with a fat soul has an eye for those who need help. The law of kindness is in their heart: "In everything I showed you [by example] that by working hard in this way you must help the weak and remember the words of the Lord Jesus, that He Himself said, 'It is more blessed [and brings greater joy] to give than to receive'" (Acts 20:35 AMP).

The best way to "water" others is with the gospel. Jesus said that if any man thirsts, he should come to him and drink, and the outcome will be that he will have rivers of living water flowing from his own heart (see John 7:37–38). This is how to gain a fat soul. Let the rivers of living water flow from you by reaching out to dying sinners with the gospel—remembering that those who water will be watered themselves. Seek first the kingdom of God and his righteousness, and God will take care of you. We have his word on it.

Father, let me put your will before mine.

Without Spot

Christ…through the eternal Spirit offered Himself.
HEBREWS 9:14

The Old Testament sacrifices offered temporal refuge from wrath. The offering of the cross was different: "How much more shall the blood of Christ, who through the eternal Spirit offered Himself without spot to God, cleanse your conscience from dead works to serve the living God?" (Hebrews 9:14). Jesus was without spot. The blood of the unblemished Lamb of God saved us from the wrath of his perfect holiness. Through that one sacrifice we see the fulfillment of John's "Lamb of God, which taketh away the sin of the world" (John 1:29 KJV).

Sin is likened to the uncleanness of leprosy, which begins with a spot and spreads over the body. Jude alludes to this contagious disease when he tells us to reach out to the unsaved: "Have mercy on some, who are doubting; save others, snatching them out of the fire; and on some have mercy but with fear, loathing even the clothing spotted and polluted by their shameless immoral freedom" (Jude 22–23 AMP). When we apply the blood of Christ to our lives, the High Priest of our salvation proclaims us as being clean. Our conscience no longer accuses us of sin. We are guilt-free in Christ. No longer do we seek refuge in the dead works of any religion. We are free in Christ to acceptably serve the living God.

Father, I can boldly face you on judgment day without guilt or fear.

Never Yield

"If your right hand causes you to sin,
cut it off and cast it from you."
MATTHEW 5:30

The Bible's admonition not to "yield" our members to sin is a good reminder that we have freedom of choice. "Neither yield ye your members as instruments of unrighteousness unto sin: but yield yourselves unto God, as those that are alive from the dead, and your members as instruments of righteousness unto God" (Romans 6:13 KJV).

This present evil age is out of our control. We can only have so much say about what happens around us. But we do have control over our own actions and the hundreds of decisions we make every day about how we act. We can yield our hands and feet to sinful actions, or we can yield them as instruments of righteousness. We can use our hands to help people. We can use our mouths to encourage our family and coworkers. We can use our minds to think on what is true, pure, and excellent (Philippians 4:8). And notice in the middle of giving us the choice as to where we go—to sin or to righteousness—Scripture reminds us that we have been saved from death. We were once dead in trespasses, and God reached down in Christ and put his life in us to save us. This gives us the incredible encouragement to sustain us in our efforts. Oh, dear Christian, we must realize what we have in Jesus—treasure and the assurance of victory.

Father, never let me surrender myself to sin.

The Frailty of Old Age

Now Joshua was old and advanced in years.
JOSHUA 13:1 AMP

None of us wants to give up our youth with its abounding energy and vitality. God told Joshua he was old, and look at what he also said: "Very substantial portions of the land remain to be possessed" (v. 1 AMP). How could an old man possess the land? But after God explained to Joshua the specifics of what he still needed to possess, Joshua said, "Look at me, I am eighty-five years old today. I am still as strong today as I was the day Moses sent me; as my strength was then, so is my strength now, for war and for going out and coming in" (14:10–11 AMP). Then he said, "Give me this hill country" (v. 12 AMP).

We still have land to possess. The world is unsaved. We have trials to overcome. Trust the God of the impossible to give you strength for any mountain of a task or trial in front of you today: "I say unto you, That whosoever shall say unto this mountain, Be thou removed, and be thou cast into the sea; and shall not doubt in his heart, but shall believe that those things which he saith shall come to pass; he shall have whatsoever he saith" (Mark 11:23 KJV).

Father, with you, nothing is impossible.

Our Choice

We will serve the LORD.
JOSHUA 24:15 KJV

The choice that every person has today is the same that Joshua presented to the children of Israel. He said, "Choose you this day whom ye will serve; whether the gods which your fathers served that were on the other side of the flood, or the gods of the Amorites, in whose land ye dwell: but as for me and my house, we will serve the LORD" (Joshua 24:15 KJV). We can either serve the Enemy—the god of this world—or we can serve the God who gave us life.

What a privilege and honor it is to serve the true and living God. Serving him brings freedom: "Having been freed from sin and enslaved to God, you derive your benefit, resulting in sanctification, and the outcome, eternal life. For the wages of sin is death, but the free gift of God is eternal life in Christ Jesus our Lord" (Romans 6:22–23 NASB95). While misery and oppression haunt those who serve the darkness, the work of serving our Lord is truly joyful. Jesus said, "Come to Me, all who are weary and heavy-laden, and I will give you rest. Take My yoke upon you and learn from Me, for I am gentle and humble in heart, and you will find rest for your souls. For My yoke is easy and My burden is light" (Matthew 11:28–30 NASB95). That's why we choose to serve the Lord. Serve him, and find rest for your soul.

Father, I love you. I choose to serve you today.

Not Forsaken

He shall judge the world in righteousness.
PSALM 9:8 KJV

More than eight hundred years BC, the psalmist gave us a glimpse of the glorious gospel: "He shall judge the world in righteousness, he shall minister judgment to the people in uprightness" (v. 8 KJV). This is the message that the apostle Paul preached in Athens to his hearers: "The times of this ignorance God winked at; but now commandeth all men every where to repent: Because he hath appointed a day, in the which he will judge the world in righteousness" (Acts 17:30–31 KJV).

Then the psalmist points to the way of salvation—to the cross and to faith in Jesus: "The LORD also will be a refuge for the oppressed, a refuge in times of trouble. And they that know thy name will put their trust in thee: for thou, LORD, hast not forsaken them that seek thee" (Psalm 9:9–10 KJV). What beautiful promises live in this passage! The Lord is a refuge, no matter what oppression or trouble you are going through. He is a worthy place to put your trust. He has not forsaken you when it comes to your biggest need: salvation. And he will not forsake you in the smaller storms of life. Seek him! Draw ever nearer to him.

Father, thank you for providing such a great way of salvation.

Always Ready

Be ready always to give an answer.
1 PETER 3:15 KJV

A soldier should always be ready to use his weapon to advance his cause, and we should always be ready to share the gospel. This means having a special attitude, and that is to make sure we know who is on the throne of our hearts: "Sanctify the Lord God in your hearts: and be ready always to give an answer to every man that asketh you a reason of the hope that is in you with meekness and fear" (v. 15 KJV).

It is because God is sanctified (separated) in our hearts that we are moved by fear, both fear for the unsaved and a fear to make sure we listen to the voice of conscience and do what we know we should. But there is another fear that can produce paralysis. And that's a fear of man. This fear is an endless source of stress in our lives. But it is a fear we should never have. Instead, it is something we need to fight daily. We should never worry about what other people will think of us. Rather, we should be concerned only with our Lord's desires for our lives. Be always ready to do his will.

Father, help me to fear you more than I do men.

Assembling Together

Let us consider one another…
not forsaking the assembling of ourselves together.
HEBREWS 10:24–25 KJV

It's not only wise to be part of a local church but also biblical. When we came to Jesus, we automatically became part of the body of Christ. We are instantly forgiven, with the knowledge that we have eternal life, by the grace of God. However, as part of our growth, we need to be involved in a local church, where we submit ourselves to the pastor and eldership. The pastor will give an account of those who are under his God-given authority. And if we're not a regular part of that local church, how can he give an account? Listen to Scripture: "Obey your [spiritual] leaders and submit to them [recognizing their authority over you], for they are keeping watch over your souls and continually guarding your spiritual welfare as those who will give an account [of their stewardship of you]. Let them do this with joy" (Hebrews 13:17 AMP).

In addition, the companionship and example of fellow believers in church is a constant source of encouragement and joy. Your Christian brothers and sisters provide advice and biblical truth. Share with them when you are worried about something. Don't deprive yourself of the power of their encouragement and their prayers. Thank God for the support of your family in Christ, and be always eager to support your church family as well.

Father, keep me safe from error and secure in Christian community.

Blessed beyond Words

He delighteth in mercy.
MICAH 7:18 KJV

Nothing and no one is anything like our God. All the combined power of nature was created by him, and it's less than nothing compared to its Maker. Yet we are blessed beyond words that with all his power and magnificence, he condescends to be sensitive to our needs, and he pardons iniquity. Scripture says, "Who is a God like unto thee, that pardoneth iniquity, and passeth by the transgression of the remnant of his heritage? he retaineth not his anger for ever, because he delighteth in mercy" (v. 18 KJV).

It was A. W. Tozer who rightly noted, "Mercy is not something God has, but something God is." If he weren't mercy itself, we would have no hope in our death. Spurgeon said, "God's mercy is so great that you may sooner drain the sea of its water, or deprive the sun of its light, or make space too narrow, than diminish the great mercy of God." It is because of that wonderful trait of his character that we shall live—because mercy passes in triumph over transgressions: "Judgment will be merciless to one who has shown no mercy; but [to the one who has shown mercy] mercy triumphs [victoriously] over judgment" (James 2:13 AMP). Mercy didn't defeat justice at the cross. Mercy satisfied justice.

Father, thank you for your wonderful mercy. Because of it, I will live.

Comfort from Jesus

"I will not leave you comfortless:
I will come to you."
JOHN 14:18 KJV

Let these words of Jesus sink into your heart. This short statement shares so much about Jesus. He sees what we are going through and understands how we feel. "I will not leave you comfortless" implies that he understands the difficulties the disciples would endure in this world. He knows they and we will need comfort. And he promises to give that comfort. Our comfort will be his return: "I will come to you." He goes on to explain, "He that hath my commandments, and keepeth them, he it is that loveth me; and he that loveth me shall be loved of my Father, and I will love him, and will manifest myself to him" (v. 21 KJV). Jesus will not leave us alone but will come back. He is with us now daily, supporting us and praying for us. And we know he will also return fully at the end of the age.

How loving of our Savior to provide this promise! He provided it to his disciples during the Upper Room discourse, right before he was betrayed and killed. How they must have needed these words of promise during that time of confusion and tragedy before Jesus rose again. And how we need those words now. Remember that Jesus will bring you comfort; he will give you himself.

Father, I long for Jesus' return. Thank you for the hope that I have.

Better than Gold

The law of the LORD is perfect,
converting the soul.
PSALM 19:7 KJV

God's law is perfect, and because of that, it converts the soul. When we see the perfection of the moral law, that it requires truth in the inward parts, it acts as a schoolmaster and brings us to the foot of the cross. Only there is the law satisfied. Then, we look back at how it brought the knowledge of sin and showed us our danger. That's when we say that it's more desirable than gold. The Commandments are sweeter than honey because it was by the Commandments that God warned us. And now that the law is satisfied in Christ, we have been given the gift of everlasting life. This is the great reward, purchased for us by Jesus on the cross.

Thank God for his law because it helped us to understand our sinfulness. And it helps us to keep our hearts free from those secret sins that we thought nobody saw—until the Lord showed us the extent of God's omniscience: "More to be desired are they than gold, yea, than much fine gold: sweeter also than honey and the honeycomb. Moreover by them is thy servant warned: and in keeping of them there is great reward. Who can understand his errors? cleanse thou me from secret faults" (vv. 10–12 KJV).

Father, thank you for satisfying the terrible demands of your law through the cross.

Soul Restoration

He makes me lie down in green pastures.
He leads me beside quiet waters.
He restores my soul.
PSALM 23:2–3 NASB95

John Lubbock said, "Rest is not idleness, and to lie sometimes on the grass under the trees on a summer's day, listening to the murmur of water, or watching the clouds float across the sky, is by no means a waste of time." Psalm 23:2 also uses nature to describe peace, but with the important reminder of where true restoration comes from: "[God] leads me beside quiet waters." David describes God's tender, shepherding care of his people in this much-loved Psalm.

It might sound overly idyllic, but in Psalm 23, David isn't peaceful because his life is calm. On the contrary, he mentions "the valley of the shadow of death" (v. 4 NASB95) and sitting at a meal "in the presence of my enemies" (v. 5 NASB95). David's soul isn't restored because there's nothing to make his stomach churn. His soul is restored despite those things because God is taking care of him—in the same way God cares for you and me today. He is a shepherd to you as well, leading, guiding, and restoring you. Trust him to care for you as he cared for David.

Father, make me trust you as David did. Please lead, restore, and comfort me as well.

Trust in God

In You, O LORD,
I put my trust.
PSALM 31:1

Would you ever trust your life to a stranger? Would you do it to the point where your life or death is dependent on that stranger's actions? You say, "Of course not. My life is very precious to me. I would never entrust it to someone I didn't know!" Have you ever traveled by plane? Then you trusted your life to the men and women who sat in the control tower. A wrong decision from them could have ended your life. You also trusted pilots you never saw as they sat in a locked cockpit. You trusted the engineers who made sure the plane in which you were flying was flight-worthy. Failure to tighten one loose bolt in a critical component could have ended your life. You have eaten meals prepared by complete strangers, who could have aspired to be mass murderers by poisoning the food and drink. But you ate and drank, with hardly a second thought, you so trusted them.

We put our lives into the hands of sinful men and women every day, such as when we drive our car with strangers flying past, separated from us only by a painted line. We do these things without a second thought. How much more then should we trust our lives into the hands of a faithful Creator who will never let us down.

Father, I completely trust you with my life and for the salvation of my soul.

The Enemy's Bow

For behold,
the wicked bend their bow.
PSALM 11:2 ESV

All kinds of things in life cause stress or fear in us. One way to combat the stress is to show up prepared. If you are a soldier and learn of an armed strike coming against you, you have to gear up and fight back. Preparation won't fully remove the fear, but it will make you better prepared to face it mentally. This is true for other stress too. Sometimes, we gear up spiritually. We lift up faith as a shield and put on the rest of the armor of God (see Ephesians 6:10–17). Other times, our preparation might seem a little more mundane. It might be putting in more study hours or waking up an hour early to get a head start on the work day.

When we see the wicked preparing against us, we turn to God. When the devil prowls around, we take up the armor of faith. When we are overwhelmed by events in our lives, we ask God for help. We look to his promises and believe them in faith. And then we act in faith, doing what we can to prepare with what God has provided for us.

Father, help me prepare for what is worrying me, and please take away unnecessary stress.

The Blessing of Family

Better is a dish of vegetables where love is
than a fattened ox served with hatred.
PROVERBS 15:17 NASB95

Today, let's think about the blessing of family. Family can be difficult. There are plenty of tragic family situations shown in the Bible, starting all the way back in the story of Cain and Abel. But family can also be one of the greatest blessings God gives us. This verse from Proverbs highlights the importance of family. God has given you a family to be your support system and your team. A loving family is preferable to all kinds of riches. Unfortunately, the people we live with and see the most often, the people who are most important to us, can be the first to get cut out of our time and to be treated the worst when we feel pressure in our lives.

Instead, we should invest in our families in the good times and the bad. Never neglect to tell your family you love them. Investing in this most central community in your life honors God and honors your family. It can also provide you with a deep base of encouragement and support. Take full advantage of this blessing from the Lord.

Father, thank you for the people you've put into my life. Help me show your love to them today.

Pity Party

Will You forget me forever?
PSALM 13:1

Psalm 13 gives us the keys to getting out of the dark room of depression. David begins with a huge pity party: "How long, O LORD? Will You forget me forever? How long will You hide Your face from me?" (v. 1). God hasn't forgotten the psalmist, nor is he in hiding. He dwells everywhere. But depression will tell you otherwise. Instead of taking counsel from the Word of God, depression takes counsel from itself, and the result is daily depression (see v. 2). Instead of telling you the enemy is under your feet, depression will tell you that you are defeated by the enemy (see v. 2). Depression will make you feel as though you are dying a slow death (see v. 3). Such a defeatist attitude makes demons rejoice (see v. 4).

But then comes the trump of victory. The cavalry of faith comes bursting in with that trumpet blast: "I have trusted in Your mercy; my heart shall rejoice in Your salvation. I will sing to the LORD, because He has dealt bountifully with me" (vv. 5–6). When Paul and Silas sat in prison, they didn't act according to their painful feelings. They sang hymns of praise. That was evidence of their trust in the Lord, and that brought deliverance. We must do the same.

Father, faith will trust you and sing for joy even though I feel like I am in a dark dungeon.

His Marvelous Lovingkindness

Shew thy marvellous lovingkindness.
PSALM 17:7 KJV

God answered David's prayer in the most loving of ways: "God clearly shows and proves His own love for us, by the fact that while we were still sinners, Christ died for us" (Romans 5:8 AMP).

He lived on the earth for thirty-three years and then displayed his wondrous love through the agony of the cross. This one verse in Psalm 17 contains the entire gospel. Behold, God did a wondrous thing, a marvelous thing, a glorious thing. He saved us by his right hand. Jesus is on the right hand of the Father. He is humanity's only Savior. He saves all who call on him, and it happens with the simplicity of childlike faith. Look at these two versus to see who it was who once rose up against us:

> Therefore, since [these His] children share in flesh and blood [the physical nature of mankind], He Himself in a similar manner also shared in the same [physical nature, but without sin], so that through [experiencing] death He might make powerless (ineffective, impotent) him who had the power of death—that is, the devil— and [that He] might free all those who through [the haunting] fear of death were held in slavery throughout their lives. (Hebrews 2:14–15 AMP)

We have been delivered from the power of Satan to the power of God, from the kingdom of darkness into the light.

Father, thank you for your lovingkindness.

The Reservation

An inheritance…[is] reserved in heaven for you.
1 PETER 1:4

This entire world is in a "bondage of corruption" (Romans 8:21). It is fallen and subject to decay and death. And yet, because of God's great love and mercy, we see a bright light shining in the darkness, "to an inheritance incorruptible and undefiled and that does not fade away, reserved in heaven for you" (v. 4). All this was made possible through the glorious gospel of Jesus Christ that gave us an inheritance that is incorruptible and is undefiled, an inheritance that is not going to fade away, ever. The apostle Paul called it "his unspeakable gift" (2 Corinthians 9:15 KJV). This free gift of God is eternal life, which came to us through Jesus Christ, our wonderful Lord, who gave himself for us on the cross so that we could break free from the power of the grave.

It's such a good feeling to go to an event holding a ticket telling you that you have a reserved seat. It's waiting for you. You know that it's all paid for and that you don't have to do anything except show up to the event. Our ticket is Jesus Christ. We don't have to do anything because it has all been paid for. "It is finished" was arguably the greatest sentence ever spoken.

Father, thank you for the hope of the future.

Everyday Blessing

The sky above proclaims his handiwork.
PSALM 19:1 ESV

The Scriptures remind us of the wonders of nature that surround us: "He gathereth the waters of the sea together as an heap: he layeth up the depth in storehouses" (Psalm 33:7 KJV).

Like a loud and daily trumpet blast, "the heavens declare the glory of God" (Psalm 19:1), but how deaf we are to that sound because we take it for granted! The sky is just there. It's part of daily life—earth, sea, and sky. But the heavens are more than a constantly changing and colorful ceiling. They are an amazingly packed storehouse, without which nothing on earth could survive. God has set in motion a process where salt water from the ocean evaporates under the heat of the sun, loses its saltiness, is kept in the storehouse of the clouds, and sporadically drops onto the earth to give it and us life. When the rain falls on soil, the land soaks it in, giving new life to its vegetation. It is the means by which fruit, grain, nuts, and vegetables find their way into our local supermarkets and then onto our tables. And this endlessly happens thanks to God's lovingkindness for his children and enemies alike. Thank God that every tiny drop of life-giving rain comes with his wonderful mercy.

Father, never let the familiarity of your blessings produce in me any sort of contempt.

The Long Wait for God

I waited patiently for the LORD.
PSALM 40:1

It was David who said, "I waited patiently for the LORD; and He inclined to me, and heard my cry. He also brought me up out of a horrible pit, out of the miry clay, and set my feet upon a rock, and established my steps" (vv. 1–2).

It's not easy to wait patiently for the Lord. We often need his immediate help, and yet we have to exercise patience while we wait for God to move. But we know that he is faithful who promised and that he inclines his ear to us and hears our cry. We have patience because we trust his great wisdom to deliver us in his perfect timing. In the meantime, we are reminded that it is God's faithfulness that took us out of the horrible pit of sin, set our feet upon the rock, and established our steps. We may be waiting for God to act for us right now, but we can remember all the past actions of God on our behalf. If you're waiting on God today, think back to specific moments when he has wonderfully, kindly helped you in the past. He has heard, answered, and rescued you so many times before, and he will do so again.

Father, give me patience and faith in you.

A New Song

He has put a new song in my mouth.
PSALM 40:3

God has put more than just a song in the mouth of those who trust him. The new "song" is a deep expression of praise and worship to our God. It is one of gratitude, of heartfelt thankfulness, all mingled with awe for our Creator. He took us out of the miry clay of the fear and power of death and established our feet upon the rock so that we would not be overcome by the storms that pound this godless world.

We have a new song of praise in our mouth because he made us new creatures in Christ. Old things are passed away, and all things have become new. When he opened our eyes to the truth, he took us out of this evil world and wrote our names in the book of life. This, then, should be the result of that new heart and new song: "Many will see it and fear, and will trust in the LORD" (v. 3). May God make our lives a constant praise to him that many will see and fear. May our lives be a reminder to them of the reality of God and the necessity of finding peace with him through the cross. May they see our faith, our fear, and our trust in the Lord.

Father, thank you for putting a new song in my heart.

The Mind of God

Many, O LORD my God,
are Your wonderful works.

PSALM 40:5

To say the wonderful works of God are "many" is true, but we tend to limit how many "many" is. Every one of the tiny atoms in the entire universe is a wonderful work of God. Then there are the many wonderful works of God we see and don't see on this great earth. In this psalm, David then considers the mind of the God who created all these wonderful works.

Our God-made minds have thoughts that line up one at a time and continually feed our subconsciousness. Occasionally, we may be able to entertain a few thoughts at one time, but anything more than that and all we have is confusion. But the thoughts of God are continually present—more than trillions of them. All at once. He not only knows how many hairs are on my head, but he also knows the thoughts of my heart and sees the thoughts of every human being who has ever lived. The mind of God is infinitely beyond human comprehension. This is a comforting thought for Christians too. While we are not able to handle everything going on in our lives and can be easily overwhelmed, our God is fully capable of seeing all and handling it.

Father, thank you for your wonderful works on my behalf.

Consider the Poor

Remember the poor.
GALATIANS 2:10

Look at these seven promises to those who care about the poor: "Blessed is he that considereth the poor: the LORD will deliver him in time of trouble. The LORD will preserve him, and keep him alive; and he shall be blessed upon the earth: and thou wilt not deliver him unto the will of his enemies. The LORD will strengthen him upon the bed of languishing: thou wilt make all his bed in his sickness" (Psalm 41:1–3 KJV).

If we remember to care for the poor, God promises to deliver us in times of trouble—to shut the mouth of lions and open the Red Sea. There are promises of preservation, of deliverance from death, to grant us his blessing, to deliver us from our enemies, to strengthen us in sickness, and to grant us recovery. We have most of these in Christ. Jesus warned that in this world we would have tribulation but to be joyous because he overcame the world (see John 16:33). In him we overcome the world, have strength, and overcome our enemies (see James 4:7), and we are preserved for his heavenly kingdom. We are more than conquerors through him who loved us (see Romans 8:37). "The Lord will deliver me from every evil work and preserve me for His heavenly kingdom. To Him be glory forever and ever. Amen!" (2 Timothy 4:18).

Father, I love your heart for the poor. Make my heart and actions align with yours.

Irrational Depression

Why are you in despair, O my soul?
PSALM 42:5 AMP

Three times in Psalm 42 David questions why he feels depressed: "Why are you in despair, O my soul? And why have you become restless and disturbed within me?…O my God, my soul is in despair within me [the burden more than I can bear]…Why are you in despair, O my soul? Why have you become restless and disquieted within me?" (vv. 5, 6, 11 AMP).

We have times when we feel irrational depression. All may be well, but we feel cast down for no reason. The answer as to why this happens is in the opening verses of the psalm: "As the deer pants [longingly] for the water brooks, so my soul pants [longingly] for You, O God. My soul (my life, my inner self) thirsts for God, for the living God" (vv. 1–2 AMP).

By loving God, we become targets for the enemy. Push to the forefront of the battle, and you are going to feel the heat of warfare. In these dark times, we have to pull ourselves up by the bootstraps, push through it, and say to our soul, "Hope in God and wait expectantly for Him, for I shall yet praise Him, the help of my countenance and my God" (v. 11 AMP). Have faith in God, and he will help to put a smile back on your countenance.

Father, thank you for the assurance that you will help me in my down times.

Our Present Help

Therefore will not we fear.

PSALM 46:2 KJV

The Scriptures say, "God is our refuge and strength, a very present help in trouble. Therefore will not we fear, though the earth be removed, and though the mountains be carried into the midst of the sea" (vv. 1–2 KJV). We need never fear that the earth will one day be removed and the mountains carried into the middle of the sea. The earth will never be removed (see Ecclesiastes 1:4), nor will mountains be "carried" into the middle of the sea. Jesus used similar hyperbole: "I say unto you, That whosoever shall say unto this mountain, Be thou removed, and be thou cast into the sea; and shall not doubt in his heart, but shall believe that those things which he saith shall come to pass; he shall have whatsoever he saith" (Mark 11:23 KJV).

He was saying that if we've got a big problem that we want removed, we should trust God by giving it to him in prayer. David then gives us a wonderful contrast: "There is a river, the streams whereof shall make glad the city of God, the holy place of the tabernacles of the most High. God is in the midst of her; she shall not be moved: God shall help her, and that right early" (Psalm 46:4–5 KJV). God is in control, and he gives peace in the storms.

Father, I will not fear because you're always with me.

Bring Them to Jesus

Men brought on a bed
a man who was paralyzed.
LUKE 5:18

Scripture tells us that the power of God was present and that four men brought a paralyzed friend for Jesus to heal. But when they couldn't get into the house because of the crowd, they got onto the roof and lowered their friend down to the feet of Jesus (see vv. 17–26). This was a wonderful act of faith and love that these four friends had for this paralyzed man.

Imitate these friends today. Bring the people you encounter to Jesus. Serve them with helpful actions, like sharing a burden with them or helping them accomplish a task. Or reach out with some encouragement—an uplifting text or a small gift of a coffee or treat. Share the gospel or a verse with someone. Or simply bring them to the Lord in prayer in your own heart. When Jesus looked at the four men and then at the paralyzed man, the Bible says he "saw their faith" (v. 20). Bringing anyone to the feet of Jesus takes faith. So when you reach out to others today, do so with faith. Remember and believe that Jesus saves and that the Holy Spirit is at work in your life, lending power to your actions and your prayers.

Father, help me to bring people to Jesus.

Lowly Beasts

A man who is in honor, yet does not understand,
is like the beasts that perish.

PSALM 49:20

Whenever we share the gospel with an unsaved person, our aim should always be to bring about the virtue of understanding. In the parable of the sower, Jesus said that the genuine convert is he who hears and understands (see Matthew 13:23). Solomon tells us that a man who doesn't understand is no better off than a lowly beast. He lives only for his appetites rather than for the will of God.

Perhaps the greatest separation of mankind from beasts is that man is capable of understanding the great truths of justice, righteousness, and equity. This is the moral law that rings true when the conscience is stirred by it. The Bible likens the law to light, saying, "The commandment is a lamp, and the law a light" (Proverbs 6:23) and alludes to it being like the rising sun that brings light to a darkened night. What a joy it is to see understanding dawn in the eyes of someone who begins to comprehend what God did through the cross. As they see their sin in its true light, they understand their terrible plight before a holy God. Then the love expressed in the cross suddenly becomes evident, and from that comes the overwhelming truth that God, in his mercy, has opened the doors of everlasting life.

Father, thank you for all you've given me as your child.

God Gave His Son

Thou hast delivered my soul from death.

PSALM 56:13 KJV

If God went to the agony of the cross to save us, then he will certainly keep our feet from falling. "For thou hast delivered my soul from death: wilt not thou deliver my feet from falling, that I may walk before God in the light of the living?" (v. 13 KJV). He gave us his Son to so wonderfully redeem us, and look at how that assures us of the benevolence of heaven: "He that spared not his own Son, but delivered him up for us all, how shall he not with him also freely give us all things?" (Romans 8:32 KJV).

If a rich man says he will give us a gift of ten million dollars, and he gives us one million now in good faith, it's a sure token of what's to come:

> In Him, you also, when you heard the word of truth, the good news of your salvation, and [as a result] believed in Him, were stamped with the seal of the promised Holy Spirit [the One promised by Christ] as owned and protected [by God]. The Spirit is the guarantee [the first installment, the pledge, a foretaste] of our inheritance until the redemption of God's own [purchased] possession [His believers], to the praise of His glory. (Ephesians 1:13–14 AMP)

Father, thank you for giving me the down payment of your Holy Spirit.

The Blessing of a Curse

He ran before, and climbed up into a sycamore tree.
LUKE 19:4 KJV

Sometimes things that we may consider a curse turn out to be a blessing. Take, for instance, a short man named Zacchaeus. He had betrayed his nation by becoming a tax collector for the Romans. Perhaps he was mocked for his lack of stature, and that caused him to hate his own people. Whatever the case, Scripture tells us that this little man couldn't see Jesus over the heads of the crowd, so he humbled himself by running ahead and climbing a tree to see him: "When Jesus came to the place, he looked up, and saw him, and said unto him, Zacchaeus, make haste, and come down; for to day I must abide at thy house" (v. 5 KJV).

When the whole world looked down on Zacchaeus, Jesus looked up to him. You and I may have handicaps in this life that we see as a curse. However, the very thing that we consider to be a curse may turn out to be a blessing. We may be shy people by nature, and we think that shyness hinders us from sharing the gospel with strangers. But, if we let it, that shyness can become the very thing that causes us to pray and trust the Lord. And that's good.

Father, may my weaknesses become my strengths.

By Night

The same came to Jesus by night.
JOHN 3:2 KJV

Three times, the Bible tells us that Nicodemus came to Jesus by night. Scripture is perhaps inferring that because he was a respected teacher in Israel, Nicodemus didn't want to be seen in public talking to Jesus. He was embarrassed of the Creator of the world. But continue reading the passage in John 3:1–21 and see how Jesus responded. He didn't reject Nicodemus or refuse to speak to him because of his fear. Instead, Jesus dove right in to discussing the new birth. He had a deep, serious conversation with Nicodemus. Jesus met Nicodemus where he was and revealed truth to him. Nicodemus was fearful, but he was still seeking Jesus.

You and I might not be reading our Bibles by night, but we may be guilty of letting embarrassment keep us from discussing Jesus in public. Or maybe our awareness of our sin keeps us from spending time with Jesus, reading our Bibles, and praying to the Father. But the story of Nicodemus is encouraging for us if that is the case. Jesus revealed truth and conversed with Nicodemus despite Nicodemus' weakness, and he will do so for you as well. God loved the world—including you—in the midst of your sin. Continue to seek him.

Father, I'm never worthy of coming to you. But Jesus paid the price for me. Help me seek you with my whole heart.

November

Peace with God

Therefore being justified by faith,
we have peace with God
through our Lord Jesus Christ.
ROMANS 5:1 KJV

This world is plagued by conflict. We see wars in the news and political conflict across our nation. We all have interpersonal conflict to different degrees, whether with our neighbors or relatives or even, tragically, in our churches.

That makes the message Paul shares in Romans 5 all the more wonderful and glorious. The most dreadful conflict we all have from birth is conflict with God. We are born his enemies and separated from him (Ephesians 2:1–3). But Romans says that now, because of Jesus' sacrifice, "we have peace with God." That is the most important peace there is. The reality of this peace should give us daily joy. We have peace with our Creator. He is our refuge for any trial we have. This peace provides the security we need to endure any other conflict we may experience. It gives us the emotional strength to turn the other cheek and to respond with kindness to those who are our enemies (see Romans 12:17–21).

Father, I am grateful that I am reconciled to you through Jesus. Please help me to be at peace with everybody in my life as much as it's in my power. Help me to show kindness and love no matter what.

Giving All

Husbands, love your wives.
EPHESIANS 5:25 KJV

Being a Christian is like being married. An important aspect of our Christian life is to place ourselves completely on the altar of God. It is to see ourselves as not being our own any longer but belonging to the Lord. Everything we do, say, and think should be done in the light of his smile or his frown. The fruit of this will be a marriage that blossoms. Love within a marriage is more than an emotional feeling. It is an act of the will, and from that, the feelings will come. We first choose to love our spouse. The fact that it is a choice is evident in that the first and greatest commandment is to love God with all your heart, mind, soul, and strength. It's a command that we choose to follow or not to follow. The Bible commands husbands to love their wives: "Husbands, love your wives, even as Christ also loved the church, and gave himself for it" (v. 25 KJV).

Again, that's a choice, and it means that the husband serves his wife. He lives for the well-being of his spouse, and she is to do the same for him. We are the bride of Christ, and as such, we imitate our groom. Being a Christian means to humbly set aside all selfishness and to "serve the LORD with gladness" (Psalm 100:2).

Father, I give my all to you today.

Good Health

Beloved, I pray that in all respects you may prosper
and be in good health, just as your soul prospers.

3 JOHN 1:2 NASB95

This verse from 3 John shows that the apostle places importance not just on the spiritual health of Gaius, the person he was writing to, but also on Gaius' physical health. Our spiritual health is of vital importance. But we should never neglect our physical bodies. In fact, the health of body and soul often go hand in hand. A strange irony is that stress of the soul can find relief through stress of the body. A quick and intense ride on an exercise bike or a hard run can often rid us of the feeling of tension caused by mental stress.

Often, anxiety in our minds and hearts can overwhelm us. Sometimes the last thing anyone wants to do with something stressful hanging over them is to go for a run or hit the gym. It's tempting instead to lie on the couch or go hang out with friends to get your mind off what's bothering you. It's also tempting to eat junk food instead of nourishing yourself with healthier food. But in the long run, the better shape your body is in, the better shape your mind and emotions will be in. Tiring yourself out with good exercise gives you more energy, mentally and physically.

Father, make me spiritually and physically healthy.

Things Change

You are not your own.
1 CORINTHIANS 6:19

After Jesus washed his disciples' feet, he said, "If you know these things, blessed are you if you do them" (John 13:17). If we know that we should humbly serve others and don't do that, we are cheating ourselves of great joy. A commitment to marriage means an end to superficial adolescent freedom of doing our own thing. A life of playing sports, endless travel, and buying what we want when we want it becomes something in the past. And when children come to the marriage, there is even more pressure to give up our rights because having children commonly means less money, less sleep, and fewer opportunities to go where you want when you want. However, if our hearts are filled with love for our family, the sacrifice will be a joy.

The same applies when we come to Christ. Suddenly, we are no longer our own. We give up our own will to do the will of our Creator. Doing our own thing becomes a thing of the past. George Mueller said, "There was a day when I died; died to self, my opinions, preferences, tastes and will; died to the world, its approval or censure; died to the approval or blame even of my brethren or friends; and since then I have studied only to show myself approved unto God."

Father, it is my privilege to live for you.

Divine Direction

"Do you understand what you are reading?"
ACTS 8:30 AMP

Philip the evangelist received divine instructions: "An angel of the Lord said to Philip, 'Get up and go south to the road that runs from Jerusalem down to Gaza.' (This is a desert road)" (v. 26 AMP). There Philip found an Ethiopian eunuch reading the book of Isaiah. Philip asked if he understood what he was reading. The Ethiopian answered Philip, "Well, how could I [understand] unless someone guides me [correctly]?" (v. 31 AMP). The Holy Spirit led Philip to be at that particular place at that particular time specifically to reach out to guide the Ethiopian.

What kindness the Lord showed! He is watching over you and me as much as he did the Ethiopian. He will provide whatever guidance we need. Most importantly, he gave us the Holy Spirit. Jesus said as much when he ascended after his resurrection: "It is to your advantage that I go away; for if I do not go away, the Helper will not come to you; but if I go, I will send Him to you…when He, the Spirit of truth, comes, He will guide you into all the truth; for He will not speak on His own initiative, but whatever He hears, He will speak; and He will disclose to you what is to come" (John 16:7, 13 NASB95). May we always be sensitive to the guidance of the Holy Spirit both as he instructs us and as he sends us to guide others.

Father, lead me to an unsaved person today. I am ready and willing.

The Power

"You will receive power and ability when the Holy Spirit comes upon you; and you will be My witnesses [to tell people about Me] both in Jerusalem and in all Judea, and Samaria, and even to the ends of the earth."

ACTS 1:8 AMP

Thank God for the book of Acts. It is packed with stories detailing all kinds of trials, tribulations, and stress endured by the early church members. We get encouraging examples of their faith, endurance, and joy no matter the circumstances. And we get story after story of God's deliverance and power in their lives.

In Acts 1:8, Jesus promised "power and ability" from the Holy Spirit. In the next chapter, the disciples received the Holy Spirit at Pentecost, and Peter preached eloquently to the crowds. This was truly a miracle of power given by the Holy Spirit. Most of these disciples, including Peter, were uneducated fishermen. Their track record throughout the gospel narratives showed an overwhelming trend of confusion and fear. Peter babbled nervously on the Mount of Transfiguration. He denied Jesus three times in a row just a few weeks before this speech at Pentecost. Peter and the other disciples were given truly miraculous power at the beginning of Acts, and we can see the effects immediately. Peter continued to be bold throughout the book of Acts. If we are in Christ, that same Holy Spirit who gave Peter such power is with us today, strengthening us with power and boldness.

Father, give me faith in the power you've given me in your Spirit.

Living Water

He had to go through Samaria.

JOHN 4:4 AMP

John chapter 4 gives us a wonderfully intimate and personal evangelism encounter of Jesus with the woman at the well. We're told that Jesus went out of his way to go through Samaria to meet with a sinful woman. She didn't know it yet, but she had a divine appointment with Jesus. She had been living with a number of different men, and like the rest of us, she was in desperate need of God's forgiveness. But notice that Jesus didn't immediately address her sinful condition. He, rather, began by talking to her about something to which she could relate. She was at a well to draw water, so Jesus first spoke to her of water and then he spoke of living water: "If you knew [about] God's gift [of eternal life], and who it is who says, 'Give Me a drink,' you would have asked Him [instead], and He would have given you living water (eternal life)" (John 4:10 AMP).

What kindness and love from Jesus. We are all sinners, just like the Samaritan woman in this story. Jesus loved us and died for us despite that. He gave his perfection to us. All we can do is respond with joy and with grateful obedience.

Father, thank you for forgiving my sin. Make me more like Jesus today.

Why We Won't Want

Present your bodies…
as a living sacrifice.
ROMANS 12:1 AMP

As mentioned in an earlier devotion, if there is one great key to Christianity, it is to present our bodies as a living sacrifice. Give everything to the Lord, and he will give everything to you. As a result, you will find God's will: "You may prove [for yourselves] what the will of God is, that which is good and acceptable and perfect [in His plan and purpose for you]" (v. 2 AMP).

If we have God's will, we won't want for anything. We will say with the psalmist, "The LORD is my shepherd; I shall not want" (Psalm 23:1 ESV). We won't allow greed into our hearts, and we will not be conformed to this world but will be transformed by the renewing of our mind (see Romans 12:2). When trials come, we won't run to weed, we will run to the Word. We don't need to get high because we have the Most High. We won't need alcohol because we have God to satisfy every thirst. So many professed Christians miss out on God's blessing because they don't yield all to him. We must not hold back with a secret love of the world and its sinful pleasures. Instead, we let the Lord be our Shepherd: when he's the one who makes us lie down in green pastures and leads us beside still waters, that is when we find peace.

Father, you are my source of peace.

It Starts with Jealousy

Am I my brother's keeper?
GENESIS 4:9 KJV

Sometimes stress is the result of harsh outside pressures, but all too often, inner unrest is self-imposed by allowing truly inexcusable feelings into our hearts. Jealousy is one such emotion. It starts small but can quickly take strong root in your heart, grow, and overthrow your peace. Cain violated a number of the Ten Commandments before God gave them on Mount Sinai. He was guilty of coveting, hatred, the first murder, and then lying to God about his sin. When questioned by God himself, Cain cynically asked if he had any responsibility at all when it came to looking out for his brother's welfare.

The answer is that he did. And so do we. Each of us is responsible for our neighbors' good. We *are* our brothers' keepers. Jesus instructed every one of us to love our neighbor as much as we love ourselves (see Mark 12:31). God's Word commands us to look out for the interests of others (see Philippians 2:4) and to esteem others better than ourselves (see v. 3). It was Cain's initial jealousy that led to hatred and then murder. That's why we must learn from him so that we let the love of God in our hearts override any temptation to be envious, jealous, or covetous of others— because that will open the door to even greater sin and rob us of our peace.

Father, help me to love others.

Joy in Service

Ye know not what ye ask.
MATTHEW 20:22 KJV

Selfishness is a bedfellow to greed and ambition. It is the enemy of personal sacrifice. It goes to the other side of the road when it sees a beaten stranger. Striving for our own wants steals our inner joy and seeks to steal from others as well. It should have no place in our lives as Christians. Benjamin Franklin is commonly attributed with the saying, "A man wrapped up in himself makes a very small bundle." The apostles James and John showed themselves to be small bundles indeed when they asked for the most prestigious positions in the kingdom of God. These grown men, without protest, let their mother speak for them. She said to Jesus, "Grant that these my two sons may sit, the one on thy right hand, and the other on the left, in thy kingdom" (v. 21 KJV). Even the other disciples were taken aback by the brazen request (see v. 24 KJV).

Selfish ambition is only concerned with self. Instead of this grasping attitude, we should have hearts full of love for others. We should focus on how we can serve the people around us. We want to find our joy in serving others, as the Lord has commanded us and modeled for us himself.

Father, help me to serve others today.

Lift Right

Blessed is a man who perseveres under trial; for once he has been approved, he will receive the crown of life which the Lord has promised to those who love Him.

JAMES 1:12 NASB95

"It's not the load that breaks you down; it's the way you carry it," said former Notre Dame football coach Lou Holtz. Many of us have been hurt by lifting loads that should not have hurt us. Hoisting heavy things carelessly or thoughtlessly can result in strains, stiffness, soreness, or even more serious injuries. The key to lifting heavy things is to use your legs and keep your spine straight. Don't yank with your back.

In the same way, when trials come, you should maintain your courage and stand up straight. Use the right spiritual muscles instead of cutting corners and hoisting with what seems easiest in the short term. Don't try to lift, much less carry, overly heavy burdens alone. What burden do you have that you are lifting the wrong way? How do you need to change your approach as you persevere? Have you been using Scripture and prayer to fortify your mind, or are you trying to coast by on some vaguely positive thinking and some will power?

Father, help me carry my trials in a way that pleases you.

The Shadow

Hide me under the shadow of thy wings.
PSALM 17:8 KJV

What a comforting word picture the psalmist gives us in
this verse. Can you imagine a more secure or cozier place
to be than under the wings of God, like a baby bird under
its mother's wings? It gives a sense of warmth, protection,
and care. Shadows can be a negative thing, but in this case,
it is a good shadow. It's like protection that you can't feel but
that hovers above you nevertheless wherever you walk. Have
you ever walked along under the eaves of a row of shops on
a rainy day? The rain is pouring elsewhere, but under the
shadow of the overhang, you're dry. In the same way, under
God's shadow, you're secure.

Every aspect of your life is under God's protecting
shadow. This security brings joy and rest. We are often
worried about the what-ifs and what will happen to
ourselves or those we love. But this verse reminds us that all
these things are under God's care. He is protective of us. We
are hidden in him.

Father, keep me in the shadow of your wings.

Only One Thing

The Lord answered and said to her, "Martha, Martha, you are worried and bothered about so many things; but only one thing is necessary, for Mary has chosen the good part, which shall not be taken away from her."

LUKE 10:41–42 NASB95

"How beautiful it is to do nothing, and then to rest afterward." This Spanish proverb is a humorous saying, but it hits on a universal point: you're less likely to be stressed when there's nothing on your plate. We shouldn't sit around doing nothing, but when we are overloaded with stress, it might be a good time to look around and see if everything we're scurrying about to accomplish is truly necessary. Even things that are good and useful we might need to lay aside in certain seasons.

Martha learned this lesson in Luke 10. Jesus came to visit her house, and while her sister Mary sat listening at the feet of Jesus, Martha hurried about, busily working at being a hostess. Then she became agitated and asked Jesus to tell Mary to come and help her. But Jesus rebuked Martha for her stress. Of course it is a good thing to cook and prepare for Jesus himself! But Martha didn't need to be doing all that, and much less did she need to be worrying about getting it all done. It's wise to stop and look at what takes up our time and thoughts. Is it all necessary? What are our priorities? We want to listen to Jesus' words and share his priorities each and every day.

Father, keep me from being distracted by good things of less importance.

Good versus Evil

Do not be overcome by evil,
but overcome evil with good.
ROMANS 12:21

Almost every story has a similar theme. From the classics of "Snow White" to "Little Red Riding Hood" to modern action movies, it is a battle between good and evil. The good guy gets the girl, and the bad guy gets the bullet. Such stories resonate with us because we love it when the bully gets his face rubbed in the mud. This is because we are made in the image of God, and at our core, we love to see righteousness triumph. This great battle between good and evil in the human race began in the garden of Eden when the serpent tempted Eve to experience not only good but also evil.

While it is true that we want good to win in our entertainment, in the reality of life, humanity is not the good guy but the evil one. God is the victorious cavalry coming on horseback with the sound of a trumpet to win the battle against evil. Conversion to Jesus Christ is the holding up of a white flag. It is saying to God, "I surrender all to Jesus." Although we are seen as "turncoats" in the eyes of this world, it is a good thing to surrender and exchange leprous rags for robes of righteousness, leaving evil behind and standing for what is good, holy, and just.

Father, I am your surrendered servant.

The Good Thing

It is a good thing
to give thanks unto the LORD.
PSALM 92:1 KJV

It is not only a good thing to give thanks to the Lord. It is also only right that we do. No one likes an unthankful brat who snatches a gift and runs off. Thanksgiving is an obligation. There is so much to thank God for. Even in this dark world, we are still surrounded by blessing and common grace every day. Thank him for a warm house. Thank him for the food you eat today. Thank him for a day of sunshine or of rain.

A hallmark of a Christian is that our hearts are filled with joyful thanksgiving. Sometimes that joy and gratitude don't come easy. But we give thanks to the Lord whether we feel like it or not. It is a defining feature of a Christian because we work to give thanks day in and day out. We have so much to be grateful for: not only for the blessings of this life but also for the cross and for the promise and glorious hope of the next. "O give thanks unto the LORD; for he is good; for his mercy endureth for ever" (1 Chronicles 16:34 KJV).

Father, my heart overflows with thanksgiving.

The Joyful Sound

Justice and judgment are the habitation of thy throne: mercy and truth shall go before thy face. Blessed is the people that know the joyful sound: they shall walk, O LORD, in the light of thy countenance.

PSALM 89:14–15 KJV

The entire message of the Bible has been condensed in these two verses in Psalm 89. Pillars of God's character are justice, judgment, mercy, and truth. So many times people like to think that someone can be either just or merciful. We think of stern and upright judges who don't let anything slip by or of merciful, loving people who are pushovers and let everyone get away with everything. But that his not true of God. He's just *and* merciful. Fully and completely, all the time.

It is because of the weightier matters of the law—matters such as judgment—that we need mercy to live. And the way we obtain mercy is through the medium of faith. The psalmist then addresses those who taste of that mercy by saying, "Blessed is the people that know the joyful sound: they shall walk, O LORD, in the light of thy countenance" (vv. 15 KJV). Our God is truly worthy of joyful rejoicing. There are many examples of the Lord's mercy and truth in our lives. Walk in the light of his countenance today.

Father, help me to be true and faithful.

Sending the Crowds Away

After He had sent the crowds away,
He went up on the mountain by Himself to pray;
and when it was evening, He was there alone.

MATTHEW 14:23 NASB95

When Jesus was on earth, he had many demands upon his time. In the passage leading up to our verse today, he had been busy with crowds of people who came to hear him and experience miracles. He had been healing all the sick people that came (v .14). He miraculously fed the five thousand from a few loaves (vv. 15–21). Then we read verse 23: "After He had sent the crowds away, He went up on the mountain by Himself to pray." Surely there were more people to heal and more of God's truth to share with the lost world. But Jesus was tired, and he needed communion with his Father. He sent the crowds away.

This is an important reminder for us. We should never grow tired of doing good (Galatians 6:9). But we need to take care of ourselves as well. It's okay to say no to some things, and it is right to take time to rest and to restore our souls. We need to prioritize time in prayer with our Father. If Jesus did so, how much more should we!

Father, thank you for Jesus' example of hard work and rest. Help me use my time wisely.

Object of Delight

"I delight to do Your will."
PSALM 40:8 AMP

Oftentimes, we can be guilty of having misplaced priorities. Scripture says of the Messiah: "Then I said, 'Behold, I come [to the throne]; In the scroll of the book it is written of me. I delight to do Your will, O my God; Your law is within my heart.' I have proclaimed good news of righteousness [and the joy that comes from obedience to You] in the great assembly" (vv. 7–9 AMP). Our desires, on the other hand, are all over the place. We become anxious when our desires seem at risk. We become angry when they are thwarted. Since Jesus' greatest priority is in doing God's will, that is where he finds his joy as well. In the same way, if our priority is to help God's priorities succeed, we will find our joy there. Our joy won't be shaken when other things don't go our way. Our priorities will be in the right place.

And guess what? God's will always prevails. We never need to worry that things won't go God's way. That is a continual source of joy and security for his children. Seek his will and rejoice when his will is done on earth as in heaven.

Father, give me delight in your will before all else.

Draw Near

Draw near to God
and He will draw near to you.
JAMES 4:8 NASB95

The amount of stress that we have during a time of trial is a barometer of our godly maturity. We should use such a time as a catalyst to draw nearer to God (see James 4:8). Country music legend Dolly Parton said, "We cannot direct the wind, but we can adjust the sails." We usually can't just rid ourselves of the difficult circumstances in our lives. But we can choose to make the most of them and direct how they affect our hearts and our minds. One effect stress should have is to make you lean on the Lord and draw near to him because of the uncertainty stress brings. The psalmist touches on this: "Before I was afflicted I went astray, But now I keep Your word" (Psalm 119:67 NASB95).

Trials show us the reality of how much we need the Lord. They make us realize how little control we have. But that emphasizes how sufficient and powerful our great God is. These seasons lead us to repent of our pride in leaning on ourselves. Spend time with him and ask him to grow your relationship with him.

Father, what I'm going through is hard. But please use it to make me closer to you.

Small Stuff

"He quieted the sea with His power, And by His understanding He shattered Rahab…Behold, these are the fringes of His ways; And how faint a word we hear of Him! But His mighty thunder, who can understand?"

JOB 26:12, 14 NASB95

Cardiologist and author Robert Eliot famously said, "Rule number one is, don't sweat the small stuff. Rule number two is, it's all small stuff." This is true, but only to the Lord. He can handle our mountains. These awe-inspiring verses from Job are just a few of the many passages throughout Scripture that display God's mighty, incomprehensible power. These verses discuss God's dominion over nature. Try as we might, we can't control nature. We can't even accurately predict it. We build houses to stay sheltered and furnaces to stay warm, but that's not controlling nature; that's surviving it. But God made this world and everything in it and thus has total control over that creation: the weather, the mighty creatures, and yes, the people and their circumstances.

"These are the fringes of his ways." How incredible is our mighty God. The power of nature's storms that we see is but a glimpse of his power. It's small stuff. Praise him for his majesty and power in the world and in your life.

Father, help me to trust your power in every area of my life.

Those Who Hunger

"Blessed are those who hunger and thirst for righteousness, for they shall be satisfied."

MATTHEW 5:6 NASB95

This is one of the most comforting verses in the Bible. All of us who are in Christ have come to him because we see our sin and long to be made clean. Thanks to Jesus' sacrifice on the cross, God freely forgives us and washes us clean. But our hunger for righteousness remains because we still are subject to sin in this life. With the help of the Spirit, we strive for holiness. But sometimes it seems like the more sin we kill, the more sin we see in our lives. How kind of Jesus to remind us that we will be made fully righteous. We will one day receive the God-glorifying righteousness that we long for.

Thank God for Jesus' righteous life and that you already have the full credit of Jesus' righteousness. Thank him that someday you will be completely delivered from sin. And look for other hungry sinners that you can share this promise with.

Father, thank you for Jesus' righteousness.

The Blessing of the Word

The law of the LORD is perfect,
restoring the soul.
PSALM 19:7 NASB95

Psalm 19 is a beautiful psalm. It's full of praise and joy in the way God reveals himself to us in the world and the Word. The psalmist begins with the way "the heavens are telling of the glory of God" (v. 1 NASB95). It then goes on to describe God's law. It is "perfect," "sure," "right," "pure," and "true" (vv. 7–9 NASB95). Think about what this means. The Bible and God's commandments are accurate and dependable. So much of this world is debatable, questionable, uncertain, or shifting. But God's Word is sure. It's right. It's true. You can stake your life—and your afterlife—on what it says.

There's even more! God's law restores souls, makes simple people wise, rejoices hearts, enlightens eyes, and is wholly righteous (vv. 7–9). Isn't that what we all need, especially in times of stress? Restoration, wisdom, joy. God's Word is where we should go for these things. Turn to him and his Word for peace and joy and guidance.

Father, thank you for the blessing of your Word.

Let It Shine

Ye are the light of the world.
MATTHEW 5:14 KJV

When Jesus called believers "the light of the world," perhaps his disciples did a double take. This is because Jesus said that he was the light of the world (see John 8:12). However, he said it because we have been entrusted with the light of the glorious gospel and instructed to reach those who sit in the shadow of death—those whose minds have been blinded by the god of this world. We are their light because it's only through the gospel that they can come out of the darkness. Then Jesus gave a challenging analogy. He said that no one lights a candle and then hides it (see Matthew 5:14–16). The reason we light it is so that it gives light. We must let our light shine before the world.

Jesus then said that we should shine our light by having our faith accompanied by good works. A kind word, a small gift, or a good deed can often speak louder than a thousand sermons. In seasons of stress, it is tempting to turn inward. Witnessing to others or reaching out to them in any way can be the last thing we want to do. But we must remain outward focused at all times. We must share our light. So this day, let your light shine before men and be rich in good works so that those who can't see our faith by our words will see it by our works.

Father, help me to let my light shine by being rich in good works.

The Same Message

We should live soberly, righteously,
and godly, in this present world.
TITUS 2:12 KJV

The instruction to live godly in this present world was
written to Titus two thousand years ago—when the world
was vastly different from the present world in which we
live. Different though it was, human nature was the same
as it is today, and the message of the gospel hasn't changed.
Scripture tells us that if we have tasted of the grace of God,
certain things should be happening in our lives. The book
of Titus tells us that we should strive to live righteously and
avoid the sin and temptations of the world, the flesh, and
the devil. We're no longer to be attracted to the vanities and
the moral filth of this godless world. We are to take up the
cross daily and deny ourselves the pleasures of sin—living
"soberly, righteously, and godly, in this present world."

And the motivation for all this is because we have the
same blessed and glorious hope—the appearing of the great
God and our Savior Jesus Christ. This is how the Amplified
Bible expresses it: "The [remarkable, undeserved] grace of
God that brings salvation has appeared to all men" (Titus 2:11
AMP).

Father, help me to live soberly, sensibly, and sincerely.

Do It Heartily

Whatsoever ye do,
do it heartily.
COLOSSIANS 3:23 KJV

It is good to be enthusiastic about life—whether it is in our marriage, our workplace, our sport, or our friendships. Solomon said that we should do, with all our might, whatever we put our hand to (see Ecclesiastes 9:10). And he certainly did. He threw himself into everything under the sun with all of his might, but his conclusion was that whatever we do, we should be careful not to forget God. The New Testament says a similar thing: "Whatsoever ye do, do it heartily, as to the Lord, and not unto men" (Colossians 3:23 KJV).

"As to the Lord" is the great key to genuine success—as opposed to selfish success. Everything we do, we do to the glory of God, and we do that by asking if what we are doing is pleasing to God. And we know what pleases him because we have his Word to guide us. The Bible tells us how to treat others. It tells us to heartily love our spouse and our neighbor and to do all things without murmuring or complaining. This is because we have the promise that whatever happens to us, no matter how negative, is for our good (see Romans 8:28). It will become positive. That is why enthusiasm should always be our daily demeanor.

Father, may I always be zealous about you.

Silencing the Alarm

God is greater than our heart.

1 JOHN 3:20 KJV

Guilt need only be momentary for any believer. It should never plague a Christian. It should rather be a temporary alarm bell that all is not well but an alarm that is easily silenced. This is because God promised long before we sinned that he would forgive our iniquities, and with that forgiveness, he would remember our sin no more (see Jeremiah 31:34). Becoming a believer in Jesus Christ is more than having our sins forgiven—it means that we are made a completely new person in Christ: "Therefore if any man be in Christ, he is a new creature: old things are passed away; behold, all things are become new" (2 Corinthians 5:17 KJV).

We are truly born again with a new heart and new desires. That means that we are sons and daughters of the living God with instant access to mercy the second we feel the accusations of guilt. His precious blood cleanses us from all sin (see 1 John 1:7). While guilt so often drives this world to stress, anxiety, or even addictions and despair, it acts in a positive way for us in that it continually drives us to the cross, and it keeps us there. And that's a good thing. "If our heart condemn us, God is greater than our heart" (3:20 KJV). God freely gives us forgiveness and deep peace.

Father, thank you that my every sin is forgiven in Christ.

Heaven's Reality

"I go and prepare a place for you."
JOHN 14:3 AMP

Heaven is often described as a state of mind in love songs or as a nebulous location the world hopes to see upon their death. However, it is for the believer a sure destination upon our passing from this life into the next. It's our true home. Jesus said that the kingdom of heaven belongs to us: "Blessed are they which are persecuted for righteousness' sake: for theirs is the kingdom of heaven" (Matthew 5:10 KJV).

We have a home in heaven, an actual dwelling place that Jesus went ahead to prepare for us: "In My Father's house are many dwelling places. If it were not so, I would have told you, because I am going there to prepare a place for you. And if I go and prepare a place for you, I will come back again and I will take you to Myself, so that where I am you may be also" (John 14:2–3 AMP). This is why we groan. We are experiencing the pain of homesickness: "We know that if our earthly house of this tabernacle were dissolved, we have a building of God, an house not made with hands, eternal in the heavens. For in this we groan, earnestly desiring to be clothed upon with our house which is from heaven" (2 Corinthians 5:1 KJV). Every indication of the brokenness of this world—every emotional hurt and physical pain—will one day be made right in our heavenly home.

Father, the constant pains of this world make me long to go home.

A Good Sleep

He gives to his beloved sleep.
PSALM 127:2 ESV

Getting a good night's sleep is a wonderful feeling. It makes us ready to face the day. But often, we experience restlessness or insomnia during the night, or we have frightening dreams, and these things can change how we tackle the daily grind. Scientists at the University of California, Berkeley, suggest that the loss of just one hour of sleep is more than enough to influence the choice to be kind to others during the day: "By looking at a database of 3 million charitable donations between 2001 and 2016, [researchers] Ben Simon, Walker and their colleagues saw a 10% drop in donations following Daylight Saving Time. This drop was not seen in states that don't follow the one-hour transition forward."[5]

This is why being kind must be a choice rather than a mere emotion because if it's not a lack of sleep that steals our joy, it will be something else in this sad and fallen world. God does give his beloved sleep, but Scripture doesn't say how much. Meanwhile we have this promise: "You will keep in perfect and constant peace the one whose mind is steadfast [that is, committed and focused on You—in both inclination and character], because he trusts and takes refuge in You [with hope and confident expectation]" (Isaiah 26:3 AMP).

Father, today it is you in whom I trust and take refuge.

---

5   Hafsa Khalil, "Not Getting Enough Sleep? It Could Be Making You More Selfish," CNN Health, August 23, 2022, https://www.cnn.com/2022/08/23/health/sleep-selfishness-study-wellness-scli-intl/index.html.

Faithful Prayer

She coming in that instant gave thanks likewise unto
the Lord, and spake of him to all them that looked for
redemption in Jerusalem.

LUKE 2:38 KJV

The Bible gives great honor to an elderly woman named
Anna. "And there was one Anna, a prophetess, the daughter
of Phanuel, of the tribe of Aser: she was of a great age, and
had lived with an husband seven years from her virginity;
and she was a widow of about fourscore and four years,
which departed not from the temple, but served God with
fastings and prayers night and day" (vv. 36–37 KJV).

Even at the age of eighty-four, she was zealous for the
Lord. The Scriptures tell us that she lost her husband after
just seven years of marriage, but that tragedy didn't turn her
against the Lord. It did the opposite. She never left the temple,
where she carved out a ministry of serving her Creator
through prayer and fasting and speaking of him to all who
would listen. There is an example for the Christian. If tragedy
strikes, it should bring us closer to him, where we can give
ourselves to prayer without ceasing. The resulting nearness to
him will bring us such joy and peace that we will not be able
to stop ourselves from telling of it to everyone we meet.

*Father, may I constantly serve you and speak of you to all who
will listen.*

Seal My Heart

"I will make an everlasting covenant with them that I will do them good and not turn away from them; and I will put in their heart a fear and reverential awe of Me, so that they will not turn away from Me."

JEREMIAH 32:40 AMP

The Bible is packed with marvelous promises from our loving God, and the promises in Jeremiah 32:40 are some of the best. This verse should give us reason to walk around smiling uncontrollably all day. First is God's promise to do us good. That alone is a big enough promise to write a whole book about. The God of the universe, your Creator, will do you good! And he says this will be "an everlasting covenant." This isn't just a throwaway statement but a sure promise you can count on.

But the really incredible part of the verse is still to come. God promises to put "a fear and reverential awe" of him in our hearts so that we will remain with him. That is what we long for. As the old hymn says: "Prone to wander, Lord, I feel it, prone to leave the God I love." Even after we've been saved, we don't follow him as perfectly as we want to. We feel our weakness and cry with the hymnist, "Here's my heart, oh take and seal it, seal it for thy courts above." That is exactly what God promises to do. He will give us the desire to follow him in this life until we are made perfect in the next.

Father, take my heart and keep it serving only you.

December

Blessed Patience

We count them happy which endure.
JAMES 5:11 KJV

The Bible speaks of the blessedness of being patient when we are going through fiery trials. This is why patience is often referred to as a virtue. Patience during our time in the lion's den is evidence that we trust God. David said, "I waited patiently for the LORD; and he inclined unto me, and heard my cry" (Psalm 40:1 KJV). Impatience with God can be evidence that we don't believe that he is in control. However, he is always in control. Perhaps the most famous example of patience, in respect to God, is seen in the life of Job. He was happy and rich and suddenly lost everything. But instead of becoming impatient with God, Job trusted him: "Behold, we count them happy which endure. Ye have heard of the patience of Job, and have seen the end of the Lord; that the Lord is very pitiful, and of tender mercy" (James 5:11 KJV).

It is wise to learn from Job. His endurance and then his deliverance and restoration give us hope as we endure seemingly endless trials. The book of Hebrews also encourages us to cultivate a patient heart and mind: "Ye have need of patience, that, after ye have done the will of God, ye might receive the promise" (Hebrews 10:36 KJV).

Father, help me to be patient today.

The Light of the Bible

Thy word is a lamp unto my feet.
PSALM 119:105 KJV

God's Word is such a wonderful book. It is more than a book; it's a lamp to our feet and a light to our path. Without it we are in darkness as to what matters in life. The Bible tells us what to do and what not to do if we want to live. In contrast, humanity by nature is in darkness: "Their throat is an open sepulchre; with their tongues they have used deceit; the poison of asps is under their lips: whose mouth is full of cursing and bitterness: their feet are swift to shed blood" (Romans 3:13–15 KJV). The world can't tell us what to do with clarity or truth. Without God's Word, we would be left looking to ourselves or the shifting culture around us for guidance. Only in the Bible do we find reliable truth. Just like Peter said, "Lord, to whom shall we go? You have words of eternal life" (John 6:68 NASB95).

God's Word is bright, and it's true. It will lead us by safe paths to eternal life. It has guidance for personal relationships, living in community, and living as a citizen in a godless nation. Most importantly, it has guidance for how to have a relationship with your Creator through his Son. Our hearts and this world are uncertain, but we will walk rightly by judging everything according to the light of God's precious Word.

Father, thank you for the light of your Word.

He Knows His Own

"The Lord knows those who are his."
2 TIMOTHY 2:19 ESV

Ask most people to define "the church," and you will get
a number of answers. Some will reply that it is a certain
denomination. Others will point to a building where
people regularly meet to worship God. Still others see the
church as an institution that conducts baptisms, weddings,
and funerals and involves itself in taking care of the poor.
The Bible has a different definition: "Among them are
Hymenaeus and Philetus, who have swerved from the truth,
saying that the resurrection has already happened. They
are upsetting the faith of some. But God's firm foundation
stands, bearing this seal: 'The Lord knows those who are his,'
and, 'Let everyone who names the name of the Lord depart
from iniquity'" (vv. 17–19 ESV).

When God looks upon the true believer, he doesn't go
through the denominational doorway, but rather, he looks
upon the heart. And those who love God are those who are
part of the true church. They are the believers—the body
of Christ on this earth. And the way to be part of the true
church is to be born again (see John 3:3–5).

Father, thank you for knowing those who love you.

Godless Traditions

"[Make] the word of God of no effect through your tradition."
MARK 7:13

The impulse of every one of us and every man-made religion in human history is to try to save ourselves. We use comparison and justification to try to minimize our sins and vainly try to do enough good things to outweigh the bad in order to earn forgiveness. Jesus said that through their religious traditions, the Jews of his time had nullified the Word of God (see vv. 12–13). And so it is with modern church traditions that are contrary to Scripture. However, we have only to read the gospels and find the good news that the attainment of eternal life has nothing to do with religious works, but it comes to us entirely as a free gift of God through the new birth:

> It is by grace [God's remarkable compassion and favor drawing you to Christ] that you have been saved [actually delivered from judgment and given eternal life] through faith. And this [salvation] is not of yourselves [not through your own effort], but it is the [undeserved, gracious] gift of God; not as a result of [your] works [nor your attempts to keep the Law], so that no one will [be able to] boast or take credit in any way [for his salvation]. (Ephesians 2:8–9 AMP).

Notice that grace is an undeserved gift, not a result of your works. Thank the Lord for this wonderful gift today and rest in the confidence this beautiful truth gives!

Father, thank you for your amazing grace.

Boldness

Though we had already suffered and been shamefully treated
at Philippi, as you know, we had boldness in our God to
declare to you the gospel of God in the midst of much conflict.

1 Thessalonians 2:2 esv

The apostle Paul provides an incredible example for us to
follow in our Christian lives. He was a tireless follower of
Christ. If you want to be encouraged by his example, just
read the stories in Acts. He summarized some of what
he faced in one of his letters to the Corinthians: he was
imprisoned many times, "beaten times without number,
often in danger of death. Five times I received from the Jews
thirty-nine lashes. Three times I was beaten with rods, once I
was stoned, three times I was shipwrecked…in dangers from
rivers, dangers from robbers, dangers from my countrymen,
dangers from the Gentiles, dangers in the city, dangers in
the wilderness, dangers on the sea" (2 Corinthians 11:23–26
NASB95). Yet he remained bold.

You and I might not face those levels of danger in our
everyday lives. But we are still called to be bold. Maybe you
aren't a missionary like Paul, but whatever God has called
you to do is important because God has called you to do it.
Look at the examples of Paul's character and the examples
of how God sustained and delivered Paul so many times.
Be bold to live as God has called you despite your fears and
despite much conflict. In particular, be bold to share the
gospel at any opportunity.

Father, help me to daily do as Paul did.

How We Know

We know that we have passed from death unto life.
1 JOHN 3:14 KJV

The apostle Paul was bursting with both curiosity and concern when it came to the state of the Christians at Thessalonica. He said, "When we could no longer endure it, we…sent Timothy…our fellow laborer in the gospel of Christ, to establish you and encourage you concerning your faith" (1 Thessalonians 3:1–2). Paul was concerned that the Christians at Thessalonica had gone back into sin because of their many trials. Look at his deep concern and love for his brethren: "For this reason, when I could no longer endure it, I sent to know your faith, lest by some means the tempter had tempted you, and our labor might be in vain" (v. 5).

Timothy returned to Paul with good news. He spoke of their love and faith and that they had great memories of Paul (see v. 6). Then Paul said, "We were comforted concerning you by your faith. For now we live, if you stand fast in the Lord" (vv. 7–8). Evidence that someone is truly saved is that they will have faith in God, and they will love other Christians: "We know that we have passed from death unto life, because we love the brethren" (1 John 3:14 KJV). It's deeply encouraging to see evidence of God's work in your brothers and sisters in Christ. We should look for Christian love in the lives of those we see and encourage them about the evidence of growth.

Father, fill me with your love today.

The Truth

The truth will set you free.
JOHN 8:32 AMP

How true are the unique and wonderful words of Jesus. He spoke absolute truth with unprecedented authority to the point where his hearers were astonished. He said, "I assure you and most solemnly say to you, everyone who practices sin habitually is a slave of sin" (v. 34 AMP). This is contrary to how we normally think. It's human nature to believe that each person is the master of their own choices. The world thinks they are free to lash out in anger, to give in to greed, or to lie whenever they can get away with it. But in reality, they're slaves to those sins. If we serve sin, we become its slave.

The only path of freedom is repentance and faith in the Son of God, who gives us the truth that sets us free (see vv. 31–32). "But now that you have been set free from sin and have become slaves of God, the fruit you get leads to sanctification and its end, eternal life" (Romans 6:22 ESV). Praise God for this wonderful gift! Instead of spinning our wheels, slaves to sin, we are free to follow him.

Father, thank you for freeing me from the bondage of sin.

God First

Thou shalt have no other gods before me.
EXODUS 20:3 KJV

Often, when we read this commandment, we think of the physical idols the Israelites were warned against. We picture carved idols of wood or stone or metal. But we're not as free from guilt as that image would tempt us to believe. In this command, God instructs us to put first in our affections the one who gave us life. We are to love him with all of our heart, mind, soul, and strength (see Matthew 22:37). As Jesus put it: "If anyone comes to Me and does not hate his father and mother, wife and children, brothers and sisters, yes, and his own life also, he cannot be My disciple" (Luke 14:26).

None of us puts God first. Our desires for comfort or pleasure or money often control our hearts. The Scriptures say there is none who seeks after God. That's why we need a Savior. The Scriptures also say that "while we were still sinners, Christ died for us" (Romans 5:8). Christ died to save us and make us right with God. In gratitude and love, we should put him first in our hearts and minds every minute of every day.

Father, you loved me when I had my back to you.

Blessings from Trials

We glory in tribulations also:
knowing that tribulation worketh patience.
ROMANS 5:3 KJV

We have all heard that difficult things grow us and that "the testing of your faith produces endurance" (James 1:3 NASB95). Often when we are actually in a fiery trial, we forget that. Tribulations take a variety of forms. There are the trials that come with living in a fallen world, like health-related suffering, financial difficulty, and heartbreaking grief. There is also religious persecution, suffering prejudice, oppression, imprisonment, or even death for faith in Jesus. But these trials all have one thing in common: they produce patience and endurance.

Our God is gracious. He gives us blessings even in the midst of struggles—sometimes blessings we would never have otherwise. And they are blessings that we should glory in. It can be hard to wait for relief or even for silver linings while a trial rages in our lives. But God promises to give just what you need: endurance.

Father, this trial is so hard. But I thank you for blessing me with growth.

Unity

Endeavouring to keep the unity of the Spirit.

EPHESIANS 4:3 KJV

The Bible uses the word *endeavoring* when it calls us to preserve our Christian unity. However, in reality, it would be easier to herd ten thousand cats into one small room than to unify the international church. This is because there are so many differing doctrines—on prophecy, what involves sanctification, what we should wear, what we shouldn't wear, what we should eat and drink, how and what we should and shouldn't sing, and more. We can derive a lot of stress and conflict from these divisions. However, there is one purpose for which we must all strive. And that is a unity of purpose to worship God and proclaim the gospel.

Christians agree that the gospel revealed in the Bible is Christ dying for our sins and rising from the dead. True Christians agree that the world is heading for a literal place called "hell." So of all the things that should unite us, it is the proclamation of the gospel that saves us from hell. When firefighters are in their fire station, they may have disagreements about how to play certain sports, what sort of clothes to wear, or what to eat. However, they unite as one when human lives are at stake. That's the sort of unity for which we must strive as Christians. Other issues really don't matter in the light of eternity.

Father, help me to have the same priorities Jesus had while he was on this earth.

The Way of Escape

Thy word have I hid in mine heart,
that I might not sin against thee.

PSALM 119:11 KJV

This is a very famous verse that encourages us to memorize Scripture. It also reminds us that when we feel overwhelmed by temptation, there is a divinely appointed tool for us to use. This hints at a wonderful promise found elsewhere in Scripture: God has given us everything that we need to obey his commands. We are not left to follow him alone. Paul discussed this idea in 1 Corinthians 10:13: "God is faithful, who will not allow you to be tempted beyond what you are able, but with the temptation will provide the way of escape also, so that you will be able to endure it" (NASB95).

The temptations ahead of us in a day often seem daunting. But remember: God is faithful. He hasn't left you to struggle powerlessly. Look at what Peter had to say about the topic: "His divine power has granted to us everything pertaining to life and godliness, through the true knowledge of Him who called us by His own glory and excellence" (2 Peter 1:3 NASB95). True knowledge of Jesus is the key.

Father, you are so faithful. Thank you that you've given me everything I need to live a godly life.

Discouragement's Antidote

He shall not fail nor be discouraged.
ISAIAH 42:4 KJV

Life has so many obstacles and so many disappointments that it's easy to become discouraged. However, when that happens, we need to look to Jesus and understand that he was never discouraged. He never lost his courage. The Amplified Bible tells us why: "He will not be disheartened or crushed [in spirit]; [He will persevere] until He has established justice on the earth" (Isaiah 42:4–6 AMP). Jesus was never discouraged because he set his eyes on the victory, and because of that, he knew he would not fail. That happened even during the horror of the cross. He knew that even death couldn't hold him: "Whom God hath raised up, having loosed the pains of death: because it was not possible that he should be holden of it" (Acts 2:24 KJV).

Seeing the victory is the key to courage in a natural battle, and it's the key to beating discouragement in the spiritual realm. No matter what life may throw at us, we can say, "Nay, in all these things we are more than conquerors through him that loved us" (Romans 8:37 KJV). Every day we have a choice. Do we let negative circumstances steal our joy, or do we look at the promises of God and have joy because we believe them?

Father, today I am more than a conqueror in Christ. I believe it because your Word says so.

The Great Shout

Wherefore comfort one another with these words.
1 Thessalonians 4:18 KJV

The apostle Paul had just spoken of the coming of Jesus for his church. He said that the Lord himself would descend from heaven with a great shout and the sound of the trumpet of God. That shout will raise the dead. Jesus spoke of it to the Pharisees. He said the time would come when the dead will hear the voice of the Son of God and be raised from their graves (see John 5:28). Scripture then says that those who are "alive and remain shall be caught up together with them in the clouds, to meet the Lord in the air: and so shall we ever be with the Lord. Wherefore comfort one another with these words" (1 Thessalonians 4:17–18 KJV).

This is our glorious hope. It is for this we groan in expectation, and it is because of this hope that we comfort ourselves. The word *comfort* is originally from the Latin word *confortare*, which means "to strengthen greatly"—a derivative of *fortis*, meaning "strong." We are to more than console ourselves with this promise. These words should catapult us to take this glorious hope to a sad and dying world. Never lose sight of the hope we have in Christ. It is both sure and steadfast, an anchor to the soul.

Father, this day I find great comfort and strength in your precious promises.

Confess and Believe

If you confess with your mouth Jesus as Lord,
and believe in your heart that God raised Him
from the dead, you will be saved.

ROMANS 10:9 NASB95

You will be saved. What beautiful words for any sinner to hear! Many times, sinful humanity tends to complicate things. Sometimes even in the church people can pile all kinds of rules and regulations on top of new Christians to prove their legitimacy. Obedience and investing time and effort in spiritual growth are important. But the requirements to be saved are simple: confess and believe. The Bible is a wonderfully rich, complex, and deep book. It's long and packed with stories, poetry, letters, and prophecy. There are plenty of passages with a multitude of interpretations from different scholars and teachers. But its overall primary message is incredibly simple and clear: Jesus is Lord, and he died for our sins and was raised from the dead to reconcile us to God. All you have to do is believe it.

This dying world needs to hear this simple but powerful message of salvation. Proclaim the good news as Paul and Silas did to their jailer: "Believe in the Lord Jesus, and you will be saved, you and your household" (Acts 16:31 NASB95).

Father, thank you for sending your Son to save me.

More than Conquerors

There is no discharge in that war.
ECCLESIASTES 8:8 KJV

King Solomon was the wisest of men, and he often spoke of the subject of death. This was because he was perceptive. He knew that death made life utterly futile. It was like chasing the wind because he had no defense against it. He wrote, "There is no man that hath power over the spirit to retain the spirit; neither hath he power in the day of death: and there is no discharge in that war; neither shall wickedness deliver those that are given to it" (v. 8 KJV).

The fight between life and death certainly was a war right up until Jesus conquered death. Now there is a discharge for that war for all who trust in him and his victory. Death has been defeated. "The last enemy that shall be destroyed is death" (1 Corinthians 15:26 KJV). There is only one more event to take place: "God shall wipe away all tears from their eyes; and there shall be no more death, neither sorrow, nor crying, neither shall there be any more pain: for the former things are passed away" (Revelation 21:4 KJV). Remembering the past victory of the resurrection and looking forward to the peace and consolation of heaven gives us the courage to face the present with God by our side.

Father, thank you for such a great victory!

The Cause of Growth

Your faith grows exceedingly.
2 THESSALONIANS 1:3

The church of the Thessalonians was thriving. Their faith had grown exceedingly, and their love for each other was clearly evident, to the point where Paul said, "We ourselves boast of you among the churches of God" (v. 4). Then the Scriptures tell us why there was such growth in their faith. Paul reminds them that it was because of "your patience and faith in all your persecutions and tribulations that you endure" (v. 4).

Nothing sends a plant's roots deep into the soil like the sunlight of persecution. The heat causes them to search after precious moisture. In Matthew 13, when Jesus spoke of the false convert having shallow soil, he said, "When the sun rose they were scorched. And since they had no root, they withered away" (v. 6 ESV). He then gave the interpretation: "[The hearer of the word] has no root in himself, but endures for a while, and when tribulation or persecution arises on account of the word, immediately he falls away" (v. 21 ESV). The tribulation that persecution brings causes false converts to fall away but causes true converts (those with roots in good soil) to grow strong and tall. That was the experience of the church of the Thessalonians, and it will be our experience if we have come to the Lord with a good and honest heart. Praise the Lord that he redeems such things in our lives for good!

Father, thank you for only allowing trials to make me grow.

God Will Answer

He shall call upon me, and I will answer him:
I will be with him in trouble;
I will deliver him, and honour him.

PSALM 91:15 KJV

In this verse and in many others, God promises to answer his children when we pray to him. Don't rush over this jaw-dropping fact. Go back and read Psalm 91:15 again. The Maker of heaven and earth, God the Father, promises to listen to you. More than that, he promises to respond when you call upon him. We don't have to spend hours upon hours kneeling alone in a dark room to get his attention. While long conversations with the Lord in prayer are very sweet, you can also call upon him with a simple, short, and heartfelt cry. Sometimes we don't even have adequate words to lay our hearts before him. But the Holy Spirit helps us: "In the same way the Spirit also helps our weakness; for we do not know how to pray as we should, but the Spirit Himself intercedes for us with groanings too deep for words" (Romans 8:26 NASB95).

We face many things that are daunting, fearsome, or stressful. But we should never try to endure it alone. God himself listens to our prayers. In those times, we are to ask him to be with us in our trouble and deliver us.

Father, I love you. Thank you for answering me and being with me in times of trouble.

Never Forsaken

Why hast thou forsaken me?
MATTHEW 27:46 KJV

This desperate cry was one of Jesus' last sayings on the cross. When Jesus bore our sins on the cross, those sins made a separation between him and the Father. That's what sin does. The Scriptures tell us: "Your wickedness has separated you from your God, and your sins have hidden His face from you so that He does not hear" (Isaiah 59:2 AMP). That was our situation before God reached down and saved us. Because our Creator is morally pure and cannot have fellowship with sinners, every one of us is cut off from God by our sin. But since Jesus took on the sins of the world as he hung on the cross, he took on the searingly painful separation from his Father as well. His separation from the Father made possible our reconciliation with the Father.

This is a solemn event in history to contemplate. But it is also very encouraging for you and me. Jesus's separation from the Father in this passage shows he fully endured our sin and its punishment. We can be assured, beyond any doubt, that since Jesus was forsaken, we will never be. That is why we can take comfort in the promise that nothing "in all creation, will be able to separate us from the love of God in Christ Jesus our Lord" (Romans 8:39 ESV).

Father, thank you for what you did at the cross.

Fly, Walk, or Crawl

He gives power to the weak,
and to those who have no might He increases strength.
ISAIAH 40:29

Martin Luther King, Jr., once said, "If you can't fly, run. If you can't run, walk. And if you can't walk, crawl, but by all means, keep moving." This is a good motto for the Christian life. In some seasons we feel like we are getting nowhere. But we still need to keep moving and do what we can. In those times, we can take comfort in knowing the advancement of God's kingdom doesn't depend on us but on God. In fact, we all know we can't fly, walk, or even crawl by ourselves. We need God to give us wings: "Yet those who wait for the LORD will gain new strength; they will mount up with wings like eagles" (Isaiah 40:31 NASB95).

Think of the poor widow in the Gospels who offered "two small copper coins, which amount to a cent" (Mark 12:42 NASB95). This gift counted for more than huge donations from rich people. Jesus explained to his disciples that the rich people "put in out of their surplus, but she, out of her poverty, put in all she owned" (v. 44 NASB95). God doesn't judge based on the outside but based on our hearts. We continue moving forward no matter our energy and ask God to fill us with his strength.

Father, you know my every weakness. Thank you for working through me.

Timely Encouragement

A word fitly spoken is like
apples of gold in pictures of silver.
PROVERBS 25:11 KJV

We can learn a lot of great biblical truths by looking at nature. We learn to be diligent and hard-working by looking to the ant or even to be humble like the lowly donkey upon which Jesus rode. Jesus pointed to the birds to remind us of God's faithfulness. But there are other lessons we can learn from God's wonderful creation. One of those lessons comes from looking at the goose. How fascinating it is to see how they fly in a V formation. Some scientists estimate that flying in the slipstream of the flock adds 71 percent greater flying range than if each bird flew alone. There's a good lesson for having a unity of spirit with other Christians: live alone and life becomes a drag.

Perhaps you've heard the occasional honk as geese fly high overhead. We can only surmise what the honk communicates. Perhaps it means, "Move over! I'm coming through," or maybe it's a honk of encouragement. A word of encouragement spoken to other Christians can be tremendously uplifting. A quick phone call, a short text to ask how someone is doing, a honk and a wave to a friend when driving can mean a lot when life has become a drag. We all need that sort of thing daily.

Father, may my words edify and encourage others today.

Follower of Christ

Be ye followers of me,
even as I also am of Christ.
1 CORINTHIANS 11:1 KJV

While the King James Version says to be followers of Paul,
the original Greek means to imitate him as he imitated Jesus.
Jesus is our great example of godliness. He is more than a
just hero or more than a good role model. But his example
is almost impossible to imitate. He loved the father with all
of his heart, mind, soul, and strength. He loved his neighbor
as himself. He loved his enemies and did good to those who
mistreated him. He healed the sick, raised the dead, and
stood with great passion for the cause of righteousness.

Paul was also a great example because, like us, he was
a forgiven son of Adam. He also showed love and kindness to
his enemies and eventually laid down his life for the cause of
the gospel. But, like us, he had a daily battle with sin, finally
calling himself the chief of sinners (see 1 Timothy 1:15). We
also have other Christians as examples we can imitate. Some
are zealous for the lost, and others show exceptional love,
kindness, and hospitality. Then there are the godly men and
women of history—plus there are those listed in Hebrews
chapter 11, who can be a great source of cheer.

*Father, may I be a source of encouragement to my brothers
and sisters in Christ today.*

The Unspeakable Gift

Work out your own salvation with fear and trembling.
PHILIPPIANS 2:12 KJV

It's essential to note that the Scriptures say to work out our salvation, not to work *for* it. Arguably the greatest deception upon humanity is the thought that we must do something to earn everlasting life. Multitudes believe that they have to strive to hopefully merit heaven. When Jesus said to "strive to enter in at the strait gate" (Luke 13:24 KJV), he was saying to strive *to enter* the strait gate. He wasn't saying strive to earn your way to heaven. The Greek word translated *strive* in this passage is *agonizomai*, the root of the English word *agonize*. We should agonize over our sins as we repent and trust the Savior. The Bible (when addressing sinners) says to let their laughter be turned to mourning and their joy to heaviness (see James 4:9). Then the moment we are born again, we receive God's gift of everlasting life: "We know that we have passed from death unto life, because we love the brethren" (1 John 3:14 KJV).

Those who are born again know that they have everlasting life—not because of anything that they have done but because of what Jesus did on the cross. "These things have I written unto you that believe on the name of the Son of God; that ye may know that ye have eternal life" (5:13 KJV).

Father, thank you that eternal life is a free gift and that I don't have to try to earn it.

Your Sleepless Keeper

Behold, he that keepeth Israel
shall neither slumber nor sleep.

Psalm 121:4 KJV

There's a lot to worry about in this life. We can have sleepless nights over bills, relationship problems, or fears about the future. Our sinful nature tempts us to think everything is up to us. A popular view of this fallen world is, "If I don't look out for myself, no one will." But we can't see everything, and we're not made to be constantly on guard. This is not how children of the living God should live. The good news is that we don't need to live in constant fear: God is on guard for us.

This isn't to say that we should not have common sense. But we can rest peacefully at night knowing that although we can't see everything, and we can't foresee anything with certainty, God sees and foresees all. God is always paying attention. The next verse confirms that God isn't just watching but is also active: "The LORD is thy keeper" (v. 5 KJV). He watches out for you, and he has your back. There's no need to be afraid of things outside our control because everything is in God's control. God is sleepless so that you don't have to be.

Father, thank you for watching over me.

New Every Morning

Great is thy faithfulness.
LAMENTATIONS 3:23 KJV

Wickedness only continues to exist because of God's great mercy. If our Creator had been without mercy, wrath would have consumed all of humanity as fire from heaven. But mercy held wrath back from us until we found the shelter of the cross. Now that same patient mercy waits for others who are still blindly serving sin, not seeing their terrible danger: "The Lord is not slack concerning his promise, as some men count slackness; but is longsuffering to us-ward, not willing that any should perish, but that all should come to repentance" (2 Peter 3:9 KJV).

Thank God for the mercy and compassion he has for guilty sinners such as us: "Through the LORD's mercies we are not consumed, because His compassions fail not. They are new every morning; Great is Your faithfulness. 'The LORD is my portion,' says my soul, 'Therefore I hope in Him!'" (Lamentations 3:22–24). His compassions fail not; they are new every morning. Like the rays of the early morning sunrise, they reach up into the heavens. Mercy and compassion, love and grace mingle into his great faithfulness, upon which hang all of his promises. "If we endure, we shall also reign with Him. If we deny Him, He also will deny us. If we are faithless, He remains faithful; He cannot deny Himself" (2 Timothy 2:12–13).

Father, thank you for your great faithfulness.

By Our Love

"By this all will know that you are My disciples."
John 13:35

Every Christian should have three great loves. The first love we should possess is a love for the God who gave us life. We should love him with all of our heart, mind, soul, and strength. We should love him because every blessing we have comes from his gracious hand. We should love him because it is the right thing to do. The law of thanksgiving demands it. The second great love of the Christian should be for others who are in Christ. The Scriptures say that the evidence that we have passed from death is that we will love the brethren: "We know that we have passed out of death into Life, because we love the brothers and sisters. He who does not love remains in [spiritual] death" (1 John 3:14 AMP). The psalmist said, "I am a companion of all who [reverently] fear You, and of those who keep and honor Your precepts" (Psalm 119:63 AMP).

The third great love every Christian should have is a love and concern for the salvation of the lost. The thought that should consume us is that multitudes of human beings just like us, with the same love of life, are heading for hell. This love should drive us to a point where we will live to warn them, as did the apostle Paul (see Philippians 1:21).

Father, please give me the same love that Jesus had for the lost.

The Cause of Legalism

Touch not; taste not; handle not.
COLOSSIANS 2:21 KJV

Legalism is a subtlety that can pull us away from the grace of God. *Legalism* is a negative term for "the direct or indirect attachment of behaviors, disciplines, and practices to the belief in order to achieve salvation and right standing before God."[6]

This is not a problem with the law because we know God's law is perfect (see Psalm 19). It is a problem with sinners who still try to save themselves. In fact, the more we know the law, the more we understand our need for grace. Our only hope is to trust in the mercy of God. Grace is our only means of salvation. We know that nothing we do can commend us to God. Those who don't tremble under the law and find themselves stripped of self-righteousness are the ones who think that what they eat, what they do, and what they say commends them to God, and thus they stray into legalism. But those who come through the door of the law by using the key of Christ know that nothing they touch, taste, or handle has anything to do with their eternal salvation. We can only come through Christ. Thus our obedience is fueled by gratitude.

Father, nothing in my hand I bring—simply to thy cross I cling.

---

6   Benjamin Espinoza, "Legalism," in *Encyclopedia of Christianity in the United States*, eds. George Thomas Kurian and Mark A. Lamport (Washington, DC: Rowman & Littlefield, 2016), 1338.

In His Image

Man became a living being.
GENESIS 2:7

Ask any believer in evolution for the difference between man and beast, and he will probably tell you that there are very few. However, we know differently. We know that man, like the animals, has a face, eyes, ears, a nose, liver, heart, lungs, and a sophisticated brain. He also has the ability to think, to sleep, and to eat, and he has the will to live. Many animals have most or all of those features—from dogs to cats, elephants, giraffes, horses, and frogs.

But a human being has much more than any beast or amphibian. We have the ability to appreciate a blue sky, the glory of the sunrise and sunset, the vastness of the universe, and the sound of music. We also have a deep-rooted sense of justice with an intuitive passion for enforcing it. None of the animals have court systems, with judges and juries and prisons for those who transgress the law. This is because we are made in the image of him who is the very source of justice (see Psalm 89:14). However, perhaps the greatest difference between man and beasts is that mankind can have fellowship with the one who created him. The Scriptures say that God has left the animals without the unique understanding that comes with the new birth—where almighty God makes his abode in the believer.

Father, thank you for making me more than a beast.

Care for Bruised Reeds

"A bruised reed He will not break and a dimly burning wick He will not extinguish; He will faithfully bring forth justice."
ISAIAH 42:3 NASB95

It is good to think at the end of the year of our Lord's compassion for his children. Jesus said that we would have trials in this world (John 16:33). We are often bruised. Many times, our light is dimmer than it should be. But we can take comfort in this description in Isaiah of our Savior and find comfort in his gentleness. He is strong and tireless in his pursuit of justice (v. 4), but he is painstakingly gentle at the same time.

Beautiful examples of Jesus' gentleness abound in the Gospels. He refuses to give excuses for sin and is stern and harsh with corrupt leaders. But he is truly gentle with repentant sinners. He healed and talked kindly with outcasts like the Samaritan woman at the well, tax collectors, and prostitutes. He truly came to deliver the lost (Luke 19:10). He is the Good Shepherd of John 10. Hear his words from Scripture: "Come to Me, all who are weary and heavy-laden, and I will give you rest. Take My yoke upon you and learn from Me, for I am gentle and humble in heart, and you will find rest for your souls. For My yoke is easy and My burden is light" (Matthew 11:28-30 NASB95). Jesus loves you and cares for you tenderly.

Father, thank you for the gentleness of Jesus. I will follow him gladly every day.

Feel the Pain

He was moved with compassion.
MATTHEW 9:36 KJV

Every prayer we pray for others should be motivated by and soaked in empathy. Empathy is the driving force of evangelism. It is the ability to feel the pain of another. Sympathy feels sorrow and, from a distance, pities someone who is in physical or mental pain. But empathy enters the house of suffering. It is because we are part of the body of Christ that we should feel the emotion of empathy. The whole body suffers if we stub a small toe because the toe isn't independent of the body: "If one member suffers, all the parts share the suffering; if one member is honored, all rejoice with it" (1 Corinthians 12:26 AMP).

If we are able to enter into the suffering of others, we will pray with feeling, and we will passionately seek to alleviate whatever is causing the pain. We will do to others what we would have them do to us. This is the spirit behind the call to remember those who are suffering in prison: "Remember them that are in bonds, as bound with them; and them which suffer adversity, as being yourselves also in the body" (Hebrews 13:3 KJV). Remember and empathize with those strangers who are held in bonds—in the chains of sin and death. Do that and you will never lose your zeal for the lost.

Father, help me to unselfishly enter into the pains of others.

Exalting Jesus

"Come and see."
JOHN 1:46 AMP

When Jesus had found Philip, he told him to be his follower. Then, one of the first things Philip did was to find Nathanael: "Philip found Nathanael and told him, 'We have found the One Moses in the Law and also the Prophets wrote about—Jesus from Nazareth, the son of Joseph [according to public record]'" (John 1:45 AMP). If we are following Jesus, we will be concerned for the unsaved and, like Philip, boldly seek to bring others to him. However, one of the greatest hindrances to us reaching out to the unsaved is a concern that they will ask us a question we can't answer. This is what seemed to happen to Philip: "Nathanael answered him, 'Can anything good come out of Nazareth?' Philip replied, 'Come and see'" (v. 46 AMP).

Philip didn't try to answer Nathanael's question. He wasn't stumped by the thought that Jesus was raised on the wrong side of town. He didn't have to defend Jesus. He simply pointed to the Savior. He said, "Come and see." Skeptic, come and see Jesus. Never a man spoke like this Man. Never did any human being in history say the things this Man said. Come and see, listen, and hear the words that have given millions peace in so troubled a world.

Father, with your help, may I turn many toward the Savior.

Today's Stress

In my distress I called upon the LORD.
PSALM 18:6

Nowadays, we tend to call distress "stress," and because of the frailty of human nature, it's easy to become distressed when life throws us a curveball, when a sudden storm thunders and overshadows our peace. But we see our great example of stress-free living in Jesus, especially when he rested his head on a pillow and slept soundly in a great storm (see Matthew 8:23–27). We tend to look to the powerful nature of the storm rather than to the powerful nature of God. But that is our goal, and the way to attain that sleep-in-the-storm faith is to count our blessings. It is to see the track record of our faithful Creator and to trust him. And in the forefront of those counted blessings is the cross. It is the immovable written-in-stone evidence of his great love toward sinners such as us. Here now is the final verse in this devotional. May it minister to you and keep your life stress free:

Do not be anxious or worried about anything, but in everything [every circumstance and situation] by prayer and petition with thanksgiving, continue to make your [specific] requests known to God. And the peace of God [that peace which reassures the heart, that peace] which transcends all understanding, [that peace which] stands guard over your hearts and your minds in Christ Jesus [is yours]. (Philippians 4:6–7 AMP)

Father, I will trust you in every storm.

About the Author

Ray Comfort is the best-selling author of more than one hundred books. He is the cohost of an award-winning television program that airs in 190 countries and the producer of award-winning movies that have been viewed by millions (see www.FullyFreeFilms.com). He lives in Southern California with his wife, Sue, and has three grown children. For more information, visit LivingWaters.com.

Confident in God's Work

I am confident of this very thing, that He who began a good work in you will perfect it until the day of Christ Jesus.

PHILIPPIANS 1:6 NASB95

Paul wrote a wonderful letter to the Philippian church, urging them to unity and joy. This verse comes right at the start of the letter. He says that he always thanks God "in all my remembrance of you, always offering prayer with joy in my every prayer for you all" (vv. 3–4 NASB95). He was proud to see their efforts for the gospel, and then he shared this joyful assurance: "He who began a good work in you will perfect it" (v. 6 NASB95).

This is a great assurance to us as well. Sometimes it can seem like we are failing to progress in our efforts to be more like Jesus. We can feel stagnant or stuck. But Paul says that he knows God will finish that work for us. Let this assurance bring you peace and also renewed energy to fight with boldness and faith.

Father, thank you for beginning to perfect me. You will surely complete that work on the day of Christ. How I long to see you on that day!

Many Rooms

"In my Father's house are many rooms."
JOHN 14:2 ESV

Think of the welcoming, glowing windows of a friend's warm house on a dark, cold, gloomy night. Even if you've been traveling all day, the knowledge that someone is expecting you, counting on you for dinner, is a secure comfort. As soon as you get near and see the house and finally step inside, none of the exhaustion matters anymore

That's what it's like for us in the world. It's dark, difficult, full of stress and trials. But Jesus said, "Let not your hearts be troubled. Believe in God; believe also in me. In my Father's house are many rooms. If it were not so, would I have told you that I go to prepare a place for you?" (vv. 1–2 ESV). What beautiful words of hope and joy! Jesus said this on the night of the Last Supper, right before his betrayal and arrest later that night. These words must have been a particular comfort to the disciples later after Jesus had risen and ascended to heaven. They surely missed his physical presence, but they knew he was getting a room ready for each one of them. He is making ready a room for you as well.

Father, I can't wait for the day when I am with you fully in heaven.

Total Surrender

"Return to the LORD with all your hearts."
1 SAMUEL 7:3

We can easily miss this great encouragement of our faith. It is to serve God with all of our energy, all of our soul, and with all of our strength. To give him our all. This is not only the key to success as a Christian. It's also the key to success within a marriage. If we love our spouse with all our heart, he or she will give us great joy, and we will get great pleasure from serving them.

When we surrender to God, there is a greater bonus: "Samuel spoke to all the house of Israel, saying, 'If you return to the LORD with all your hearts, then put away the foreign gods and the Ashtoreths from among you, and prepare your hearts for the LORD, and serve Him only; and He will deliver you from the hand of the Philistines'" (v. 3). When we give God our everything, we put away every other affection—and the fruit of that is deliverance from the enemy. When we are completely submitted to God and then resist the devil, he will flee from us (see James 4:7). If you have never presented yourself to God as a living sacrifice, do it today. You'll never regret it.

Father, this day I give you every area of my life and will serve you with all of my heart.

The Enriched Faith

You were enriched in everything by Him.
1 CORINTHIANS 1:5

The Christian is as influenced by the presence of God as a fish is influenced by the presence of the ocean. The ocean is all around it and in it. The fish can't live without the ocean because it was created to be in that environment: "I thank my God always concerning you for the grace of God which was given to you by Christ Jesus, that you were enriched in everything by Him in all utterance and all knowledge" (vv. 4–5).

The apostle Paul continually thanked God for the amazing grace extended to the Corinthian church. They were partakers of the divine nature and of the unspeakable gift of everlasting life solely because of God's kindness toward guilty sinners. Being a Christian means being enriched by him in all utterances. Every word that comes out of our mouth is influenced by our desire to please the one who gave us life and redeemed us. We always want to say what is right. But that enrichment isn't restricted to what we say. We are also influenced by him in all knowledge. Everything that passes through our minds is enriched by the knowledge of God. And so we pray with the psalmist that everything we say and meditate on in our deepest thoughts would be acceptable to him (Psalm 19:14).

Father, may I always remember and be influenced by your omniscience.

Our Brother

Our brother Sosthenes.
1 CORINTHIANS 1:1 AMP

The apostle Paul opened his letter to the Corinthians by making a quick reference in honor of Sosthenes: "Paul, called as an apostle (special messenger, personally chosen representative) of Jesus Christ by the will of God, and our brother Sosthenes" (v. 1 AMP). We don't know why he did so, nor do we know for certain the identity of Sosthenes. He perhaps served as secretary to Paul to write down his dictation. He may have been the synagogue leader mentioned in Acts 18:17. When Gallio was the deputy of Achaia, the Jews made insurrection with one accord against Paul, brought him to the judgment seat, and made accusations against him. But Gallio quickly dismissed the case (see vv. 13–16).

But look at what then happened: "Then all the Greeks took Sosthenes, the ruler of the synagogue, and beat him before the judgment seat. And Gallio took no notice of those things" (v. 17). It seems that Sosthenes was a believer who was the victim of the Jews' frustration with Gallio. Whatever the case, Paul was honoring him with a mention to the Corinthians to whom he was writing, calling Sosthenes "our brother." Gallio may not have been concerned that an innocent man had been beaten by an angry mob, but it seems that Paul was. We should be, too, and we certainly know that God is.

Father, help me to always be concerned for my brothers and sisters who suffer persecution.

Power of Unity

Ye all speak the same thing.
1 CORINTHIANS 1:10 KJV

Paul was about to correct the Corinthian church for their superficial divisions. Like some sort of silly teenage fan club, everybody had their favorites—there was the Pauline club, the Apollyon club, the Peter and Jesus clubs. Paul said, "I beseech you, brethren, by the name of our Lord Jesus Christ, that ye all speak the same thing, and that there be no divisions among you; but that ye be perfectly joined together in the same mind and in the same judgment" (v. 10 KJV).

Paul pleaded with them, in the name of Jesus, for three things: 1. They should speak the same thing without divisions. 2. They should be perfectly joined together with the same mind. 3. They should have the same judgment. No army will win a battle when it allows the enemy to infiltrate its ranks. It is strongest when it has a unity of purpose. These admonitions are for our learning. When we are strong and unified in purpose, we will not be anxious or fearful: "Do not be anxious or worried about anything" (Philippians 4:6 AMP).

Father, help me to have a mind filled with all that is pleasing to you.

The Scarlet Thread

"Thou shalt bind this line of scarlet thread."
JOSHUA 2:18 KJV

This story is a sweet and beautiful example of God's love for anyone who wants to come to him. Rahab was a prostitute, a citizen of an evil pagan nation that was an enemy of God's people Israel. But Rahab asked to be saved from the wrath of Israel's army, and the two spies told her what she should do to be assured of her safety. They said, "Behold, when we come into the land, thou shalt bind this line of scarlet thread in the window which thou didst let us down by: and thou shalt bring thy father, and thy mother, and thy brethren, and all thy father's household, home unto thee" (v. 18 KJV).

If we want to be saved and if we want our loved ones to be saved, we must apply the crimson blood of the Savior to our lives and teach our loved ones to do the same. If we do that, we have God's word that we will be saved from his wrath. With the scarlet thread, Rahab was secure as the army of Israel marched around the city and blew their trumpets ominously day after day. She was secure even when the walls of Jericho suddenly fell all around her. In the same way, with the blood of Christ, we are secure no matter what is happening around us in this world. The most pressing problem we could ever face has been solved, and we are safe eternally.

Father, keep me trusting in the blood of the cross.

Is It I, Lord?

A fool hath no delight in understanding.

PROVERBS 18:2 KJV

The Amplified Bible interprets that verse as "A [closed-minded] fool does not delight in understanding, but only in revealing his personal opinions [unwittingly displaying his self-indulgence and his stupidity]."

When Jesus spoke of someone who was going to betray him, the disciples asked, "Is it I, Lord?" (Matthew 26:22 ESV). We should ask the same question when we read of a fool in God's Word. It is wise to soul search; a fool would never consider himself to be a fool because his close-minded foolishness would never allow it. But the wise self-reflect because they have humility and the wisdom that's from above. It is open to reason. Am I closed-minded? Am I humbly teachable? Do I delight in understanding—especially in understanding the Scriptures? When I'm with others, do I listen, or am I only interested in telling others about myself, my opinions, and my experiences? Do I seek out the truth of everything, or do I quickly believe every rumor I hear? These are good questions to ask ourselves because we want to be without fault.

Father, help me to be an honest soul-searcher, walking in humility of heart.

A New Day

Sorrow and mourning shall flee away.

ISAIAH 51:11 KJV

On the first day of the week after Jesus was crucified, Mary Magdalene went to the tomb while it was still dark. And it was certainly still dark. Those who loved Jesus had endured a time of unspeakable horror. He had been beaten, stripped, and crucified, and Mary was there to continue her mourning. Suddenly she saw that the stone had been rolled away from the tomb, and her immediate thought was that the body of Jesus had been stolen. She ran to spread the alarm: "She ran and went to Simon Peter and to the other disciple (John), whom Jesus loved (esteemed), and said to them, 'They have taken away the Lord out of the tomb, and we do not know where they have laid Him!'" (John 20:2 AMP).

Little did she know that that rolled-away stone meant an end to her nightmare. Her sorrow was about to be turned to joy. Life sometimes becomes a nightmare. Then things get worse. But we must never lose heart because the day is coming when our sorrow will turn to everlasting joy. "Therefore the redeemed of the LORD shall return, and come with singing unto Zion; and everlasting joy shall be upon their head: they shall obtain gladness and joy; and sorrow and mourning shall flee away" (Isaiah 51:11 KJV).

Father, thank you for giving me a hope that is both sure and steadfast.

God Remembers

God is not unrighteous to forget.
HEBREWS 6:10 KJV

How wonderful it is that there is an obligation for God to remember kindness shown to other human beings: "God is not unrighteous to forget your work and labour of love, which ye have shewed toward his name, in that ye have ministered to the saints, and do minister" (v. 10 KJV).

While some would maintain that God couldn't care less when we show kindness, the Bible tells us differently. He is not unrighteous to forget when we do something good. Before we came to Christ, any "good" thing that we did was as filthy, leprous rags in his sight (see Isaiah 64:6), but now, because of what Jesus did on the cross, our works are acceptable to him. Our motivation for showing kindness, loving others, and doing good works is the light of that cross. It is our inspiration. Jesus is our example. He reached out to lepers, healed the sick, gave sight to the blind, and raised the dead. While without a miracle, we don't have the ability to physically raise the dead, we can certainly bring the words of everlasting life to those who are dead in their trespasses and sins. We can reach out with loving acts. We can forgive any actions others do against us as God has forgiven us.

Father, help me to imitate Jesus today.